A FUTURE FOR AFRICA

CRITICAL ESSAYS IN CHRISTIAN SOCIAL IMAGINATION

AFRICAN THEOLOGY TODAY SERIES

VOLUME II

The African Theology Today series is intended to bring to the attention of the African continent itself and especially to the wider world, the often hidden riches of African theology. These are to be found in the frequent Inter-African theological meetings and conferences and in the stream of articles published in a variety of theological journals. Unfortunately, since neither of these initiative and sources is well known outside of Africa, the University of Scranton Press has launched this modest series of books to make them better known. It will consist of three major categories: first, carefully selected and edited selections from various African theological journals. Second, original works by African theologians. And third, reprints of valuable classic works of this type drawn from the past.

It is hoped that these contributions of ideas and culture will, to the benefit of all, add to the history, growth, and culture of Christianity itself and deepen the healthy dialogue already begun within Africa itself and with other Christian theologians, churches, and general readers around the world.

Questions concerning the African Theology Today series should be directed to the series editor:

Dr. Emmanuel Katongole
The Divinity School
Duke University
Box 90068
Durham, NC 27708
Tel: 919-660-3465
Fax: 919-660-3473
Email: ekatongole@div.duke.edu

A FUTURE FOR AFRICA

CRITICAL ESSAYS IN CHRISTIAN SOCIAL IMAGINATION

Emmanuel M. Katongole

SCRANTON: THE UNIVERSITY OF SCRANTON PRESS

Library of Congress Cataloging-in-Publication Data

Katongole, Emmanuel, 1960-
    A future for Africa : critical essays in Christian social imagination /
Emmanuel M. Katongole.
        p. cm.
    Includes bibliographical references and index.
    ISBN 1-58966-102-8
        1. Africa--Church history--20th century. 2. Christianity and culture--
Africa. 3. Church and social problems--Africa. I. Title

BR1360.K36 2004
276'.083--dc22   2004057596

Distribution:

The University of Scranton Press
Chicago Distribution Center
11030 S. Langley
Chicago   IL   60628

DEDICATION

In loving memory of Ben Ssettimba,

a priest of extraordinary love and warm hospitality,

a dear friend,

who, in death as in life, remains a cheerful beacon of hope.

TABLE OF CONTENTS

INTRODUCTION

A FUTURE FOR AFRICA
CRITICAL ESSAYS IN CHRISTIAN
SOCIAL IMAGINATION

In the recent past, we have witnessed a renewed interest in Christian social ethics in Africa. Much of this interest has been generated at the intersection of two apparently contradictory developments on the continent. On the one hand, there has been a steady, and in some places, exponential growth, in the number of Christians, a fact that helped to confirm predictions of Africa as the new center of gravity of the Christian faith in the twenty-first century. On the other hand, and going hand in hand with the confidence of Africa as a Christian continent, there has been a growing concern about the worsening social, political, and economic conditions in many parts of Africa. In some cases, the AIDS pandemic, the 1994 genocide in Rwanda, as well as the violence associated with civil war and instability in a number of countries on the continent have led some to give up on Africa, a sentiment that was well represented by the May 13th, 2000 issue of *The Economist*, with its cover depiction of Africa, "The Hopeless Continent." Given such pessimistic predictions, the search for a more hopeful social, political, and economic future for Africa has never been greater. African theologians have enthusiastically joined this search, seeking to show that there is hope for Africa, and that Christianity can be a positive factor in giving birth to a new future in Africa. This book seeks to contribute to this conversation by displaying how and what difference Christianity can make in the quest for and realization of a new future in Africa.

The book deals with concrete problems that affect social life in Africa—such issues as AIDS, violence, poverty, tribalism, corruption, and the Rwanda genocide. To be sure, these problems are not "new" in the sense that they have been on the horizon of Christian social ethics for quite a while. In fact, as I noted above, African theologians have been wrestling with these same issues for a while. And so, from this perspective, the essays in this book deal with the same "old" problems that affect Christian social life in Africa. This is true even of the essay dealing with September 11th . In fact, a key concern behind this essay is the need to resist attempts to isolate the terrorist attacks on New York and Washington from their global context, and thus present them as singular and unique manifestations of evil. The essay argues that, from an African perspective, there is something familiar about the terrorism of September 11th which, in many ways, connects the event with the despair, frustration, and violence that seems to be an everyday reality for many in Africa.

However, what is new, and where I hope the book will provide a fresh direction in the discussions of Christian ethics in Africa, is in pointing to the concrete reality of the church as the site through which a new future for Africa is both imagined and becomes a reality. The new future for Africa, the book argues, happens not so much in terms of abstract principles and recommendations, but in terms of concrete Christian communities whose way of life and practices are able to interrupt the history of violence, tribalism, and corruption. This is the argument that underlies all the chapters, but is most extensively developed in the third, and final section of the book.

That this constructive argument is only more explicitly laid out in the final Section means that the overall tenor and orientation of the book is critical. It is critical, first of all of Africa's social history, which makes the various problems of social existence—such issues as tribalism, violence, instability, and corruption endemic in Africa. More specifically, the book is critical of the assumptions and approaches that Christian social ethics has adopted in confronting these problems. Simply stated, my quarrel with the way Christian social ethics has developed in Africa comes to this. Christian ethics in Africa has been predominantly preoccupied with the search for *realistic* and *pragmatic* considerations and solutions. I am sure, for many, this sounds like a good thing, a very positive feature of Christian ethics, which just confirms that the church can contribute relevantly to the task of social reconstruction. There are, however, many drawbacks to this realistic and pragmatic preoccupation. First, the failure to question or re-narrate the popular assessments or characterization of Africa's social problems ultimately leads to thin prescriptions that not only fail to alleviate the problem, but instead lead to the replication of these same problems, often in more egregious forms. Secondly, the preoccupation with strategies, recommendations, and solutions often encourages an occasional and thus isolated approach to the social problems in Africa, and fails to highlight the fact that the various problems are sustained by the same underlying imagination. Thirdly, by focusing on recommendations, Christian ethics does not fully and critically engage the reality of politics in Africa, especially the fact that politics involves the formation of identities. A preoccupation with prescriptions does not, therefore, highlight the specific type of identities formed within post-colonial politics. Lastly, the preoccupation with guidelines and recommendations cannot do justice to the full range of Christian life as a political way of life, but only encourages a very superficial and moralistic view of the Christian life. These are some of the shortcomings that the book critically highlights in order to suggest an alternative starting-point for Christian social ethics in Africa.

To put the issue differently, what I try to do in this book is to show that various problems of social existence in Africa—poverty, violence, instability, tribalism, and so forth—are not just incidental problems which Christian social ethics can easily fix by coming up with relevant recommendations. These problems are wired within the imaginative landscape of Africa. That is why, even when political regimes change or new programs and processes are adopted, the problems of poverty, tribalism, and violence do not disappear. Rather, these social challenges persist unchanged, or simply reformat themselves under new labels, as they become more retrenched within the African imagination. In the various chapters of the book, I draw attention to different facets of this imagination, and show that by not questioning or at least drawing attention to this imagination, social-ethical recommendations for a way forward, simply orbit around and within the same imagination.

What I therefore hope will be clear to the reader is the fact that if the problems of social existence in Africa are wired within the imaginative landscape of Africa, the wiring does not take place in abstract. It happens through stories and practices that are embodied within the various social and political institutions of modern Africa. It is through these stories and practices that a people's vision and collective memory—identity—is shaped. This is a very crucial observation, one once realized, forces us to attend to the full range of Christian stories and practices as concrete and real alternatives, through which a different imagination can begin to take shape through the life of the church.

The argument of the book revolves around three very closely interrelated notions of memory, performance, and imagination and is developed through ten essays. The essays were independently conceived and written in a variety of contexts and for a variety of audiences, extending over a period of three years. Six of the essays have been previously published, and are reproduced here with the permission of the original publishers.[1] Except where it was felt that major editorial changes were necessary for clarity and brevity, the essays have been reproduced only with slight editorial revisions. Preserving the original context, it was felt, would allow the essays to retain their original sharpness, while illuminating the argument of each essay in its historical context. The drawback, of course, is that the reader will have to put up with variation in style as well as some minor repetitions. Given the overall advantages, however, we thought this might be a worthwhile price.

Even though independently conceived, all the essays move in the same direction. In fact, as I thought through the connections of the essays, it became obvious that the attempt to highlight the significance of Christian social imagination has been the driving motivation behind much of my scholarly contribution. Thus, arranging the essays around the notions of memory, performance, and imagination not only helps to highlight the limitations of the current approaches to Christian social ethics in Africa, it makes more clearly evident the difference a distinctive Christian imagination can make for the future of Africa, as well as the form such an imagination needs to take for the new future to become a reality.

The first three chapters are organized around the notion of memory. The first chapter, "Remembering Idi Amin," is particularly important in understanding the significance that memory, plays within the moral life, as well as the interconnection between memory, performance, and imagination. In this first chapter, I deal with the reality of everyday violence, corruption, and the growing trend of ragged individualism in Ugandan social life. When I first thought about these social problems, I realized that the majority of Christian ethical discussions on these issues did not offer much more than recommendations drawn from Scripture and the Christian tradition of how to deal with them. It is this approach that I consciously try to avoid in this essay. For I realize that any rush to offer Christian guidelines for dealing with violence, for instance, would simply leave the complex nature of violence not sufficiently described. It is this shortcoming that I address in this chapter by narrating how we got into the particular straits in which a culture of violence, corruption, and individualism seems to have become part of the "normal" way of life in Uganda. Such a narrative not only helps to make obvious the nature of violence, corruption, and individualism in Uganda, it confirms that these are not simply general social problems, but performances that are grounded in a particular social history. In the language of the essay, I display these social problems as distinctive memories—geographies of memory—formed by the story of Idi Amin.

Accordingly, "Remembering Idi Amin" makes explicit the connections between memory and the moral life, and at the same time provides a good example of the direction which Christian social-ethical reflection needs to take. For I suggest, it is the same sort of narrative display as is engaged in this essay that needs to be employed in relation to other social problems in Africa. But Chapter One not only helps to make the case for a narrative approach to Christian ethics, it shows that once a narrative approach to the social problems within Africa is engaged, the Christian social challenge displays itself with fresh and vivid clarity. Once the problems of corruption, violence, and individualism have been shown to be memories set within a particular social imagination, the theological challenge can no longer simply be one of offering recommendations or prescriptions for what the church can or ought to do to fight these. The challenge now becomes one of narrating or displaying how the church and her practices can be, and in fact, are geographies of memories of a unique and distinctive social imagination. Accordingly, the more the church can live true to that memory, the more it can become a community that is capable of providing a critique to, but also a concrete and visible social interruption to, a history of violence, corruption, and individualism.

Chapter Two, "AIDS, Condomization, and Christian Ethics" proceeds along a similar line of argument. In this essay, I seek to move beyond the standard discussions of the morality of condom use in the fight against AIDS, in an attempt to explore "the sort of people we are becoming" in the wake of the AIDS pandemic in Africa. I show that the reality, controversies, and practices surrounding AIDS are grounded in, confirm, and advance a particular vision of Africa and Africans. That is why, the essay argues, a far more productive discussion than one about the morality of condom use in the fight against AIDS is one that displays the specific individual and social imagination that is emerging in Africa in the wake of AIDS. More specifically, the essay points to Christian practices like the Eucharist which, because they are grounded within a different memory, can sustain alternative visions of well-being and flourishing in the wake of AIDS.

A similar argument underlies Chapter Three, "September 11th: Why do they Hate Us?," which was originally written for a public lecture at Molloy College, exactly five months after the terrorist attacks on Washington and New York. The essay argues that the best way to go on in the wake of September 11th is to connect this event with other "memories" of terror, violence, and despair around the world, particularly in Africa. In this case, the biblical story of Job offers not only resources with which to begin to formulate a Christian response to September 11th, it shapes a distinctive imagination of the world different from the one in which terrorism and its counterviolence seems to be the only alternative.

Thus, what the three chapters in Section One seek to do is to recover the significance of memory for moral-theological reflection, a notion that has been completely overlooked within African theological and ethical discussions. What becomes clear from this section is the fact that attending to the issue of memory in Africa is important because it helps to align the various social problems facing African Christians with their histories—through which not only a people's vision of the world, but their very identities in that world have been shaped. But that is why, I also hope that this section helps to confirm that, contrary to the usual impression, the notion of memory does not primarily refer to a mental category. In fact, one of the problems of modern rationalism in this respect has been to psychologize the category of memory and reduce it to individual processes of mental recollection. What, however, the three chapters in Section One help to illuminate is that that memory, at least in the sense I use it here, is not primarily something we have in our minds. Rather, memory has to do with specific habits and patterns of life that are performed and reproduced by the stories through which we see the world.

This sense of memory is picked up and explored more extensively in Section Two on "Performance." What the three chapters in this section seek to show is the fact that both our vision of the world and our way of being in it are shaped by particular stories. Stories, in other words, shape us, or to put it differently, form distinct identities in the world. Chapter Four, "Postmodern Illusions," particularly makes this claim evident by pointing to the much celebrated advance of Postmodernism, and displaying the type of characters or identities such a story like postmodernism performs in Africa. Nowhere, however, is the power of stories to form identities more evident that in Rwanda in 1994. As I show in Chapter Five, "Christianity, Tribalism, and the Rwanda Genocide," the 1994 Genocide in Rwanda was clearly the result of Hutu-Tutsi tribalism. Contrary to popular opinion, however, in this chapter I argue that tribalism in Rwanda, as well as in other parts of Africa, does not arise out of the "natural" animosity between tribes, and does not reflect hatreds that have existed from "time immemorial." The type of tribalism that is evident in Africa is a very recent, and in fact, a very modern phenomenon, which has to do with the stories through which Africans and African societies have been inserted within the modern nation-state project. What the Rwanda genocide confirms is that stories do, in fact, shape identities in the world, and that different stories perform different identities or characters.

This observation involves serious consequences for how one understands the challenge of Christian ethics in relation to issues of tribalism and racism. For if the Hamitic story succeeded in creating, two distinct "tribes" marred by intense animosity for each other, out of a people who spoke the same language, then the challenge is whether we can afford different stories, which can perform different identities. It is for this reason that I make the strange claim that the primary challenge facing the church in Africa in the face of tribalism is not one of tribal or ethnic reconciliation. To accept racial or tribal reconciliation as the primary theological challenge is already to accept "tribes" and "races" as natural identities, and fail to see them as the result of distinct performances grounded in particular stories. The primary ethical challenge has to do with understanding the stories and processes through which we have come, to be preformed into the tribal identities that we have come to assume as "natural." Only then does it become possible to see in a fresh light the stories and practices that shape the church's imagination as the sort of stories that are capable of forming different identities and shaping alternative patterns of living in a world marked by tribalism.

Once the issue has been put in this way, then Christian social ethics becomes less focused on offering the usual recommendations to advance democracy, development, and justice—recommendations that prop up nation-state politics and policies. Instead, it now understands its key challenge in terms of displaying the church as a story or set of stories and practices that reflect a different social vision of politics. This is what Chapter Six, on "Kannungu and the MRTCG," helps to make explicit. Moving from a critical angle, the essay argues that unless the church in Africa is willing to take seriously the social imagination implicit within the Christian stories and practices, it risks being preformed in the same patterns of violence, corruption, and despair characteristic of nation-state politics in Africa. The tragic end of the members of the group who saw themselves as *The Movement for Restoration of the Ten Commandments of God* (MRTCG) at Kannungu in Uganda simply confirms this.

Sections One and Two constitute the critical foil around which the central argument of the book revolves. Accordingly, these two sections help to make clear that the primary aim of the book is not to show what Christians believe can help the search for democracy, development, or the political task of reconstruction in Africa. While this might be the case, in this book I am engaged in a far more substantive task of redefining the very meaning of "Christian social responsibility." I do so by pointing to the so-often unexamined assumptions and stories that sustain social-political life in Africa. I hope it is also clear even as the book does offer insights on how Christians can deal with the problems of AIDS, poverty, terrorism, tribalism, and violence in Africa, that this is not my primary aim. My primary contribution in this book is in trying to change the way we think about or understand these social problems, by narrating or re-narrating them within the imaginative landscape of Africa's social history. In doing so, I hope to invite the reader to see that the task facing us in the face various social challenges is not simply one of prescription, but has to do primarily with description. It is this task of description that I engage in this book by pointing to the underlying stories and visions of life within which these problems are grounded as distinct memories or performances.

To claim that the primary challenge for Christian social ethics is description—and not prescription—does not mean that Christian ethics ceases to be the practical discipline it ought to be. The hope is that in re-describing the challenges facing us, new possibilities for Christian social ethics are opened up and displayed. For instance, by showing how the various social problems arise out of a particular social imagination, one is able to see the church, more clearly, as a set of stories and practices that reflect an alternative, or at least different imagination and vision of society. This is what makes the Christian life a unique form of politics whose significance is not simply to prepare, motivate, or help Christians deal with the political challenges of the day, but itself is the most decisive way of seeing the world and living in it. In other words, within the stories and practices that constitute Christian life, the very meaning of notions like power, service, success,

and freedom—in a word, what a peaceful society is—is being redefined. This is the constructive argument that the chapter on "Kannungu
and MRTCG" develop by highlighting three Christian practices, which
could have provided the members of the MRTCG resources with
which to creatively and truthfully reimage social life in Uganda.

It is this practical, *ecclesiological* nature of Christian ethics, which
is the focus on Section Three. The four chapters within this Section all
point to the church's way of life, and practices as the site within which
a Christian social imagination is shaped and renewed through the formation of truthful lives. The argument takes many forms. In Chapter
Seven, "A Different World Right Here," an explicit argument is developed for the need to draw attention to the nature and reality of the
church in African theological reflection. In this chapter I discuss the
work of three leading African theologians, and show that Kwame
Bediako's and Jessi Mugambi's respective descriptions of the challenges facing African Christians are lacking to the extent that the
nature and reality of the church is obscured in their writings. In contrast, I show that Jean Marc Éla provides a more credible display of the
challenges facing African Christians precisely because he makes the
reality and nature of the church central to his theological reflection. A
similar argument underpins Chapter Eight, "Faces of Jesus and *The
Poisonwood Bible*," as well as Chapter Nine, on "Racism: Christian
Resources Beyond Reconciliation." Even though they come from different angles and respond to different challenges, both essays arrive at
the same conclusion: namely, that without attending to the reality,
work, and concrete practices of the church, one cannot offer an adequate assessment of the status, challenges, and promise of Christianity
within Africa.

What the discussion on racism (Chapter Nine) also helps to confirm is the fact that it is within the concrete practices of the church's
life—such practices as worship, the Eucharist, Scripture reading, hospitality, and forgiveness—that the distinctive social vision or imagination of the Christian life is concretely embodied and displayed. In fact,
it is through and within such concrete practices that the church embodies a concrete and visible alternative to a social history of racism and
tribalism. It is through these concrete practices, as they arise out and in
turn inform the life of Christian communities, that the church becomes
the sign and hope of a new future in Africa.

After I had put together the collection of essays, I was asked to
write an essay for a *festschrift* celebrating Stanley Hauerwas' sixty-

fifth birthday. I have decided to throw in this essay at the end, for I think it serves well as a conclusion to the collection. By reading "Hauerwasian Hooks," after all the other essays, the reader will have a better picture of why I have come to think about the challenges of Christian ethics in Africa in the way I do. Blame it on the work of Stanley Hauerwas. This last essay is therefore a tribute to Stanley Hauerwas and an acknowledgment of the great influence his work has had on me. By making explicit this influence, the essay not only helps the reader to see where I am coming from, but the direction in which my work is moving in relation to the challenge of Christian social imagination. More specifically, the essay helps to make clear that the recent demographic shifts and projections firmly place Africa as the new center of gravity of World Christianity. Following these projections many have noted how the future of the church is in Africa. What I try to do in this essay, and indeed in the book as a whole, is to show that for such a future to be credible—that is, for its impact to be effectively felt within the social, political, economic, and cultural spheres of life in Africa—it cannot be based merely on the statistical growth of Christianity in Africa. Rather, such a future must be embodied within actual church communities, which are shaped by visions and practices that stem from a different imagination, and are thus able to interrupt the dominant performances of politics and economics in Africa. That is why, given the recent explosion of the Prosperity Gospel associated with forms of neo-Pentecostal Christianity in Africa, the need for the church to recover its unique and distinct social imagination has become even more urgent. It is through such a recovery that one might begin to actually see not just the fact that the future of the church is in Africa, but also a more hopeful future for this great continent.

Finally, a word of thanks to various people who have made the writing of this book possible. I am grateful to Greg Jones, the Dean of the Duke Divinity School, and to Willie Jennings, the Associate Dean, for their invitation to me to join the faculty of Duke Divinity School in a full-time position. I am equally grateful for their support as well as for their patience and willingness to work with me as I move back and forth between Uganda and Duke. I am equally grateful for the support I have received from all my colleagues at the Divinity School. Special thanks go to Professor Stanley Hauerwas. His work continues to inspire and inform my work in so many ways. That he was able to take the time to read the manuscript of the book and suggest ways of improvement just confirms how lucky I am to have him as a colleague and even more so, as a friend. I am equally grateful to Professor Teresa Berger—"the other short Catholic at the Divinity School"—for her comments on the draft of the book, but more so for the inspiration of her life and work, particularly her determination not to give up on the church. My research assistant James Corbett worked tirelessly on the manuscript to make it more readable. He not only spent endless hours proofreading the text, but he also offered invaluable recommendations and insights regarding the structure and the argument of the book. Because James is a lawyer and a recent graduate of the Divinity School, he pushed me to state clearly what I needed to say in order to convey the theological point I wanted to make. I will miss him as a research assistant and as a friend. And finally I am grateful to Fr. Richard Rousseau, Jeff Gainey, Patty Mecadon, and the entire staff of the University of Scranton Press for their support and hard work in bringing this book to publication.

Emmanuel M. Katongole
Duke Divinity School
September 9, 2004.

Notes

[1] "Remembering Idi Amin: On Violence, Ethics and Social Memory in Africa," was originally published under the same title in *Mtafiti Mwafrika*, 11 (2004), 1–30; "Aids, Condomization, and Christian Ethics" was originally published as "Christian Ethics and AIDS in Africa Today: Exploring the Limits of a Culture of Suspicion and Despair," in *Missionalia* 29/2 (2001), 144–160; "Postmodern Illusions and Performances," published as "Postmodern Illusions and the Challenges of African Theology: The Ecclesial Tactics of Resistance," in *Modern Theology*, 16/2 (2000); "Kannungu and the Movement for the Restoration of the Ten Commandments of God," published as "Kannungu and the Movement for the Restoration of the Ten Commandments of God: A Challenge for Christian Social Imagination," in *Logos*, 6/3 (2003), 108–144; "A Different World Right Here: The Church within African Theological Imagination," published as "A Different World Right Here, a World Being Gestated in the Deeds of the Everyday: The Church within African Theological Imagination" in *Missionalia* 30/2 (2002), 206–234; "Racism: Christian Resources Beyond Reconciliation," published as "Greeting: Beyond Racial Reconciliation" *Blackwell Companion to Christian Ethics*. Eds. Stanley Hauerwas and Samuel Wells, (Malden, MA: Blackwell Publishing, 2004).

SECTION ONE:

Memory

CHAPTER ONE

REMEMBERING IDI AMIN
ON VIOLENCE, ETHICS, AND
SOCIAL MEMORY
IN AFRICA

*The culture of silence then, is not just the absence of
speaking out against intimidation and repression. It is
a complex mix of fear, avoidance, and compromise
that is often entangled with confused ideas from the
regime's propaganda. In many cases the primary message that has been absorbed is the process message—
that power confers the right to abuse.*

— Terry Dowdall,
Remember to Heal

I. "WHERE IS IDI AMIN?"

"Uganda!" The immigration officer said as he examined
my passport. "Where is Idi Amin?" he asked, looking at
me. "I do not know," I replied, and then jokingly added,
"I thought he was somewhere in the United States."

He laughed as he stamped my passport, handed it back to me, and
wished me a very nice stay in the United States. As I gathered my
papers I told him what I knew as a matter of fact: namely, that Amin
was in exile in Saudi Arabia. He asked me if any of his relatives were
still in the country, and I told him yes.

That was June 1991 at Chicago's O'Hare International Airport, my
very first visit to the United States. As I came to think about this incident later, I thought it strange that my first 'conversation' in the United
States would be about a former dictator who had since left Uganda and
who had ceased, so I thought, to have any influence over Ugandans.
And yet here I was far away from Uganda, being asked the whereabouts of Idi Amin.

3

Forced to Live with Amin's Ghost

Over the years, I have encountered similar questions and grown
increasingly frustrated by many who, for various reasons, seem to be
unwilling to let go of the subject of Idi Amin. Every time I have introduced myself to an American or European audience as someone from
Uganda, there has been the usual barrage of questions about Idi Amin.
"Where is Idi Amin?" many ask. And how was it to live in Uganda during Amin's time? Was Amin still the president? Was he in Uganda? Did
I know him personally? Was I related to Amin? So the questions went.
I remember how one time, out of frustration with such questions, I jokingly told my friend Michael Russo from New York that Amin was my
uncle. It took me over four years to convince him that this was just a
joke. I also remember how, in 1994, a reporter on a Fort Wayne television station interviewed me about my impressions as an African visiting the United States. However, when he realized I was from Uganda,
all he wanted me to talk about was Idi Amin. Out of exasperation, I
half-jokingly told him that perhaps the only good thing that Amin
accomplished was to put Uganda on the world map. Of the entire inter-
view, this was the one line that was directly quoted.

I am sure other Ugandans living abroad, particularly in Europe and
the United States, find themselves in a similar situation of being
'forced' to think and talk about Amin. And so, try hard as many of us
do, it seems difficult, if not impossible to put the ghost of Idi Amin
behind us. On the contrary, it looks like part of what it means to be a
Ugandan living abroad is to be forced to live with the memory of
Amin. To be sure, I found this forced memory of Idi Amin to be annoying at first. For I, like many other Ugandans, had come to think that
Uganda had moved on since the days of Idi Amin. Accordingly, I
increasingly became frustrated and annoyed by my audience's interest
in Amin. In fact, I took the fascination with Amin as a clear example
of how the West generally, Europeans and Americans in particular, are
selective in their knowledge about developments in Africa and only
associate Africa with dictators, bad news, and disasters like war,
famine, and warfare. Yes, Amin *was* a brutal and senseless dictator, but
that was a long time ago, and a chapter long closed. Uganda has since
moved on, so I often felt like telling my audience, and in fact, sometime did tell them so.

But since my audiences' interest in the subject of Amin did not
wane, and questions about him did not stop, I had to find ways of deal-

ing with the topic of Idi Amin. Since I had come to anticipate questions about Amin, I began to take them as a good opportunity for me to share some old jokes about him. Many of these jokes make fun of Amin's English (not surprisingly given his Primary Four background) and which was quite 'original'. My favorite joke is the one where Amin, at a royal dinner in England, is asked to propose a toast to the queen. He reaches into his pocket for his spectacles as he says: "Before I undress (address) the queen, I must first put on my testicles (meaning spectacles). He then proceeds to tell the queen how completely disgusted (satisfied) he was, and how he (Amin) will have revenge when the queen visited Uganda! In another joke, (this one apparently true) Amin is interviewed by a French journalist. They are standing at the swimming pool and Amin, in his swimsuit, is surrounded by a number of his children, many of whom are almost the same age. Amin points to each of them in turn as he says, "This one is mine, this one too, and this one here," and then he adds, "You see, I am a very good marksman!"

But even as I told these and similar jokes about Idi Amin, I was left with a nagging feeling that there was something odd about reducing the subject of Amin to a joking matter. Perhaps it was the realization that Amin would have been a big joke but for the fact that during his eight years in power many Ugandans lost their lives and the country that Churchill had called "the pearl of Africa" was completely reduced to ruins. I was therefore beginning to feel that by reverting to jokes to deal with questions about Amin, I was not only trying to avoid the reality of Idi Amin, I was inadvertently using the same tactic—ironic humor—that many of us had used to survive Amin's brutal dictatorship. For, as Amin's regime of terror and violence gripped the country, and as any hope of meaningful opposition was lost, the telling of jokes became a way to distract ourselves and thus survive the fear and silence of Amin's violence.[1] The realization that more than twenty years later I was still using a similar tactic to deal with Amin had a sobering effect on me and led me to realize that contrary to what I thought or wished to admit, Amin still exercised influence on my life.

Help from King Leopold and His "Ghost"

Then I read *King Leopold's Ghost*, Hoschild's gripping account of King Leopold of Belgium and his regime of violence, terror, and plunder in the Belgian Congo.[2] If *King Leopold's Ghost* was a deeply disturbing book, it was also therapeutic in that it forced me to see the importance of social memory and to realize how it is impossible to understand the present without seeing it in some historical continuity with the past. For now, in the light of Leopold's rubber terror, not only did I begin to make some sense of the constant fighting and looting in the Congo, I was for the first time able to "understand" the dictatorial and kleptomaniac policies of Mobutu's regime.[3]

One sentence in particular helped to make the connection clear for me. The fourteenth century philosopher Ibn Khaldhn observed, Hoschild notes: "Those who are conquered, always want to imitate the conqueror in his main characteristics—in his clothing, his crafts, and in all his distinctive traits and characteristics."[4] In this connection, Hoschild adds that, apart from the color of the skin, there were few ways in which Mobutu did not resemble King Leopold:

> *His one man rule. His great wealth taken from the land. His naming a lake after himself. His yacht. His appropriation of state possessions as his own. His huge shareholdings in private corporations doing business in his territory. Just as Leopold, using his privately controlled state, shared most of his rubber profits with no one, so Mobutu acquired his personal group of gold mines—and rubber plantations. Mobutu's habit of printing more money when he needed it resembled nothing so much as Leopold's printing of Congo bonds . . . Mobutu's luxurious Villa del Mare . . . on the French Riviera, complete with indoor and outdoor swimming pools, gold-fitted bathrooms, and heliport, lay a mere dozen miles down the coast from the estates Leopold once owned at Cap Ferrat.[5]*

Given this revelation, when later I had a chance to read Michael Wrong's account of life in Zaire under Mobutu—it just confirmed what I had began to suspect: namely, that as far as the Congo was concerned, King Leopold was not dead; that he lived on not only in the policies of Mobutu, but in the lives and everyday reactions and responses of ordinary Congolese.[6] It was this realization that finally forced me to see the need to attend to the violence that has been part of the social memory of many Africans. For it was now clear that without confronting this memory, there was no way to understand, let alone to confront the violence within Africa's history. But left unattended to, the violence could only reproduce and reformat itself endlessly in the present. To put it differently, I had come to realize that unless we are, as individuals and as communities, able to examine our present patterns of life and choices, and locate them within a comprehensive narrative of social history, we are neither able to understand who we are in the present nor clearly able to see the alternatives that might be available to us. Only by confronting the past, which still somehow lives on in the present, are we able to envision or imagine meaningful and viable alternatives for the future.

The more I thought about these connections the more I realized that the question "Where is Idi Amin?" required more serious attention than I had been willing to give it. Moreover, I now realized that confronting this question required more than the simple knowledge of Amin's current domicile. For by now I had began to suspect that a closer look at some of the habits and patterns of life in Uganda today might reveal that we have not moved on from Amin's days as much as many of us would like to think. On the contrary, it might be that many of our current patterns and habits reflect Amin's continuing grip over the imagination and lives of Ugandans.

Thus, from being a nuisance and an annoying distraction, questions about Amin's whereabouts had now led me to see the ethical and social significance of memory, but even more specifically, they were forcing me to remember Idi Amin. It is then that the question "Where is Idi Amin?" took on a new significance and urgency for me, and in fact even began to haunt me. My main problem, however, was that I was not sure how or where to look in order to discover the memory of Idi Amin, since as I have noted, for many Ugandans including myself, Idi Amin was a closed chapter, about which there was almost near silence in Uganda.

Desperately Searching for Amin's Memory

This realization was confirmed to me three years ago in a class discussion of political philosophy with my seminary students at Katigondo when I asked the students what they knew or remembered about Amin. I was of course aware that many of these students were born after Amin, but I thought they would share the stories about Amin which they would have heard from their parents and/or grandparents. It soon became very clear, however, that very few knew anything about Idi Amin, except perhaps as a fact of history—a former president of Uganda, 1971–1979. But what was even more disturbing was the realization that even fewer students seemed to be genuinely interested in the topic. For many, Amin was a chapter of the past, a problem that my generation and those older than I faced. They had their own problems to face, so I understood their general lack of interest in the topic.

With my peers, the situation was different, but not much helpful either. The way I went about it was to bring up the topic of Idi Amin whenever I had a chance to meet with a contemporary, especially those I had not seen in a while. At other times, I specifically invited one or two friends out for a drink in order to engage them in a conversation about Idi Amin. While with a few of my contemporaries we were able to talk about some events we remembered about Amin and his time, more often we just ended up cracking jokes about Amin . . . like his "opening a new bus park of airplanes." At many other times we just mused about the man's many titles: Ali Haji, Field Marshall Idi Amin Dada, VC, DSO, MC, CBE, and Life President of Uganda! Or about his eccentricities, like when he allowed himself to be carried shoulder high by four Britons, thus adding another title, "Conqueror of the British Empire," to his ever increasing litany of titles.

I also brought up the topic of Amin every time I had a chance to visit my mother and her village community. It soon became apparent that while many of my mother's generation remembered and talked about the Luweero war of the 1980s with great details, they were quite vague when it came to the time of Amin. True, one or the other remembered the hardships of those days and mentioned a name of a person or relative who had disappeared. But even within this group there was no explicit attempt to connect their present lives and the events of those days. It was therefore clear that if I was looking for a conversation that would constructively engage Amin's memory I would have to do more than simply depend on what was "remembered" of Idi Amin. This was the same conclusion I got when I attended to my own recollections of Amin and his days.

Of Distinct and Vague Recollections

As I attended to my own recollections, I was amazed at how vague my own memories of Amin and his days had become in my mind. Well, this is not quite true, for my childhood memories of Amin as a happy and generous man are quite distinct. For instance, I have very distinct and clear recollections of 25 January 1971, the day of the military coup that brought Amin to power. I was ten years old and in

Primary Four. I remember how on arriving at school that morning we were told there would be no school because there had been a *coup d'e-tat*, and an army general—Idi Amin Dada—had become our new president. I was happy to go back home that day at 10 A.M., neither fully realizing what was going on nor aware that it was going to affect my life, or the lives of anyone I knew. In fact, when my brothers and I returned early from school that morning and told our parents what had happened, they just invited us to join them in the work in the fields. The news of a new president did not seem to affect my parents or the way they carried on with their ordinary business.

I also remember my first opportunity to see Amin in person. Sometime in June or July of that same year, Amin had been visiting troops at a barracks in Mubende and was scheduled to return to Kampala by the highway near my school. All the children in my school and other neighboring schools had been told to line up along the highway to wave to the president. We waited for over three hours, and when Amin's motorcade finally drove by around 5:30 in the evening, it slowed down considerably. This way, I was able to get a clear view of Amin in his full military uniform, as he smiled and confidently waved at us from a military jeep. He looked like a very strong and kind man.

The following year when my class went on a class tour of the State House at Entebbe, Amin was in Kampala, but we were informed that he had left a telephone message that he would be back at the State House in the late afternoon to visit with us. After touring the State House we were however told that Amin had telephoned to give his apologies that he would not be able to meet us as he was delayed in a cabinet meeting, but that he had instructed that we be entertained. We were accordingly served soda and cakes on the State House lawn. We each had all the cake we could eat, and each had at least two bottles of soda. I came back home that evening with renewed sense of Amin as a very loving and generous man, not of course realizing that this was the standard way the State House chief of protocol dealt with tours of school children.

This was 1972, and from then on my recollections of Amin and his regime become vague and indistinct. I have recollections of Amin's secret agents and of the military; recollections of stories of missing persons; of people being bundled and carried away in car trunks; stories of people tortured in the cells of Amin's famous State Research Bureau. I have vague recollections of the public firing squads that we listened to on the radio, and recollections of dead bodies carelessly thrown on the side of roads. I also remember incidents where mobs and soldiers publicly beat up suspected criminals. I have passing recollections of my parents and neighbors speaking in whispered voices; of a general state of fear and boredom, as well as recollections of scarcity and the virtual unavailability of such basic commodities as sugar, salt, and paraffin. I have passing recollections of the "liberation" war that ousted Amin; of the endless bombing and the sound of falling bombs and the cracking of gunshots at night. I remember walking to the front line and enlisting in the liberation war and being turned back because I was sick. I have memories of becoming even sicker during the war; of being unable to go to hospital, and thinking I was going to die. Overall, the memory I have especially of Amin's last years in office is one of fear, and of anger and frustration giving way to despair.

But why were these recollections of Amin's last years neither as vivid nor as clear as my "happy" childhood recollections of Amin? Could it be that the desire to move on from the troubles of those days has involved a more or less unconscious attempt to forget the pain, fear, and violence of Amin's time? Could this also be the reason why there has been very little interest and talk about Amin in Uganda? I suspect that this is no doubt the case. However, the more I probed the silence around Idi Amin, the more I began to be haunted by the possibility of another explanation: namely, that perhaps the fear, pain, suffering, and violence of those days has just become so deeply embedded and embodied in our patterns of life that they have just become part of us. If this was the case, as I was now beginning to suspect it was, then a constructive conversation about memory (of Idi Amin) must move beyond a focus on recollections in our mind, to an examination of concrete habits and patterns of life. It was then that I realized that memory, at least the sort of memory that ought to be a crucial part of ethical reflection, was not just something that takes place in our minds, but that our bodies and overall patterns of life are themselves sites of memory. And that, in the case of Idi Amin, it is by pointing to such concrete (to use an expression from Greg Jones) "geographies of memories" that one is able to realistically face the question, "Where is Idi Amin?"[7]

Memory and Social Imagination: Surviving Idi Amin.

Even then I must confess, it was not until I read Simopoulos' wonderful article, "David's Kingdom: The Congo's Inferno. An Examination of Power from the Underside of History," that I began to see more
clearly the connection between the use of power and the shaping of
memory.[8] In this essay, Simopoulos intertextually and interestingly
weaves the biblical story of King David together with the story of Mr.
Kurtz of Conrad's *Heart of Darkness*, in order to display the effect of
power on those on whom it is used. In this connection, Simopoulos is
able to show that even though the accounts of King David and Mr.
Kurtz are radically different, both men use their power in similar ways
in order to draw the compliance or obedience of their subjects. Both
David and Kurtz, Simopoulos argues, "exercised their powers in three
forms: (1) coercive power—causing others to submit through force or
threat of harm; (2) reciprocal power—securing objectives by means of
exchange; (3) moral power—altering others' behavior and beliefs
through ideas or persuasion." These powers, she notes, have sometimes been called, respectively, the power of the sword, the power of
the purse, and the power of the pen.[9] A key aim of Simopoulos' analysis is to show that the combined effect of these three uses of power was
to create, whether in David's enemies or Kurtz's Congolese natives,
the same desired effect of total compliance or obedience through a
combination of fear and admiration. It is through this combination of
fear and admiration that both King David's enemies and Kurtz's
Congolese natives are gradually drawn in as the willing participants in
their own subjugation.

I found Simopoulos' analysis quite fascinating and in fact instructive on a number of points, especially as it led me to see that unpopular and hated leaders are able to stay in power not just because they are
able to intimidate their subjects or buy them off, but by drawing them
into a particular vision or imagination. But what does this have to do
with Amin and his memory? It means that at least one way to discover Amin's memory today is to examine the many aspects of Amin's
power—especially how he was able to use this power to sustain his
regime. It is in fact this connection, well analyzed by Simopoulos,
between power and the shaping of a community's imagination, that
explains the puzzling fact that unpopular though he was, Amin was
able to stay in power for almost a decade. The puzzle is well captured
by Tony Avirgan and Martha Honey, two journalists who covered the

1979 Liberation War from Tanzania. Particularly to outsiders, Avirgan and Honey note, the solution in Uganda seemed to be remarkably straightforward:

> *Someone with courage needed only to pump a few bullets into Amin's great hulk and the country would be free from oppression. But this never happened. Instead, it took an eight-month war by forty-five thousand Tanzanian and two thousand Ugandan Liberation soldiers to topple the regime. Even for the Tanzanian soldiers who fought and walked their way across Uganda, Amin's survival and, the other side of the coin, the seeming lack of popular resistance to his overwhelmingly unpopular regime, was perplexing.*[10]

But even though Avirgan and Honey capture the puzzle very well, they are unable to offer a thorough and convincing explanation simply because they do not make the connection between power and the shaping of social imagination. In their attempt to throw light on the seeming lack of popular resistance to Amin's unpopular regime, they point to Amin's internal base of support as well as his foreign props in the CIA and the Muslim League. Important as Avirgan's and Honey's explanation is, it nevertheless fails to take into consideration the key insight from Simopoulos' analysis: namely, that unpopular leaders— King David, Kurtz, Amin—do not stay in power simply because they are able to exercise control and fear among their subjects, but also by drawing them into a particular social and practical imagination.[11]

I think this is a very crucial observation, one that is able to explain the fact that Amin, his unpopularity notwithstanding, was able to stay in power for almost ten years. Even more importantly, however, it is this observation that helps to establish a connection between the social imagination of Amin's reign and the geographies of Amin's memory. The connection is simple enough to see. Living under Idi Amin and trying to survive his reign of terror involved, on the part of Ugandans, more than just keeping out of Amin's way. It involved adjustments in terms of practical and moral ideals, in the expectations of what is possible and good, and in the vision of what is true, as well as in forming everyday habits—habits that are still part of the practical and social imagination of Ugandans today. And so in the following section, by drawing attention to three aspects of life in Uganda during Amin's time, I provide a tentative exploration of the geographies of Amin's memory as a way of engaging the question, "Where is Idi Amin?"

II. GEOGRAPHIES OF MEMORY: AMIN LIVES ON

Amin's State of Blood: A Memory of Violence

That Amin was a ruthless and brutal dictator needs no elaboration. By the time he was overthrown in 1979, it is estimated that between 250,000 and 500,000 Ugandans had lost their lives, many of them through torture and disappearance.[12] Among the victims was the Anglican archbishop Janan Luwum, as well as a number of Amin's ministers, and Kay, one of Amin's wives, whose badly mutilated body was shown by Amin to his children and his other wives as an example of what happened to anyone who dared to cross, cheat, or stand up to Amin.[13]

The case of Amin's wife is particularly significant because it shows how Amin's regime was sustained by violence, but even more importantly, how Amin had a way of making the violence visible through a display of his victims. And so, whether it was by the public execution of criminals, or by the manner in which Amin's special agents carelessly dumped their victims on roadsides, in swamps, forests and rivers, Amin's violence was everywhere to be seen. This routine display of violence did, I am sure, achieve the desired effect of instilling grave and ominous fear of Amin in all of us. This fact alone might explain the "culture of silence" and the apparent lack of popular resistance to Amin's otherwise unpopular regime. But, as Terry Dowdall notes, the primary message that is absorbed within this complex mix of fear, avoidance, and compromise is the process message— that power confers right to abuse![14]

What the culture of silence masks, however, is its true character— namely, the gradual naturalization of terror and violence as part of the "normal" way of life in Uganda. Nobody has captured this truth as well as the Cambridge historian Louise Pirouet, who worked in Uganda for eight years. In her analysis of "Religion in Uganda under Amin," she makes an interesting observation to the effect that the church did so little when the security forces harassed the people and threatened their civil liberties. One reason for this reticence on the part of the church, Pirouet suggests, is that "it was easy to take for granted a certain amount of violence because it was part of the pattern of life in Uganda."[15]

That this pattern of violence is still so much the case today is clear from a recent story carried by the Ugandan leading daily the *New Vision* (February 4, 2003) with the headline: "60% of Ugandans are Violent." The story quoted the vice chairperson of the Uganda Red Cross Society, Robert Ssebunnya, who had noted with concern the physical harm frequently inflicted on people and animals in Uganda. According to the Uganda Bureau of Statistics, Ssebunnya noted, the majority of Ugandans preferred listening to or reading stories of disasters like bomb blasts and acid attacks to news of peaceful acts.

Although Ssebunnya did not make the direct connection, I see the truth of his observations reflected in such local newspapers as the Luganda daily, *Bukedde*, which regularly carries, on its front page, graphic pictures of dismembered bodies of victims of auto accidents, acid attacks, murder, and/or domestic violence. Moreover, it seems that the more graphic and gruesome the pictures are, the more *Bukedde* sells. Such graphic images not only reflect the infrastructure of violence on which Ugandan society is built, it shows how in our getting used to violence we have come full circle. In 1972, when the public executions started, Amin had to command the population to watch these public executions. If the display of violence in *Bukedde* and other local papers is anything to go by, it is obvious that we do not have to be forced to watch the violence—we demand and crave to see the violence. And the fact that the Ministry of Ethics and Integrity in Uganda has not even commented on this diet of violence in the local papers just goes to show that violence and its display are simply part of the "normal" way of life in Uganda.

The Christian churches have also failed to draw attention to the issue of everyday violence in their preaching. This is perhaps not surprising, since the Christian churches themselves have learned to take violence for granted, which is clear from the way churches too now easily resort to violence as a way of resolving conflicts. One example will be sufficient to illuminate the point here. When in the 1990s there was a standoff between the bishop and many priests in the Catholic diocese of Kabale (the standoff lasted for over five years until a new bishop was appointed by Rome in 1994), a number of priests who disagreed with bishop Halem'imaana openly threatened to beat, kill, or "finish him off" if he visited their parishes. One can dismiss the case of the Kabale Diocese as just an isolated and exceptional manifestation of violence within the church, but that would be to overlook many other instances, all of which seem to indicate a gradual naturalization of violence within the Christian imagination.[16]

Amin's *Mafuta Mingi*: A Memory of "Falling into Things"

Amin was able to stay in power also as a result of the intricate network of partnerships and alliances within the country. It is these alliances that provided, broadly speaking, the bulwark of collaborators, those who supported and in turn directly benefited from Amin's stay in power. Closest among these were members of the armed forces as well as his secret service agents. Both of these groups were generously rewarded by Amin with fat salaries, beautiful cars, houses, and all sorts of luxuries. It is perhaps not surprising that one of the reasons that the Tanzanian forces that ousted Amin did not find much resistance was the fact that Amin's generals and commanders, who by now were used to a comfortable life, could no longer stand the discipline and hardship of a conventional war. During the war, they drove around in jeeps and armored personnel carriers at a safe distance from the front line and then returned to their mansions in the capital.

Amin's secret service agents were also very well-rewarded for their loyalty. One could always tell them from the dark glasses, the well-tailored bell-bottomed Kaunda suits, the high heeled Bongo shoes (popularized by the then president Bongo of Gabon), and by the brand-new white Honda Civic cars they drove. In their distinctive style, Amin's secret agents were thus as much popular trendsetters as they were loathed and feared. Moreover, since many of these were young men, it was clear that their being part of Amin's inner circle owed less to their long years of training or hard work, and more to their belonging to a particular inner ethnic background or to their having the right connection in the government. In the Ugandan expression, many had just "fallen into things." This was also the case with those who were allocated the property and businesses of the departing Asians in 1972. For this class too, their transformation from village paupers to millionaires was overnight. Quite often the transformation was reflected in their new trademark: a potbelly, the result of instant weight gain. They became members of the new class of *mafuta mingi* (literally meaning plenty of oil—a reference to the oil within their new rich diet).

Even as they were both loathed and envied, the *mafuta mingi* soon became a cultural icon, with many hoping if not to become one, at least to have some kind of connection with one. For only with such a connection could one stand a chance of being appointed headmaster, District Veterinary Officer, or a local agent for essential commodities. If, through the Economic War (see below), Amin promised Ugandans a life of wealth and success, the *mafuta mingi* embodied the fact that becoming rich was not only possible: the journey to success was either instant or a very quick one. All it took was luck and the right connection.

One can see how this cultural pattern is at odds with the long-standing ethical and moral view of life as a journey that requires formation of character and virtue, through a process of gradual transformation. It is also perhaps not surprising that one of the key institutions that came to suffer greatly from the expectation of "eating" and "falling into things" was education. For in as much as education is grounded on an assumption of success through hard work and gradual achievement, this was greatly at odds not only with the logic of instant success, but also with the life experience of many of the *mafuta mingi* who, like Amin himself, were themselves primary school dropouts. In fact, a popular expression of the *mafuta mingi* was *ndi soma wapi* or its Luganda equivalent, *nze atasoma sirya*—which translated liberally comes to the same: there is no need to go to school to be successful (to eat well). The result was visible not only through the collapse of Uganda's hitherto well-organized and competitive education system, but by the many young people who abandoned education and the pursuit of a career for the streets in search for "connections" that would assure them quick success, whether this was through a black market trade (*magendo*) or through some other forms of shady deals popularly known in Uganda as *mipango*. Just like with the *mafuta mingi*, these deals were built on a dream of instant success—at the same time formatting into a cultural pattern this dream—one not built on patient and enduring hard work, but on luck. In many ways, the expectation of instant success is a large part of Ugandan popular culture. Ugandans still believe they can become rich quickly. Sometimes they hope this will come to them if they are lucky and chance on money (*kuteeba*); at other times they hope they will get a benefactor (*muzungu wange*) as was the case of many servants who inherited the property and businesses of their departing Asian or European bosses in 1972.[17] One only needs to watch Ugandans in their desperate search for "connections" or the number of times words like *kupanga* (dealing), *kulya* (eating), and *kugwa mu bintu* (falling into things) come up in any given conversation to realize how well-entrenched the cultural patterns of instant success are. Needless to say, the expectation of effortless success, success not based on enduring hard work and gradual transformation, helps to make corruption and embezzlement an ever-constant reality in Ugandan business and government circles.

Amin's Economic War: A Memory of Survival

No single idea provided more of a moral focus to Amin's regime than the famous Economic War, the ideological and policy reforms by which Amin sought to create a prosperous Uganda for Ugandans. As part of this Economic War, Amin decided early in 1972 to expel the Ugandan Asians, who up to this point, had played a key role within the Ugandan economy as businessmen, traders, and manufacturers.[18] In a dream, Amin had been warned that these Ugandan Asians were exploiters, and were draining the country of the much-needed foreign exchange. Accordingly, Amin gave them 90 days to leave the country. Economically, this was a disastrous decision, as the combination of gross mismanagement by Ugandan businessmen, the lack of skills and technical know-how in manufacturing, as well as the economic sanctions imposed on Uganda by the international community, soon brought the economy to a standstill. By 1977, even such essential commodities like sugar, salt, soap, and paraffin become very rare or completely unavailable to many families. Hospitals ran out of drugs, and as the fuel situation became extreme, all public transportation was grounded. I remember for instance how at the end of the school term in 1976, we had to walk over 18 miles to return home for holidays.

From this point it is therefore clear that if Amin's Economic War was a dream of a prosperous Uganda, it was a glorious failure. Yet, from another point of view, the hardships of Amin's Economic War also created one of the most lasting legacies in terms of creative dynamism of Ugandans. The creativity not only required learning to get by with or survive on as little as possible, but learning to do with whatever was at hand. In the absence of sugar, for instance, many families pounded sugar canes and used the juice as a substitute. Given the unavailability of soap, many discovered that, while not as efficient, papaw leaves added to water provided foam that made the washing of clothes possible. If improvisation is the hallmark of African societies in general, the Economic War turned it into a necessary aspect of life in Uganda.

One of the most enduring aspects of the Economic War, however, was the fact that its hardships easily combined with the prevailing state of insecurity to make survival the only goal for many people. In this way, the hardships of the Economic War ironically encouraged a cultural pattern of "celebration." The reason is not difficult to understand. Since many had come to expect very little in life, even finding oneself alive at the end of a day became an occasion for celebration. At the same time, given the harsh realities of survival, looking forward to and actually treating oneself at the end of a day made existence bearable for many people.

It is against this background that one can understand the popularity and success of the Umbrella (outdoor pub) in Ugandan towns and cities and the *malwa* and *wargai* clubs in the rural areas. Ugandans typically like to celebrate and party. They will throw a party for the slightest reason, and spend anything they have (and even borrow money) to have one. Saving is not a typically Ugandan thing. If we can be uncalculating in the determination to have a good time, it is somehow not unconnected to the fact that we are not afraid to have nothing at all. We have been here before. But even when Ugandans are not partying, they constantly talk about giving themselves and each other a treat (*okuwaamu*). Even for those without regular employment, the favorite meeting place in the evening is one of the many outdoor pubs dotting the suburbs of Kampala as well as other towns in Uganda. It is around here that Ugandans spend the long hours "treating themselves" or asking to be treated to rounds of Nile beer and *muchomo* (roasted goat or chicken). For many, including those who can hardly make ends meet, a stop for what Ugandans call "one-one" under the Umbrella has become as much a part of the daily routine as much as anything else they do.

III. REMEMBERING IDI AMIN:
THE ETHICAL AND THEOLOGICAL CHALLENGE

What emerges from this tentative exploration of the geographies of Amin's memory is a firm realization that memory is not just something we have in "our heads." In fact, while our minds can and, in fact, do often forget, our bodies quite often "remember." This is to say that our bodies as well as the personal and social habits we embody are important sites of memory, or to use the same expression from Gregory Jones, they are interesting "geographies of memories." This observation has far-reaching implications. For one, our bodies are shown to be geographies of memory, it becomes obvious that the topic or memory cannot be limited to the field of history since ethics, Christian ethics in particular, would have a lot at stake in the topic. This of course does not mean that the learning of history is not necessary to the task of memory. The learning of history, or historical consciousness in general, can provide a unique opportunity for a conversation regarding the events and processes that have shaped our past, and which therefore shape our memory, or the concrete practices and habits we live by. When, however, the learning of history turns out to be, as is often the case in many African institutions of learning, nothing more than a restatement of "facts" about the *past* (what happened) and a presentation of disconnected dates to be memorized, such an exercise cannot help but become boring, and ironically, even contribute to a certain amnesia: a collective identity of forgetfulness.

What I have however sought to do by exploring some geographies of Amin's memory is to show that the task of memory is in fact a conversation about the *present*. It involves taking a closer look at who we are in the present—our current responses, reactions, and patterns of life—and trying to situate that within a narrative of social/political history.[19] To put it differently, I have attempted to show that since memory is the embodied performance of the past into the present, the ethical task of remembering is nothing but living with a certain attentiveness to the stories, habits, and practices that shape our lives today and form us into the sort of characters or people we are. I can think of no more crucial and more urgent ethical challenge and task.

It is a crucial task, since without such attentiveness to the stories and imagination that have shaped us, we can neither understand who we are today in relation to the past, nor limit the grip this past continues to have on us, and thus be able to envisage a different, more life-giving future. This is particularly the case given the violence that grips many African societies. The violence takes many forms, which range from outright military brutality to civil unrest; from ethnic violence that was recently witnessed in Eastern Congo to the sort of rebel madness in northern Uganda, where rebels routinely attack villages and cut off people's limbs, lips, noses, and genitals. The violence also takes the form of carnage on public roads, which results from careless road accidents to frequent cases of domestic violence and abuse. The frequency, casualness (or is it playfulness?) with which violence is reported and displayed in the local media is just an indication of the simmering infrastructure of violence on which many African societies are built. A key aim of this paper has been to understand this culture of violence in Uganda by locating it within a narrative of social history in which Amin was a key actor. By doing so, I do not want to claim that Amin is responsible for introducing violence to Ugandan society. Violence in one form, degree, or rate might exist in all societies. However, to understand this type of pathological violence that carries a certain casualness about it, one needs to view it as a memory of settled practices and habits of violence embedded within a people's social history.

Amin is certainly a key actor within this history of violence in Uganda, even though he is not the only one, or even the most important one. In fact, a key assumption of this paper, one, however, that has not been directly or explicitly explored given the scope of this paper, is that Amin's violence itself cannot be understood without an understanding of the wide history of colonial violence in which Amin was formed, trained, and became a functionary. What Amin's regime managed to reveal and bring to a logical conclusion was the underlying imagination of violence in which Amin firmly stood. It is nevertheless important to make this historical connection. For abstracted from the history that formed him, Amin's violence might just appear as a personal eccentricity or even an expression of a native African trait. This is of course not to excuse Amin, but to make the general point that, abstracted from its social history, the violence that is rampant in many parts of Africa might begin to appear to some as either "natural" or just another of those "African cultural traits." Such intellectually simplistic and lazy characterizations help to engender negative stereotypes of Africans and are behind the misuse or value laden words like "tribalism."

Accordingly, my exercise of remembering Idi Amin is meant to be an invitation and indication as to the type of inquiry that needs to be done in relation to the major epochs of Africa's history: to events like colonialism, apartheid, and slavery. It is a similar process of inquiry that needs to be invoked in relation to such key figures within Africa's history, such as Mwanga, Captain Lugard, Jomo Kenyatta, and King Leopold. In this connection, "Where is Captain Lugard" might be an interesting starting point for an exploration into the culture of militarism in Uganda, more specifically into a conversation about the conflict in northern Uganda.[20]

Thus, the task of memory is not only crucial—it is an urgent requirement. It is a particularly urgent task given the current modes of social ethics, most of which involve a calculated forgetfulness of the past and a naïve optimism and invitation to "move on." The point I am making is simple. In the face of Africa's distressing social and economic crises, social ethics has moved in a rather predictable fashion. It usually begins by depicting the situation: of civil unrest, poverty, refugees, warring factions, dictatorships, refugees, and so forth, and then proceeds to offer suggestions and recommendations on what Africans need (ought) to do to overcome those crises. Interesting as many of these recommendations are, they give an impression that Africans will be able to overcome these problems if they can bring themselves to think more clearly, become more spiritual, learn the right ethical principles, adopt the relevant economical policies, and/or choose the right political system. In this respect, Africa abounds with many technical advisors and "experts" who administer the nicely pre-packaged prescriptions from the IMF, World Bank, or other donor agencies. All of them promise a solution to Africa's problem in the manner: "What Africa needs (ought) to do is . . . ." In the face of these recommendations, ethics increasingly looks like just another prescription. Perhaps this is what explains the recent interest and explosion in the number of centers and institutes of ethics across Africa. All of them are meant to empower Africans with the relevant ethical principles which, once applied correctly, are meant to save Africa from its current social and political crises.

The problem, of course, is not simply that many of these prescriptions make no reference to previous prescriptions, programs and histories. They leave the reality of "Africa, Uganda, and Africans"—the subjects for whom the prescriptions are meant—unexplored in terms of the specific memories that make "Africa" and "Africans" the way they are. In other words, by not making a serious attempt to connect the present to Africa's past through the notion of social memory, the prescriptions ironically encourage a certain form of forgetfulness and an unwillingness to confront the imagination and memory that is embodied within the present. But to the extent that this is a memory of violence, then such memory remains a loaded gun that goes off ever so frequently.

That is one reason why terms like "postcolonial" and "post-apartheid" can be misleadingly deceptive, especially when many people uncritically adopt these terms as a good description of our situation. What is deceptive about these terms is that they often involve a naïve optimism of having moved on from the bad past (colonialism, apartheid), and are now living within a new dispensation: "a new South Africa." To be sure, there might be a lot that is new within the postcolonial or postapartheid establishment, but if there is no serious effort to confront the stories and imaginations that sustained the colonial or apartheid establishments, it is often the same imagination which will live on, even as the external formalities change. But since the memory of colonialism and apartheid is a memory of violence, perhaps it is not surprising that quite often violence becomes an ever-present performance in the so-called postcolonial and postapartheid societies.[21]

The point I am making—simply put—is that social ethics in Africa has tended to be overly prescriptive and not sufficiently descriptive. The ethical challenge of memory is, in the first place, one of narrative, which is to say, one of providing thick accounts of Africa in general, and of different African societies and communities—Zaire, Uganda, and South Africa and so on—in order to display the distinctive imaginations and memories that sustain these societies. Only once such a narrative task has been engaged can it become clear as to the sort of persons or communities we have become, given the history we embody. Only then can we begin to realize that the more urgent social and theological challenge might be one of *unlearning* particular memories associated with the histories, be it the history of colonialism, Amin, apartheid, or AIDS.

In other words, providing thick accounts of the memories that have shaped us and with which we live is only the first step in the overall ethical task of memory. An even far more demanding aspect of the same challenge is *unlearning* some of those memories, so as to allow ourselves to be formed by different habits—habits more conducive to the pursuit of happiness, peace, and the common good. I do, of course, realize that this way of putting the issue is misleading, since it might give an impression that we first unlearn one set of habits and then learn a new set of habits. This, however, is not how it happens in real life. Take the example of falling in and out of love. Quite often one does not first lose interest in the person they love, and then fall in love with another person. The reverse often happens. When one falls in love with a new person, they begin to realize that they do not have the same love and commitment to their original love as they once had.

That is why, for people committed to one another, a decision they must constantly make involves not allowing themselves, to the extent they are able to, to fall in love with someone else. At any rate, unlearning particular memories proceeds along similar lines. It requires the existence of, and in fact familiarity or coming in contact with, other practices and habits which are grounded in alternative memories, and therefore form alternative possibilities and visions of life.

It is for this reason that I see a high theological stake in the task of memory, or to put it differently, why I think the task of memory is specifically a task for Christian social ethics. For Christians are not only invited to be a people of memory; their lives are shaped around and by concrete geographies of memories, which engender particular habits, visions, and expectations. Two such geographies of memory for the Christian are scripture and the Eucharist. Let me explain.

Christians are invited to be a people of memory. Among other things this means that to be a Christian is to be able to locate one's life within the ongoing drama of God's action in the world, through Israel and through the Church. In other words, to be a people of memory for Christians is to remember that they are who they have become in the present because of what God has done, and the promises God has realized in the lives of others who have gone before them. That is why Scripture is central to Christian life to the extent it makes available the stories and events that have shaped lives of those who have long gone before, but whose part the Christians have become. Thus, to be a Christian is to be part of a community of memory, a community that includes people like Abraham, Moses, Jeremiah, Jesus, Peter, Paul . . . all the people whose stories scripture recounts. Accordingly, by reading and listening to scripture, Christians not only remember the stories of God in relation to these many witnesses, they learn to stand within the same imagination as the one that formed Abraham, Isaac, Moses, Isaiah, Jeremiah, Jesus, and Paul. And as they do, they are shaped by the same visions, expectations, faith, hope, and habits of faithful living as the biblical characters. In this way they can claim that they honestly know and indeed worship the same God of Abraham, Isaac, Moses, Jeremiah, and Jesus.

It is therefore misleading to think about the Bible simply as a moral guide: a holy book that is consulted for guidelines of what is right and what is wrong. No doubt one does find in the Bible a number of insights, principles, recommendations, and even explicit commandments for moral living. However, these moral guidelines contained in the Bible must be seen as the outer boundaries that shape and form our memory (more like boundaries that cannot be crossed if we have to remember the story rightly). In other words, their purpose, just like the whole of Scripture, is to shape our current habits and expectations in such a way that they "fit" within the memory and imagination that Scripture unfolds.[22] And so, to abstract these guidelines from the story of the community and of the lives whose memory it continues to shape is to misleadingly turn the Bible into a magical source of salvation or manual for personal sanctification. It is more accurate to view the Bible as a concrete geography of memory, and the reading of scripture as an opportunity to constructively engage the memory that shapes the Christian life.

The Eucharist is another key geography of memory within Christian life. For while Christians are invited to be a people of memory, they are specifically invited to locate their lives within what the German theologian John Baptist Metz has accurately termed "the dangerous memory of Jesus Christ."[23] What Metz means is that the memory of the death and resurrection of Christ is the very identity of Christians. The community of men and women followers of Christ, in the beginning as in the present, is formed on the basis of calling to mind the life, passion, and death of Jesus Christ, and of the experience of salvation that burst forth in the resurrection as the promise of the final and eschatological liberation for all. This memory of Jesus is a dangerous memory because it constantly assaults the present with its unfulfilled demands, with its repressed conflicts and open wounds; calls it into question, and opens up possibilities and a new future of reconciliation and hope. Such hope and future of forgiveness and self-sacrificing love cannot but appear dangerous to a world that is accustomed to living with fear and the pursuit of self-interest.

But it is exactly this dangerous memory that Christians are engaging when they celebrate the Eucharist. As they celebrate the Eucharist, Christians are invited not only to remember Jesus' life, death, and resurrection ("Do this in remembrance of me"), but to be the bearers of a particular memory—of forgiveness and the self-sacrificing love of their Savior. Moreover, it is this memory of forgiveness and self-sacrificing love that grounds all their hope. It allows them to face the past without fear, and to envision the future with hope. In other words, through the memory that the Eucharist shapes, Christians can afford to remember the past with all its violence, betrayal, and pain, because they realize that as they remember the story of God's love, they are in turn remembered by the very same forgiving and reconciling love of God. Their being remembered is nothing but their being made into members of a new community—a transformed community of forgiven sinners.

What this means in relation to Amin and his memory, is that by making the story of God's self-sacrificing love and forgiveness central to their lives, and allowing it to shape their view of the world and their responses in it, Christians turn their energy and vision to the formation of communities that reflect and embody this memory. It is these Christian communities, living in and by the Eucharistic praxis, that become the nucleus of a new future of a transformed society in which the memory of violence begins to give way to a practices of peace and reconciliation. Again within these communities, Christians are set forth onto a journey (of baptism) that involves gradual transformation through the practices of hope and courage. It is through such a journey that the practices of hope, friendship, and happiness begin to take root where once a culture of violence, of individual survival, and of superficial and instant thrill once prevailed.

Notes

[1] On ironic humor as a way to survive Amin's dictatorship and violence see Kevin Ward, "The Church of Uganda Amidst Conflict," in Twaddle and Hansen, *Religion and Politics in East Africa*, (London: James Curry, 1995), cited at Paul Gifford, *African Christianity: Its Public Role* (Bloomington, IN: Replica Books, 1998), p. 119.

[2] Adam Hoschild, *King Leopold's Ghost. A Story of Greed, Terror, and Heroism in Colonial Africa* (Boston: Houghton Mifflin, 1998).

[3] It would be interesting and productive, even though this is not the time, to explore the connections between Idi Amin and King Leopold, especially the fact that Amin's rise to power is somehow connected to his being implicated in the looting and sale of ivory and gold from the Congo. On this and other related details of Amin's rise to power see P. A. Olok-Apire, *Amin's Rise to Power: The Inside Story* (London: Lawrence and Hill, 1983). In terms of the challenge of memory I am exploring here, what is significant to note is that these and other connections place Amin firmly in the same history and imagination as King Leopold. Accordingly, Amin's rise to power as well as his exercise of it cannot be understood without reference to the story embodied and advanced by King Leopold: namely, the story of colonial violence and dispossession. In fact, I shall be arguing that given Amin's role as a soldier in the King's African Rifles, he serves as a crucial link between Uganda's colonial past and the post-independence history of Uganda. As a crucial link and midpoint within this history, Amin both helped to display and perpetuate the violence embodied within this history.

[4] Hoschild, *King Leopold's Ghost*, p.304.

[5] *Ibid.*, p. 304.

[6] Michela Wrong, *In the Footsteps of Mr. Kurtz: Living on the Brink of Disaster in Mobutu's Congo* (New York: Harper Collins, 2001).

[7] Greg Jones, "Geographies of Memories," *Christian Century*, (August 30– September 6, 2000), p. 874. Overall, I find Jones' recovery of the significance of memory for Christian reflection as well as his insistence on the concrete forms memory takes within the Christian tradition quite helpful and essential to a theological discussion of memory. See particularly his *Embodying Forgiveness: A Theological Analysis* (Grand Rapids: Eerdmans, 1995), and his "Healing the Wounds of Memory," *Journal of Theology* 103 (Summer 1999), pp. 35–51.

[8] Nicole Simopoulos, "David's Kingdom: The Congo's Inferno. An Examination of Power from the Underside of History," *Bulletin for Contextual Theology in Southern Africa and Africa.* 4/3 (1979), pp. 9–25.

[9] *Ibid.*, p.13.

[10] Tony Avirgan and Martha Honey, *War in Uganda: The Legacy of Idi Amin.* (Westport, CT: Lawrence Hill and Co., 1982), p. 3.

[11] A comparison between Amin and the character of Kurtz in Conrad's *The Heart of Darkness* could prove very instructive, even though such an analysis lies beyond the scope of this paper. I suspect, however, that Amin's brutality, especially the rumors about the decapitated heads that were discovered stashed away in a freezer in Amin's house, fanciful as these rumors might be, indicate that Amin and Kurtz (at least in the popular imagination) are connected into the same imagination and narrative of colonial violence and terror.

[12] Avirgan and Honey, *War in Uganda*, p. 72.

[13] Henry Kyemba. *A State of Blood. The Inside Story of Idi Amin* (New York: Ace Books, 1977), pp. 152–158.

[14] Terry Dowdall, "Psychological Aspects of the Truth and Reconciliation Commission," in *To Remember and to Heal*, ed. Russel Botman and Robin Peterson (Cape Town: Human and Rousseau, 1996), pp. 31–32.

[15] See Louise Pirouet, "Religion in Uganda under Amin," *Journal of Religion in Africa* 11 (1980), pp. 13–29 (p. 16). What Pirouet's analysis also helps to make clear is the fact that although Amin might have been responsible for radicalizing and thus making explicit violence as a way of political control, its roots precede Amin and its expression was already somehow evident in the erosion of civil liberties before Amin's coup.

[16] On the crisis involving Bishop Cyprian Bamwoze, the Anglican bishop of Busoga, see Gifford, *African Christianity: Its Public Role* (Bloomington, IN: 1995), pp. 124–130. The Kannungu cult saga provides another obvious example. See *The Kanungu Cult-Saga: Suicide, Murder or Salvation*, ed. Kabazzi-Kisirinnya, Nkurunziza Deusdedit and Gerard Banura (Kampala: Makerere University, 2002). For my reflection on the same see Chapter Six, in this volume, "Kannungu and the Movement for the Restoration of the Ten Commandments of God in Uganda. A Challenge for Christian Social Imagination."

[17] With the popularization of terms like *muzungu wange* (white benefactor), one begins to suspect, and rightly so, that the *mafuta mingi*, to the extend that they embodied a life of effortless success, were attempting to appropriate for themselves, and thus imitate the assumed effortless ease of the *muzungu* (i.e., the life style of the white,

colonial officer). In other words, the *mafuta mingi* were the very memory of the colonial exploitation they were supposed to overturn through Amin's Economical War.

[18] Asians were first brought to East Africa in the 1930s from her Asian colonies by Britain to help in the construction of East African railway. With the Independence, while many opted to become British citizens, a number became citizens of the independent countries of East Africa, even as these were part of the British Commonwealth. Even though the sizeable Asian community fared well economically and were thus the backbone of much of the local economies of the newly independent countries of East Africa (setting up businesses, plantations, and factories), racially they were never fully integrated into the African communities. Most of the time they kept to their own group, often perceiving themselves as a buffer between the racial hierarchy of Africans and Europeans.

[19] Peter Kanyandago makes a similar point by drawing a distinction between, on the one hand, history, which tends to emphasize the "diachronic dimension in human affairs by looking at events as spaced out in the past," and on the other hand, anthropology, "which talks about culture in synchronic terms, looking at it as it is at a given moment." His intention in making this distinction is to invite us to move beyond mere history into the area of "anthropological history" to underscore the fact that what happens in the past is relayed into the present through policies and traditions of different kinds. In this connection, Kanyandago argues, the past is not dead, but erupts and exists in the present. "The way we deal with each other, and the way we perceive others influences our and their behavior negatively or positively. For example, the tendency among Africans to cower before white people is not inborn, but a result of the socialization and internalization of violence against African cultures and people." What happened in the past (history) is observable and has effects in the present." Kanyandago Peter, "Anthropological History and Interpreting African History and Culture," unpublished paper, p. 5.

[20] A highly informative resource on the origins of the conflict in northern Uganda is Heike Beherend, *Alice Lakwena and the Holy Spirits: War in Northern Uganda, 1986–1997* (Kampala: Fountain Publishers, 1999).

[21] Frantz Fanon captures this fact very well when he notes that since the colonial establishment is built on violence, it both requires and begets violence, which comes to be ingrained into the colonized imagination as a way of life. That is why, Fanon argues, even long after the colonial regime has packed off, violence remains one of the characteristic marks of the so-called postcolonial society. This is also one reason Fanon notes that the last war of the colonies will not be a war of the colonized and the colonizer, but of the colonized against the colonized (See Frantz Fanon, *The Wretched of the Earth*, trans. Constance Farrington (New York: Grove, 1968).

[22] My reflections on the role of Scripture in shaping Christian memory as well as on the overall significance of memory within Christian life owes a great deal to the work of Stanley Hauerwas. See particularly his "The Moral Authority of Scripture. The Politics and Ethics of Remembering," in *A Community of Character Toward a Constructive Christian Social Ethics* (Notre Dame: University of Notre Dame Press, 1981), pp. 53–71.

[23] See Alberto Moreira, "The Dangerous Memory of Jesus Christ in a Post-Traditional Society," in *Concilium* 4 (1999): *Faith in a Society of Instant Gratification*.

CHAPTER TWO

AIDS, CONDOMIZATION, AND CHRISTIAN ETHICS

INTRODUCTION

Quite often, theological and ethical discussions concerning HIV/AIDS in Africa are too narrowly focused on sex or condom use. Not that AIDS has nothing to do with either sex or the condom. It has everything to do with both, particularly in Africa, where over 95% of all AIDS infections are sex related, and where we are witnessing an unprecedented promotion of the condom as the only way to slow down the further spread of the disease. What, therefore, makes the usual ethical discussions on AIDS narrow is not simply the fact that they are about sex and the condom, but the fact that they usually end in discussions concerning the morality of "protected" sex, or, in other words, the right or wrong of condom use. Individuals (couples) wanting to make sure they do the right thing, as well as institutions seeking to work out an institutional position on this matter, often appeal to their priests or theologians for guidance.

However, given the narrow scope of the discussions, any attempt to bring theology into the picture generally ends in frustration. The introduction of theology often polarizes the discussions into two theological camps, with "liberals" on the one side, and "conservatives" on the other. While liberals tend to look at the advantages of the condom in halting the spread of AIDS (and often cite the recent "scientific" and WHO statistics in support of their position), conservatives seem to be stuck with moralistic statements about the will of God regarding the ends of sexual union. An extremist view within this conservative camp might even read into the spread of AIDS on the continent a clear sign of God's punishment on a society that has failed to heed his commands regarding sex and marriage. Within this extremely frustrating and boring discussion there seems to be no middle ground, which leaves the theological field not only polarized and confused, but also without any meaningful way in which we can talk theologically about AIDS in Africa.

What is particularly misleading about theological discussions relating to AIDS in Africa is the failure to realize that both liberals and conservatives share the same narrow view of ethics as primarily a prescriptive discipline, whose objective is to set guidelines for what is right or wrong, good or bad, acceptable or unacceptable by society in general, and communities or groups of individuals in particular. Their disagreement is only about whether such considerations should be based on "utilitarian" considerations of the benefits of the action, or on religious considerations of the "revealed" will of God.

Even though ethics and theology should no doubt contribute to a clarification of what is right and wrong, of what should be done or avoided, there is need to invoke a wider notion of ethics as a total vision of life. This means that beyond deciding on what is right or wrong, ethical discussions are meant to help us understand ourselves and the sort of people we become as we make particular decisions and choices, even as these are a response to the crises, anxieties, and tensions within our everyday life struggles. For it is not just the direct choices and decisions that people make or fail to make that form people into particular sorts of individuals. Rather, our anxieties, expectations, and the fears we bear, and the strategies we adopt to negotiate particular challenges in life all contribute to shape our vision of ourselves, others, and the world. In essence, they all contribute to making us the sort of people we are. But if this is so, then the task of ethics is not simply prescriptive, but more determinedly descriptive or narrative. This is not just in the plain sense of telling stories, but in the critical sense of offering interpretive frameworks and descriptions that help us to understand and critically assess the sort of people we are becoming as we live with and try to negotiate the challenges we face, such as, in this case, the AIDS pandemic.

The argument I develop in this paper is fairly simple, For the last 20 years or so we the people of Africa have increasingly come under an AIDS blanket. The statistics continue to give an alarming picture: 25 million Africans already infected, and the numbers are expected to rise to over 35 million by the year 2003.[1] Given the magnitude of the crisis, it looks as if, to date, everybody in Africa is already either infected or affected by AIDS. Individually and socially we have tried to comprehend its magnitude as well as its uncertain origins and modes of transmission. We have tried to absorb its fear and cope with its deadly seriousness by adopting certain strategies and policies. However, beyond these observable negotiations, something far more enduring is happening to us. We are *becoming different people*, assuming a different social and individual character or identity. Such a transformation is marked not only by a shift in our understanding of sex and marriage, but also in the way we look at ourselves, at others, and the very conception of what we consider important or meaningful in life. I suggest that ethical and theological discussions about AIDS should not only help us understand the sort of people we are becoming in the face of the AIDS pandemic; they must also provide alternative symbols, images, and practices to those currently available. Otherwise these discussions become sterile and detached from the real suffering experienced by the subjects of discourse.

More specifically, I argue that one of the most distracting effects of the AIDS blanket over Africa is that it is succeeding in turning suspicion into a cultural pattern of life. This, to me, is going to be one of the most lasting legacies of the AIDS pandemic in Africa. Long after AIDS has been wiped off the face of the globe, we shall find ourselves struggling to cope with the self-destructive nihilism and cynicism generated by the AIDS pandemic. I developed this argument in four sections.

First, I show how the AIDS epidemic has pushed the negative characterization of Africa in the eyes of the West to its worst extreme. This suspicion, however, is being reciprocated by Africans, who are increasingly questioning Western goals and intentions for Africa. I develop this argument in the second section by showing that, in the face of the uncertainties surrounding AIDS, the suspicion of the West, which in the past was limited to a small circle of African intellectuals, is increasingly becoming a cultural pattern for many Africans. While the egregious history of Western influence in Africa warrants a certain degree of suspicion toward Western intentions, suspicion, like cynicism, sooner or later turns on itself. I pick up this argument in the third section of the paper. Using the transformation of the understanding of sex as a paradigm, I show how the radical suspicion generated by AIDS gnaws at the very core of our self-understanding, and thus threatens the basic trust on which our individual and societal existence is based. In the final section I argue that the current spate of condomization is both an expression and an attempt to cope with, the despair and suspicion (now turned into cynicism) which AIDS underwrites. This, in effect, transforms all of us into free-floating postmodern individuals, lacking any serious commitments and attachments, but driven by forms of nihilistic playfulness. I conclude by pointing out some ethical and theological challenges.

AIDS, THE WEST, AND AFRICA
ANYTHING GOOD OUT OF AFRICA?

If the standard view of Africa within Western imagination has tended to associate Africa with "blackness," darkness, and barbarism, the AIDS pandemic has helped to push this negative characterization of both the continent and Africans to its radical extreme. With statistics showing that as many as 30% of the adult population of some countries may be infected, and with projected statistics showing an even grimmer picture, AIDS is increasingly becoming a defining characteristic of African countries.[2] But given what appears to be the long list of Africa's endless woes—floods, famine, poverty, disease, tribalism, political instability, bad leadership—AIDS seems to be the final straw that Afro pessimists needed to write off the continent.[3]

Given these alarming statistics, it not only appears that Africa is the center of the AIDS pandemic, but also that AIDS is largely an African *thing*. Unfortunately, the medical research establishment has a lot to do with this perception. Even though the first known incidents of AIDS in the early 1980s were among gay communities in Los Angeles, the scientific community was quick to "locate" the origin of the virus in the dense forests of Africa. Many variations of this story of the African origin of AIDS exist, with the most common one pointing to a "leap" of the virus from chimpanzees to the human community, through some kind of association.[4] While the validity of such a connection has been questioned, it is perhaps not surprising that even without sufficient basis for the claim, the scientific community was quick to trace the origin of AIDS to Africa. Such an association is quite consistent with the standard (Western) imagination concerning the supposedly licentious life of Africans.[5] Moreover, the African origin of AIDS fits in neatly with long-standing Western views and constructions of Africa as a "dark and savage" continent ravaged by wild animals, warfare, disease, and untamed barbaric instinct.

In the middle of the nineteenth century the German philosopher Hegel declared that Africa had no part in world history, thus exacerbating and raising this negative characterization to a respectable science or *episteme*. According to Hegel, world history is the history of rational development. Africa, Hegel mythologized, is the "land of childhood which, lying beyond the day of self-conscious history," is devoid of any positive manifestation of history, culture, or Spirit, but remains tragically "enveloped in the dark mantle of the night."[6] Accordingly, whatever is good in Africa must be traced back to some "outside" or European influence: "Historical movement in it—that is, in its northern part—belongs to the Asiatic or European World."[7]

In the wake of this Hegelian perspective on Africa, European explorers, missionaries, and anthropologists would feel the need to "explain" or account for the various positive developments that they (not infrequently) stumbled upon on the African continent. As Valery Mudimbe notes, they simply assumed that:

> Since Africans could produce nothing of value, the tech-
> nique of Yoruba statuary must have come from Egyptians;
> Benin art must be a Portuguese creation; the architectural
> achievements of Zimbabwe was due to Arab technicians;
> and Hausa and Buganda statecraft were inventions of white
> invaders.[8]

Similarly, European explorers and historians could not imagine that such a good thing as cereal crop agriculture could be original to sub Saharan Africa. Instead, they reasoned it must be "the product of human migration or some form of culture diffusion or stimulus deriving from south west Asia."[9] And as late as the 1930s European anthropologists, historians, and scientists were busy assembling theories to explain the Tutsis in central Africa in terms of an "outside" origin: as Black Aryans; as Hamites or "Jews of Africa"; as descendants of ancient Egyptians; as coming from either Melanesia or Asia Minor—in any case as *unAfrican*: "their intelligent and delicate appearance, their love of money, their capacity to adapt to any situation—all seem to indicate a Semitic origin."[10]

If the Western sciences have always felt a need to account for the good on the African continent in terms of an outside (i.e., Western influence), they have also been quick to trace deadly viruses and diseases to Africa. It is, in fact, within this "politics" of knowledge that one must understand why it comes naturally to assume the African origin of not just of AIDS, but of Ebola, meningitis, and the West Nile virus.

The overall effect of this long tradition of suspicion and negative characterization has been one of stigmatization of the continent and of Africans generally. The stigmatization has been further complicated by the recent decision of the U.S. State Department to add AIDS to the list of national security threats (the other two major threats being drugs and terrorism). Such a decision, I am sure, will have far reaching consequences in the way Africans are viewed and treated in the United States.[11] To the extent that AIDS is still viewed largely as an African thing, it is Africa and Africans that are being "constructed" (and targeted?) as a threat to the U.S. national security. They are, accordingly, immediately suspected to be the carriers, not of drugs or terrorist weapons and bombs, but of the deadly AIDS virus.

SALVATION FROM THE WEST?
QUESTIONING WESTERN INTENTIONS FOR AFRICA

1. An Intellectual Suspicion

Africans have not accepted Western prejudices, constructions, or suspicions of Africa without question. At least in African intellectual circles, there has always been a lurking suspicion that the descriptions and categories employed by the West in talking about Africa are misleading at best, and outright racist at worst. For instance, in the work already cited, the Congolese scholar Valery Mudimbe[12] has argued that the standard Western view of Africa as a "dark," pagan, primitive, savage, or undeveloped continent is a construction: an "invention" by the Enlightenment-inspired disciplines of knowledge, whose motivation is the need to confirm the identity of the West as a Christian, developed, and civilized continent.[13] Mudimbe's work is finding more echoes in the growing circle of postliberal, postmodern, or postcolonial African scholars. The result is that more African voices are adding their chorus to the questioning of what have hitherto passed as objective claims of the Western disciplines of theology, philosophy, anthropology, sociology, and even science itself. The overall effect of these postcolonial moves has been to make people more aware that beneath the various disciplines of the academe lie specific Western interests and designs through which the West continues to colonize the economic, political, and intellectual heritage of non-Western societies in general and Africa in particular.

But it would be misleading to read (and therefore dismiss) this intellectual suspicion simply as an inconsequential fad accompanying the popularization of postcolonial studies. The suspicion has been marginal, nevertheless a long-standing element within African intellectual circles. In these circles, there has always been a degree of mistrust not simply of the human sciences, but of Western-inspired ideals of civilization, enlightenment, progress, and even of Christianity. As early as 1887 the West Indian-born Liberian citizen, Edward Wilmot Blyden, raised doubts about Christianity and education—the two pillars of Western philanthropy—and their effect on Africa. Writing against the background of racism in America, Blyden noted the debilitating effects of Western education on the African. The intelligent Negro child, Blyden wrote:

> *revolts against the descriptions given in elementary books —geographies, travels, histories—of the Negro; but though he experiences an instinctive revulsion from these caricatures and misrepresentations, he is obliged to continue, as he grows in years, to study such pernicious teachings; After leaving school, he finds the same things in newspapers, in reviews, in novels, in quasi scientific works; and after a while—saepe cadendo—they begin to seem to him the proper things to say and to feel about his race.*[14]

But it is not only Western education and its purported benefits for the Africans that Blyden questioned. He was equally disturbed by what he saw as the "innumerable woes which have attended the African race for the last three hundred years in Christian lands."[15] Blyden wrote: "Very few among races alien to the European believe in the genuineness of the Christianity of the white man."[16] Blyden was accordingly concerned that the Western desire to teach Christianity to the Negro could have the same effect as education: leading to the demoralization of the African, to the erosion of his self-confidence, and to instilling a sense of inferiority and self-hatred.[17]

Almost eighty years later, the late Ugandan poet and playwright, Okot p'Bitek, noted the same effect of alienation and self-hatred, which he portrayed through the tragic character of Ocol.[18] A product of Western "civilization," Ocol has learned to despise everything African and sees no value in the traditions of his people. When his illiterate wife Lawino pleads with him, showing him the futility of cutting oneself loose from the traditions of one's ancestors, Ocol responds with dismissive arrogance:

> *Africa*
> *What is Africa to me?*
> *Blackness*
> *Deep, deep fathomless Darkness . . .*
> *Mother, Mother, why was I born black?*[19]

And, just like Blyden, p'Bitek suspects that the source of Ocol's alienation and self-hatred is somehow connected to "the shyness you ate in the church,"[20] but more so to Western education. For, as Lawino laments, it is in the classroom that all "our young men were finished . . . their testicles smashed with large books."[21]

To be sure, there have been other African scholars who have similarly questioned the effect of Western institutions on the African, and Western intentions towards Africa in general.[22] On the whole, however, genuine as the concerns generally are, this limited group of African scholars have not been able to exercise any significant persuasive power within intellectual circles, and have accordingly been unable to effect any marked cultural patterns. On the contrary, given the hegemony which Western intellectual disciplines and ideals of civilization have generally enjoyed, the limited group of African scholars who questioned these disciplines have often enough been easily dismissed, both by the West and their African counterparts in orthodoxy, as either eccentric, extreme, Marxist, or disfranchised scholars. This meant that, for the rest, the average African continued to have a quasi-religious faith and trust in Western intellectual disciplines of theology, anthropology, philosophy, sociology, and science, as well as Western institutions, ideals, and overall goodwill for Africa. After all, the education system, the social and economic infrastructure, as well as the humanitarian and religious interventions on the continent, all seemed to depend on this trust and conviction that, if Africa did as the West said, Africans would see themselves and their societies transformed into civilized, Christian, or developed nations.

2. Elements of a Growing Cultural Suspicion

With the coming of AIDS, however, this picture is rapidly changing, particularly since a lot of unanswered questions still remain concerning the origin, determination, status, and possible causes of HIV/AIDS. Concerning the origin of HIV/AIDS, for instance, I have already noted how standard scientific opinion has focused on Africa. This "orthodox" view has, however, become increasingly controversial even within the scientific community, with a number of "dissident" scientists showing that the evidence concerning the African origin of AIDS is at best clumsy and inconclusive—at worst mere science fiction motivated by racist ideologies.[23] Coming from a different angle, President Thabo Mbeki of South Africa has complicated the scenario by raising doubts about the determination of HIV/AIDS in Africa, which so narrowly focuses on "viral infection" and overlooks the wider economic, political, and general health conditions in Africa. To be sure, Mbeki's views on AIDS have caused a bit of a stir in the political and scientific establishment beyond South Africa. Unfortunately, Mbeki's views have not led to the required rethinking of AIDS which he is calling for, but have instead simply been dismissed by the medical establishment as "irresponsible" utterances by a leader who should be more worried that his country has one of the highest incidences of AIDS. It is, in fact, with a similar attitude that "orthodox" science has dismissed any further questions (by "dissident" scientists) relating to the origin or determination of HIV/AIDS as "mere idle speculation," whose effect is to distract from the more urgent challenge of controlling the spread of the AIDS!

Call it whatever you wish, the "idle speculation" has not only gone on, it has greatly captured the imagination of many Africans who are hardest hit by the AIDS epidemic. The speculation involves many possibilities. Could it be that HIV/AIDS was the unintended result of some vaccination experiments in Africa that got out of hand? Might it have been the result of some scientific conspiracy, some kind of germ warfare against unsuspecting Africans? For some, even the coincidence between homosexuals, drug addicts, and Africans (the groups, which together with Hippies and Jews make the "hate" list of Hitler's Nazi machinery) as the groups most affected by HIV/AIDS lends itself to high speculation.

One may dismiss these suspicions as unfounded, unscientific, and nothing but "idle speculation." But that is to miss the real point—namely, that the suspicions are, at the core, suspicions about science itself and its claimed objectivity, and about the goals and overall goodwill of the West towards Africa. Viewed in this manner, the speculation is a clear indication of the extent to which the uncertainties about

HIV/AIDS are pushing suspicion of the West by Africans to new extremes, and releasing into the general culture what used to be the preserve of a limited group of intellectuals. As an example of the growing suspicion, consider the following two cases.

First: the 1994 UN Cairo Conference on Population and Development. In the discussions preceding and following this conference, a number of ordinary Africans become distrustful of the main premises (and intentions) on which the conference was based—namely, that the poverty of the so-called Third World, and of Africa in particular, was due in great part to the growing population (high fertility rates) of Africans. If these countries could limit the size of their families, so it was argued, the income of the families and the general development of the Third World would be assured. In short, the U.S.-led coalition of Western or "developed" countries sought to empower women in the "developing" countries with "reproductive rights," which would allow them the right to determine (control) the number of children they produced. If the Third World in general "resisted" the drift of this conference, it was not just because of the force of Islamic and Catholic fundamentalism (the two groups most often accused of sabotaging the conference), but because a number of Africans rightly suspected that the conference was an attempt by the West to avoid confronting issues of economic justice in a global economy unfairly skewed to the advantage of the North. In other words, like Mbeki's call not to de-economize or depoliticize the issues related to AIDS, the very notion of population growth requires a wider historical, political, and economic context for it to become meaningful.

The second, and even more obvious, indication of the mood of widespread suspicion of Western intentions for Africa can be seen in the 1997–1999 UNO and WHO sponsored campaign to "Kick Polio Off the Face of Globe." The campaign involved free and compulsory immunization of all children under the age of three. I personally was amazed to see a number of mothers in Uganda (I suspect that was true in a number of other African countries) stubbornly refusing to take their children for the free vaccination. As a result, a number of mothers were prepared to face government penalties, including imprisonment, for their subversive "lack of cooperation." Behind such explicit resistance by which many mothers intentionally hid their children away from vaccination centers, one can detect a distrust of not just Western (UNO, WHO) inspired vaccinations, but of the "generosity"of Western humanitarian concern in general. For, to many African mothers, it was not clear why polio would receive so much funding and publicity, particularly because polio was not, by their reckoning, a big threat to the health of their babies, certainly not as big a threat as measles or malaria.

Perhaps without explicitly saying so, many were wondering what the effect would have been if similar goodwill, attention, and funding were to be directed to the control of malaria, or measles, the provision of clean drinking water, the improvement of nutrition, and sanitation. Was the isolation of polio just a case of misplaced priorities, or were some other sinister motives behind the campaign against polio? In the wake of suspicions associated with the AIDS pandemic, these are not mere idle speculations, but concrete indications of how the distrust of Western science—of the intentions of Western humanitarian intervention on the one hand, and on the other, the overall goodwill of the West toward Africa—has been pushed to its extreme. I suspect that this distrust will become even more widespread as a result of increasing marginalization of the rural poor in the wake of economic globalization.

SEX, AIDS, AND SUSPICION
ON LOVING "CAREFULLY"

It might well be that as human beings we need a certain measure of suspicion as part of the practical wisdom of everyday life and human interaction. The challenge, of course, is to ensure that such suspicion is kept within moral bounds, or as Aristotle would say, the challenge is to make sure that the suspicion remains part of an enduring disposition or character, which forms and directs the suspicion to the right object and in the right measure. Cut loose from these moral moorings, suspicion easily turns into cynicism, which is nothing but the self-justifying and chronic distrust—not just of the good intentions of others, but of one's own intentions. I think the suspicions associated with HIV/AIDS have already passed through this transformation, and are therefore no longer limited to the mutual suspicion between the West and Africa. Consequently, suspicion has come to characterize each and every one of our dispositions and relationships. That the suspicion has already turned inward, threatening to undermine the basis and fabric of social existence in Africa, is evident from the change in the way in which we have come to think about sex and to manage sexual relations in the face of AIDS.

Human societies in general, and interpersonal interactions in particular, are all founded on the key virtue of trust. No human act provides for a more radical realization and expression of this feeling of trust than the sexual act. For even though pop culture tends to promote and fantasize about sex in biological terms, like the "body," "functioning," and "technique," sex is at its core a "spiritual" event: the communication of love and total trust between partners. In that naked embrace called love-making, what is communicated between partners includes not just sparks and fluids, but the helplessness of surrender, total self-giving, and total trust. There in lies both the depth and vulnerability of conjugal friendship or love, which makes marriage not just a community based on trust, but the epitome of all human communities.

With the AIDS pandemic, such total trust has increasingly become strained. Today there is much talk about "protected" sex, particularly warnings about the dangers of "unprotected" sex. What is perhaps not realized is the fact that this way of looking at sex represents just a final stage in the working out of suspicion at the heart of this basic and yet noble form of human interaction. One can see the transformation reflected on the billboards bearing anti-AIDS slogans and messages intended to warn the general public of the dangers of AIDS. Here, Uganda might prove a helpful case in point as one of the countries which has, from the start, opted for an open policy in its awareness campaigns, as well as in the policies to fight against the further spread of AIDS. Already by the mid-1980s there were a number of billboards and posters in many parts of the country warning against the spread of HIV infection. The posters carried the picture of what was obviously a married couple with their three young children, and bore the caption: "Love Faithfully. Avoid AIDS." By the early 1990s the Uganda AIDS Commission had replaced most of these posters with what were deemed to be more appropriate posters: a picture of two young lovers in embrace, with the caption: "Love Carefully." What the Uganda AIDS Commission might not have realized, but what in fact it was confirming, was the realization that with AIDS even lovers could not trust each other faithfully, but must instead learn the art of loving "carefully," that is, suspiciously. Apparently it did not take a long time to realize that such "careful" love involves regarding the partner as a potential danger from which one had to "protect" oneself. Thus, by the mid-1990s the caption had changed once again, this time from "Love Carefully" to "Use a Condom to Avoid AIDS." "Love" had completely dropped out of the picture, as the ultimate symbol (and message) of sex came to be increasingly identified with that seductively misleading piece of rubber: the "protector" condom. Good sex, so it seems, is "protected" sex!

What, of course, becomes evident here is the fact that the changes in pictures and captions in the anti-AIDS drive are not simply about the adoption of new and perhaps more adequate strategies to fight AIDS. Rather the changes reflect an ongoing (de)evaluation of the depth of the trust and commitment necessary to sustain sexual relations. Viewed in this manner, the "protector" condom is both an expression and a way of managing the radical suspicion that has already inserted itself at the core of this most intimate of human relationships. To be sure, there seems to be much more at stake in the aggressive way in which condom use—as a way to save Africa from the of AIDS pandemic—is promoted. But, as I have argued elsewhere, the overall effect of this spate of condomization has been to make the condom one of the most available cultural symbols of postmodern Africa. As a cultural symbol, its subliminal message is clear: the other is a potential danger against whom you need protection. You cannot afford to trust anyone! Moreover, because the condom is one of the most popular cultural symbols, it underwrites the belief that Africans are obsessed with sex.

I think it is only a matter of time before such suspicion, as well as the art of learning not to trust anyone, which it calls into being, becomes self-destructive. One who is unwilling to trust anyone sooner or later discovers that one cannot even cannot trust oneself. It is here that the "protector" plays a double role: as the ultimate expression of the suspicion we live with in the wake of the AIDS pandemic, and also as a way of coping with that suspicion now turned into cynicism and despair.

CYNICISM AND DESPAIR
CONDOMIZATION AS NIHILISTIC PLAYFULNESS

One cannot meaningfully talk about AIDS/HIV in Africa without drawing attention to the social, material, political, and ideological conditions in which Africans live. In fact, any attempt to isolate AIDS from this wider context and simply reduce the issue to one of a "viral infection" is not only misleading, it is an ideological trap whose effect is to perpetuate the myth of Africans as incurably promiscuous. This in turn provides a self-justifying promotion for condomization as the only way to curb the spread of the disease. Accordingly, the prevalence of AIDS in Africa is part of a "package" in which malnutrition, the lack of basic health and hygienic conditions, unemployment, political instability, and material poverty form the infrastructure of life for many Africans. In other words, the prevalence of AIDS in Africa is perhaps not surprising, since the disease is ravaging an exhausted population. Writing about life in Mobutu's Zaire, Michela Wrong notes the extent of the "exhaustion" we are talking about here. She describes how the distressing conditions of life in Zaire provided a sort of existence in which ordinary Zaireans were reduced to a "permanent state of 'Low Batt,' surviving rather than living—ticking over without ever flaring into life."[24] Unfortunately, her words ring true for many Africans in other countries, a fact confirmed by Manthia Diawara's even more apt description of life in postindependence Guinea. Here, as in most other African countries, the social, material, and political contradictions and frustrations underwrite a cultural pattern of despair and cynicism for which the "deflated" is a type:

> [They] constitute a race unto themselves. I do not mean the unemployed. A deflated person is someone beyond good and evil, beyond feeling the blues of unemployment. He has reached a point where he says to himself, "They don't need me because I don't know how to do anything. They don't know me. They don't see me." . . . He knows that no matter what he does, he will not get anywhere. The statistics are against him: he will die young. He sits down and looks to see if people see him. He sees from the others' gaze that he is transparent. He does not know how to do anything, and he does not want to do anything.[25]

I am suggesting that it is against such a background of distressing conditions of life in Africa that the prevalence of AIDS makes sense. What often may not be realized, however, is that the way in which the constant production and assembling of statistics showing the widespread of AIDS in Africa—all constantly thrown into the face of a people for whom survival has become their chief and perhaps only project—has the effect of generating yet more despair and cynicism: "Everybody is sick. I am sick. I shall die young." There is something like a circular movement of a double take involved here. First, the alarming statistics not only confirm, but also somehow create the sense of desperation.

Secondly, within this context of despair, condomization becomes not just a strategy to fight against the further spread of AIDS, but a way of coping with the despair and cynicism already upon us. To a person for whom the possibility or hope for accomplishing any long-term goals in life has been lost, perhaps the only thing left is the pursuit of whatever satisfaction one can salvage out of life, however, risky and ephemeral the satisfaction might be. It is in this context that one must understand both the appeal and misleading facade of condomization in Africa.

The way to understand the "politics" driving the current spate of condomization in Africa is not simply in terms of the claimed benefits of condom use in halting the spread of AIDS, but rather in terms of the culture which such a practice both discloses and promotes. For instance, one reason why condomization seems to be successful in Africa has to do with a key appeal of the condom: its disposable nature. Such disposability, which makes the condom another item of the same consumer culture as *Coca-Cola* cans, disposable diapers, and throwaway razors, fits in quite well with a postmodern culture of endless "progress" without any stable or permanent base. For disposability, not simply of goods, but of relationships and particular attachments of any kind, seems to be the hallmark of postmodern society. If this is the case, then condomization is not just about the convenience of disposable condoms, but more importantly, it is about the popularization of a certain form of sexual activity, one detached from any serious attachment or stable commitment. In other words, condomization encourages one to view both sex and one's sex partner(s) as essentially disposable, and at the same time to realize, as one *Radio Uganda* commercial promoting a brand of condoms declares, "this feels so good!" While it is one thing to live in a world where there are no serious or stable commitments and where relationships and partners are disposable, to think that this is a good thing too (one that feels so good) is the ultimate sign of despair.

That is one reason why condomization seems to reflect and promote a form of nihilistic playfulness. No doubt sex always involves a certain "play." The sort of playfulness condomization promotes, however, is one detached not only from any stable relationship, but from any meaningful social, material, or economic life goals. Abstracted from *any* context and lacking any real justification except perhaps that "it feels good," the playfulness becomes it own end. Accordingly the popularization of such playfulness bears witness to an underlying culture of despair and nihilism which has learned to vent its frustration through forms of superficial "feeling good" playfulness.

THE THEOLOGICAL AND ETHICAL CHALLENGE

If my analysis is correct, then the theological and ethical challenges that face us are enormous. The challenges are far more demanding than making decision about the "ethics" (right or wrong) of condom use. The challenge involves the need to confront and provide an alternative to the cynicism and playful nihilism generated or exacerbated by the AIDS blanket over Africa. It is therefore at this level of culture, especially the present culture of "deflation" and despair, that all ethical and theological discussions need to focus. Moreover, if the current spate of condomization is an indication of the extent to which suspicion, cynicism, and despair mark the life of many Africans, then there can be no greater challenge than the construction of a counter-narrative and counter-practices through which Africans can regain a sense of hope and self-worth. This, of course, is easier said than done. And so, in order to face this challenge, the churches in Africa will find that they will need to adopt a number of new priorities and strategies. Let me, in broad strokes, point to the direction in which theological practice and reflection needs to move if we are to face this challenge.

More than anything else, the AIDS challenge calls for a revision in the way in which the church understands herself and her mission. The church needs to change from being a moral and spiritual umpire, to engendering a practice of cultural empowerment. Among other things, this means that the church begins to see herself in terms of providing not so much "spiritual" guidance and consolation, but a new culture through which Christians see themselves and relate to the world. Accordingly, in the context of Africa, cultural empowerment does not simply mean the retrieval and affirmation of African traditional culture (although this is indeed a part of it). It is also about the provision of alternative cultural symbols and images to displace the present power that AIDS seems to hold over Africa. This is not to deny the reality or seriousness of AIDS, but it is to realize that by allowing condomization to become the key cultural image for our time, we have allowed AIDS to become the major grid through which others define us, and through which we in turn see ourselves and others. As Christians we cannot allow this to happen, particularly since, as I have argued, this is a story which simply draws us ever more increasingly into a cycle of

cynicism, despair, and playful nihilism. Condomization cannot therefore save us. In fact, as Acts 4:12 reminds us, there is no other name
through which we can be saved but the name of Jesus. That is why the
call for cultural empowerment involves in the first place an attempt to
reclaim the story of the death and resurrection of Christ as the primary
grid through which we narrate our existence.

Similarly, it is important to realize that this story of the gospel does
in fact provide rich images, symbols, and practices which are, in
essence, credible alternatives to condomization. One such practice is
the Eucharist. For if condomization, as has been shown, bears witness
to despair and cynicism which tends to form us into individuals without any serious commitments or attachments, the Eucharist exercises a
force in the opposite direction. It bespeaks commitment and love (even
in the face of betrayal), of despair turned into hope, and of fear transformed into strength. And all these take place within the space of
everyday activities and realities: of bread and wine. It is therefore at
the Eucharist that our first resistance to the drift into cynicism is
sparked, while at the same time the building-up of a new community
of hope and its empowerment is effected. If, as African Christians, we
can dare to see the Eucharist as an everyday event, indeed the paradigm of all everyday events, then we can begin to feel its dynamism as
it recharges the rest of everyday events into "High Batt."[26] Then the
seeds of a new culture will already have become obvious.

Notes

[1] http://www.avert.org/worlstatinfo.htm.

[2] According to UNAIDS Report of December 2000, the most affected countries are:
Botswana 35%; Zimbabwe 25%; Swaziland 25%; South Africa 19%; Kenya 13%;
Cote d'Ivoire, 11 %. See also http://www.avert.org/subaadults.htm.

[3] See e.g., "The Hopeless Continent" in the *Economist* (May 13–19, 2000): 17, 22, 24,
45.

[4] See http://www.avert.org/origins.htm; http:// www.avert.org/his81_86.htm.

[5] The belief that Africans are incurably sexually promiscuous is a myth. As Kanyan-
dago notes, "apart from the fact that the first European Christian missionaries in Africa
held this belief, there is absolutely no scientific evidence for this view. Peter
Kanyandago, "The Role of Culture, Poverty, Eradication," in the *Challenge of
Eradicating Poverty in the World: An African Response*. Eds. Carabine and Reilly
(Nkozi: Uganda Martyrs University Press, 1998), 119–152. On the contrary,
Americans lead the world as far as changing sexual partners is concerned. They are
followed by France, Australia, and Germany. South Africa, like Thailand, is well back
in the middle of the sex league. . . . But there is, of course, a long Christian tradition
of fantasizing about the supposedly licentious life of Africans.'" C. Fiala, *Dirty Tricks:*

How the WHO Gels its AIDS Figures, (New African), 36–38. Africans forced into the slave trade and brought to the Americas also were victimized by the same myth. African women, in particular, were viewed as sexual seductresses that somehow enraptured the innocent white slaveholders. This explanation conveniently allowed white slaveholders to be held blameless for the rape of slaves. This supposed sexual prowess of African-American males also has its genesis in this same myth. See Kelly Brown Douglas' *Sexuality and the Black Church: A Womanist Perspective* (Maryknoll, NY: Orbis Books, 1999).

[6] G.W.F. Hegel, *Lectures on Philosophy of History* (New York: Dover, 1956), 91–93.

[7] *Ibid.*, 99.

[8] Valery Mudimbe, *The Invention of Africa: Gnosis, Philosophy, and the Order of Knowledge* (Bloomington, IN: Indiana University Press, 1988), 13.

[9] *Ibid.*, 99.

[10] Gerard Prunier, *The Rwanda Crisis 1959-1994: History of a Genocide* (Kampala: Fountain, 1995), 7–8 and Fergel Keane, *Season of Blood: A Rwandan Journey* (London: Penguin, 1966).

[11] I am not sure how this decision will, in the long run, affect race relations in America. An immediate effect for immigrants and those seeking asylum is a mandatory HIV test.

[12] Valery Mudimbe, *The Invention of Africa: Gnosis, Philosophy, and the Order of Knowledge* (Bloomington, IN: Indiana University Press, 1988), and *The Idea of Africa* (Bloomington, IN: Indiana University Press).

[13] Coming from a slightly different angle, McGrane makes the same point by noting how it is within this politics of identity that one has to understand the discipline of anthropology, particularly its fascination with "primitive" cultures and societies. Given this fascination, anthropology, McGrane argues, operates like a kind of "terrestrial science fiction," whose overall effect has been to maintain belief in the existence of exotic and alien others. Bernard McGrane, *Beyond Anthropology: Society and the Other.* (New York: Columbia University Press, 1998).

[14] Edward W. Blyden, *Christianity, Islam, and the Negro Race, Edition 2* (New York: Black Classics Press, 1998), p. 88.

[15] *Ibid.*

[16] *Ibid.*, as cited by Valery Mudimbe in *The Invention of Africa*, 126.

[17] Blyden's view and relation to Christianity would remain ambivalent. While he was aware that Christianity could contribute to the regeneration of Africa, he did not wish to include in his program for liberal education those "theories—theological, social, and political—(which) were invented for the degradation and proscription of the Negro . . . ." However, in the "religious work of the college, the Bible will be our textbook, the Bible without note or comment." Edward W. Blyden, *Christianity, Islam, and the Negro Race*, Edition 2. (New York: Black Classics Press, 1998), p. 103.

[18] Okot P'Bitek, *Song of Lawino and Song of Ocol.* (London: East African Writers Series, 1994).

[19] *Ibid.*, 125–126.

[20] *Ibid.*, 118.

[21] *Ibid.*, 117.

[22] The Senegalese scholar Cheikh Anta Diop was a key influence in this critical direction, as his work provided new light on African history—a history that, under the ban-

ner of European enlightenment, was summarily dismissed as non-existent. See eg.,
Checkh Anta Diop's *Nations Negres et Culture* (1955), *The Cultural Unity of Negro
Africa* (1959), the *African Origin of Civilization: Myth or Reality* (1974).

[23] Richard & Rosalind Chirumuuta, *AIDS, Africa, and Racism* (London: Free
Association Press, 1989), and Edward Hooper, *The River: A Journey to the Source of
HIV and AIDS*, (NY: Little Brown, 1989).

[24] Michela Wrong, *In the Footsteps of Mr. Kurtz: Living on the Brink of Disaster in
Mbotu's Congo.* (New York: Harper Collins, 2001) 134.

[25] Manthia Diawara, *In Search of Africa*, (Cambridge, MA: Harvard University Press,
1998), 50–51.

[26] Michela Wrong, 134.

CHAPTER THREE

SEPTEMBER 11TH
"WHY DO THEY HATE US SO MUCH?"

A joke is told about a report at an international meeting at which there was a concern regarding food shortage in the rest of the world. The report was circulated among delegates from Africa, Europe, and America, all of whom found it confusing. The African delegation looked at the report and said, "Food? What is food"? The European delegation wanted to know the meaning of shortage. "The American delegation returned the report to the secretariat with a note: "Could someone please explain the phrase "rest of the world'!"

INTRODUCTION

I t is so nice to be back at Molloy.[1] I thank my wonderful colleague and friend Mike Russo, the Center for Ethics and Society, and the administration of Molloy College for inviting me to address you on this day, exactly five months after September 11th. Many people, a great many of them "experts" in one field or other, have attempted to disentangle the reality, reasons, and implications behind the terrorist attacks on New York and Washington. The more I have read and listened to these explanations, the more I have come to realize how *complex* the events of September 11th are. Even more complex is the world we must now live in and try to shape into a more hopeful future following the terrorist attacks on September 11th.

I underline "complex" because we must be careful so as not to be tempted by the clarity of simple explanations regarding September 11th. Perhaps I should say at the start that I do not intend to provide an explanation or a theory for September 11th. All I would like to do is to initiate a conversation about the event by offering brief remarks about the challenges I see emerging out of September 11th. I am, of course, aware that my biography and status as a nonresident alien in this country make me a rather awkward partner in the conversation—a sort of outsider on the inside. What I am about to say, therefore, may sound to some as nothing more than the fragmented and incoherent ramblings of an African tribesman, who does not fully understand the intricate logic of geopolitical and economic realities.

But that itself might be a good thing. For perhaps more than ever, no greater ethical and theological challenge faces us in the wake of the terrorist attacks than to listen to the strangers in our midst. It is they, the strangers, that might help us to take the much-needed critical introspection into the practices and identities we embody, and which many times we just take for granted. Only when we do are we able to recognize the extent to which our lives, and indeed our quest for meaning and well-being, are located within a network of global connections and relations. Thus, without attending to these connections, the frustration, pain, and suffering of September 11th, as well as the hope for a future world free of terrorism simply cannot make sense. That is why I have come to realize that in the wake of September 11th, there is perhaps no greater ethical and theological challenge than the cultivation of a global imagination.

My awareness of this challenge, as well as its urgency as it relates to September 11th, has been sharpened by two related and yet somehow contradictory events or impulses. First, there was the event of September 11th itself, particularly the experience of global solidarity and the human connection that was felt that day. Secondly, there are the attempts to explain this event, and my increasing frustration by the way in which these attempts to explain September 11th obscure the experiences of global solidarity, and connectedness. Let me explain.

GLOBAL SOLIDARITY

One of the most impressive aspects of September 11th was the global solidarity that it evoked. It was deeply touching to see the solidarity and spontaneous outpouring of empathy and support for the victims, their families, and Americans in general following the terrorist attacks on New York and Washington. This show of solidarity came not only from within America, but from all corners of the world, including traditional "enemies" of America (like Cuba and Libya) and far-flung countries like my own: Uganda.

In this spontaneous show of solidarity, there was something of a deep human connection that transcended ethnic, national, and geographical boundaries. For a brief period of time following the terrorist attacks on New York and Washington, it did not seem to matter whether one was white or black; Democrat or Republican; American, European, or African. We were all united in the anguish, shock, and anxiety that was unleashed by the terrorist attacks. This is the sort of global imagination that I have in mind: an imagination that is able to draw us into a deep human embrace of solidarity—one that is able to cut across any national, geographical, or racial boundaries.

I must also note that for someone from Africa, the reason I found myself immediately connecting with Americans in a way much deeper than I had before, could be that the experience of pain, vulnerability, anxiety, suffering, and tragedy was the same experience that I have so many times had to experienced in Africa. It could therefore be that for many people in the so-called Third World, the spontaneous show of solidarity and empathy was not only borne of this human connection, but also by the fact that in that moment of vulnerability, they felt that America was part of their world and they were part of America's world.

For this is not always the case. In fact, the impression of many, at least in the so-called Third World, is that the world of America is different from "our world." But that is also how many Americans feel, since many times America tends to maintain aloofness from the rest of the world. As the Harvard professor Stephen Walt has noted, America's involvement in the world is often characterized by a "Muhammad Ali syndrome." Ever since the end of the Cold War, Walt notes, the United States has used its great wealth and influence to insulate itself from the troubles of the world. "They wanted to be strong but hover above the rest of the world. Their model was Muhammad Ali: float like a butterfly; sting like a bee—and then fly away."[2]

But if September 11th, as I have noted, seems to have reconnected America to the world, the rhetoric and official explanations that have since followed have increasingly drawn America back into to a pre-September 11th "Muhammad Ali syndrome." Most of the rhetoric and explanations have focused on trying to unravel the motives behind the attacks. The guiding question in this attempt has been the same question that I have been asked to address tonight: namely, "Why do they hate us?" In what follows, I will show how this question has given rise to a poor conversation and suggest ways to move beyond it so as to be able to appreciate the need for and respond to the challenges of a global imagination.

THE RELIGIOUS CONNECTION: THE SUFFERING OF JOB

I have found the book of Job to be a very interesting starting point, and a helpful grid through which to articulate the challenges of a global imagination for a post-September 11th America. I do not know what drew me to the book of Job in the first place. It could have been the theme of God's blessing on the one hand and Job's undeserved suffering on the other. However, the more I reflected on Job's situation, the more I saw the parallels between Job's and America's situation following the terrorist attacks. And the more I explored these connections and parallels, the more I was clearly able to realize the challenge and need for the cultivation of a global imagination in the wake of the terrorist attacks.

The story of Job is the story of an innocent man who suffered terrible and undeserved suffering. The story opens by noting that Job was a God-fearing man who was greatly blessed by God, and as a result "was greater than any man in the East" (Job 1:3). Among his blessings: seven sons and three daughters, seven thousand sheep, three thousand camels, five hundred yoke of oxen, five hundred she-asses, and a great number of work animals.

The parallel between Job and America may not be difficult to see here. For even though there may not be many outside of America who still believe that America is a God-fearing country, no one doubts America's current status as a superpower, and how, in the mind of many, this status confirms God's special blessings on America. It was therefore impressive to watch, in the wake of September 11th, the fervor with which Americans took to the churches and other places of worship in order to pray for God's protection and at the same time affirm God's special blessings. At many of these services, songs like "America the Beautiful" and "God Bless America"—songs that either affirm or ask God's special blessings to America—formed a central part of worship on that day and after. In fact, that many "naturally" took to the churches and other places of worship in the wake of the attacks may reveal yet another parallel with Job: namely, the continued trust in God's providence in the face of suffering. Even though Job is greatly tested when he loses all his wealth and family, he does not lose faith in God. He instead turns to God in complete surrender and affirmation of God's will: "Naked I came from my mother's womb," he says. "Naked I shall return. The Lord gave; the Lord has taken away. Blessed be the name of Lord" (Job 1:21).

However, the more interesting and by far the more productive parallel between Job and a post-September 11th America has to do with the question which has been the focus of many discussions: namely, "Why do they hate us so much?" A similar question is at the heart of the book of Job. In fact, the great bulk of the story of Job (3–37) is a series of speeches between Job and his three friends as they search for an explanation for Job's suffering. While Job's wife and three friends suggest that Job has sinned and his suffering is in line with God's justice, Job on his part insists that he is innocent. What, however, makes Job a model of patience and religious submission for many is the fact that although he pleads with God to take away his suffering, God doesn't even reveal to Job the reasons for it or the purpose it serves.

This sounds like a very fair and reasonable request by Job. It therefore comes as a surprise to learn that God not only refuses to provide any explanation to Job, but is extremely angered by Job's search for one. Thus, when God finally comes to answer Job (out of the whirlwind) his anger is undisguised: "Who is this obscuring my intentions with his ignorant words?" God asks. "Brace yourself, for now I will speak . . ." (Job 38: 1–3). I have always found it strange and surprising that God would respond to Job with such indignant fury. After all, Job was not even asking God to heal him, but only that He (it is definitely a He God here) may make known His plans to his friend Job.

I have now come to realize that what triggers God's indignation is not so much Job's search for an explanation, but the tone and drift that the "conversation" between Job and his friend has been taking. *It is all about Job.* This indeed, as the opening lines of Job suggests, is the story of Job. Job is an upright man; Job is blessed by God; Job loses everything; Job remains firm; Job is inflicted by pain; and Job's friends explain to Job the reasons for Job's suffering. Job insists that he (Job) is innocent; he (Job) only wishes God would reveal God's plan to him (Job) and explain why he (Job)—the just and God-fearing man—is suffering.

Looked at from this angle, the "conversation" between Job and his friends turns out to be nothing but a monologue—a very long (over 36 chapters) and extremely boring monologue—in which Job is both subject and object. What is therefore instructive is that when God finally speaks (38–41), His speech is not really an answer to Job but a series of questions about creation and different creatures—questions that really have no apparent or direct bearing to Job's current plight. "Where were you," God asks Job, "when I founded the earth?"

> *Who determined its size, do you know?*
> *And who shut within doors the sea,*
> *when it burst forth from the womb?*
> *Have you ever in your lifetime commanded the morning*
> *and shown the dawn its place?*
> *Which is the way to the dwelling place of light,*
> *and where is the abode of darkness?*
> *Has the rain a father?*
> *Can you raise your voice among the clouds?*
> *Do you hunt the prey for the lioness?*
> *Do you know about the birth of the mountain goats?*
> *Who gives the wild ass his freedom? (Job 38–39)*

And so many other similar questions in the same vain. To be sure, this barrage of questions that God confronts Job with seem unfair, especially to a man that is facing issues of life and death. As far as Job and his friends are concerned it is Job's life and God's justice that are on the line. This is what God must clarify. But this is what God fails to do. Instead, God responds by asking Job about such things as wild donkeys and mountain goats: things that apparently have nothing to do with Job's predicament. Can you not just hear Job screaming back to God, "Who cares about mountain goats and stupid wild asses? You tell me why I am going through such undeserved suffering. Then, perhaps then, we can talk about the rain and donkeys and lionesses!"

Job however does not scream back. He does not because he realizes that the questions God asks are not the sort of questions that require an answer. They are instead God's way of telling Job and his friends to shut up—to snap out if it, so to say. Job recognizes this and he accordingly capitulates, "I have been speaking without knowledge; I have uttered what I did not understand: marvels which are beyond me. I retract what I have said, and repent in dust and ashes" (Job 42:1–6).

But God's questions are therapeutic for Job in more than one way. First, I have noted, they interrupt the boring and unproductive monologue between Job and his friends. Secondly, and as a result of the interruption, they draw Job's imagination away from himself and lead him to realize that he (Job) is not the center of the universe. In fact, Job's life cannot make sense unless it is placed within the wider context of wild donkeys and mountain goats! But that means that Job and his friends must even given up their cherished language of justice and begin to see that Job's life is bound up with the life of mountain goats and wild donkeys in ways that go beyond the claims of "justice"— human or divine.

The final section of the book of Job (42: 7–17) depicts a humbled and silenced Job—one more attentive to the global connection between all God's creation, who is blessed even more abundantly than ever before. To put it differently, only when Job has been drawn into a new vision of life, a critical and attentive global imagination, does his life become genuinely and abundantly blessed.

THE MONOLOGUE OF SEPTEMBER 11TH: WHY DO THEY HATE US SO MUCH?

In many ways America faces the same challenge as Job. Following the terrorist attacks, the question that has been asked over and over again has been, "Why do they hate us?" What, however, has been disappointing is the fact that far from providing a much-needed discussion about the world in which we live, the question has generated a very unfruitful, misleading, and boring monologue. Both the way the question has been posed and the answers that have been provided, it is all about America and Americans. American experts and opinion leaders ask the question, and they supply the answers to fellow Americans. The effect is that anyone genuinely interested in the discussion is not only left with a very unclear sense of who the "they" (in "why do they hate us?") are, one is offered even less insight into how a constructive engagement or conversation with the "them" might look. On the contrary, the "conversation" about "Why do they hate us?" just reproduces and confirms to Americans the usual assumptions that Americans have of themselves and their country.

That is why the very nature of the question, "Why do they hate us?" reflects a surprise, for many Americans believe that America is the most generous nation and that a great deal of American taxpayers' money is spent by the government assisting people in the outside world. Thus many are surprised that the people they have been so good to ("we saved the Russians from Communism; we saved Afghanistan from Russia; we saved Somalia from starving . . .") can carry out such malicious acts. To be sure, Americans are generous people, but it is not true that the government spends a great deal of their taxes assisting people in the outside world. On the contrary, America's global out-reach in terms of overseas assistance ranks miserably below that of most developed nations (See Appendixes 1 and 2).

Also, many Americans believe that people everywhere want to live like the Americans. This feeling is based on the assumption that global (liberal) capitalism is the only way of organizing a modern econo-my; it represents the hope and promise of all nations. Within this assumption, all societies are bound, sooner or later, to converge on the same liberal capitalistic values and views of the world; that religious, cultural, and historical differences are only peripheral, destined to dis-appear or shrink into the private sphere. Thus, the illusion is sustained that since the American economic and political system represent the highest form of liberal, capitalist, social organization, everybody would like to live either in America or like the Americans. Thus again the surprise, "Why do they hate us?"

A look at the answers is also revealing. For, given the assumptions above, the only conceivable explanation to the question "Why do they hate us?" is to see anybody's hatred of America as utterly incompre-hensible, their acts unimaginable, and their motivations senseless. Thus the terrorist acts cannot but be the acts of "madmen," of "evil" men (part of the axis of evil) or of fundamentalists.[3] In other words, the terrorists cannot but be fanatics who are either "envious of our free-dom," misled by their religious traditions, or are simply perverted indi-viduals such as Osama bin Laden.[4]

Whereas there might be some truth in each of these explanations their real effect is to make Americans feel good about themselves, since the explanations all come to this: "our success is the object of attack by envious fanatics." In this way, the explanations for September 11th, not unlike Job's search for an explanation to his suf-fering, simply generate into a monologue by America about America and the assumed success and goodwill of America. The media has been crucial in both shaping and reflecting the monologue back to us—in its coverage of September 11th and its aftermath. As always, CNN provid-ed a good lead in explaining what was at stake through its headlines: "America Under Attack" "America Fights Back"; "America Recovers"; "America Wins!"

I can therefore think of no greater and more urgent ethical challenge in the wake of September 11th, than the need to interrupt this dangerous, boring, and unproductive monologue, whose real effect is to drown out any meaningful conversation about the nature and challenges of terrorism. In fact, just as the answer to Job's suffering lay partly in Job learning to see connections between his life and the life of mountain goats, I would like to suggest that we can only begin to make sense of September 11th by making connections between this event and other human tragedies that affect those who might be the equivalent of the mountain goats of our time.

THE LIFE OF MOUNTAIN GOATS

What kind of conversation, therefore, can locate September 11th within the violence and tragedy that is part of the world today? For starters, it is important that even as one recognizes the uniqueness of this date, violence and tragedy did not enter the world on September 11th. On September 10th for instance:

- 30 thousand children died from hunger-related causes and preventable diseases; 30 thousand died on September 11th, and September 12th, and every day since then.
- Malaria alone kills one million people each year; 75% of these are children under 5.
- Almost 2 million people died of AIDS in Africa alone in 2001.
- Close to a million Rwandans died in the genocide in 1994.
- Land mines continue to maim over 26,000 people every year; that is 500 per week, 71 per day.

My aim in bringing these facts into focus is not to take away the sinister uniqueness of the terrorist attacks on the World Trade Center and Pentagon. Neither do I thereby intend to offer any explanation for these attacks. All I intend to do is locate September 11th within a global context of suffering, and connect it to the lives of "mountain goats." Doing so at least allows us to see and rightly name the innocent people who died in the attacks as *victims* (not heroes) of a tragedy. It is this acknowledgement of tragedy that allows a deeper understanding of human life and calls for all sorts of affective connections and response to other forms of pain and suffering in the world. We must therefore resist the attempt to singularize September 11th and thus create a distance between the innocent victims of New York and the Pentagon (by terming them heroes) from other victims throughout the world who are caught in tragedies and suffering not of their own making or choosing.

Similarly, any constructive conversation on the events of that day cannot isolate the terrorist attacks from the despair, violence, and death that is increasingly becoming a way of life for millions of people. A look at some statistics might prove shocking.

- 23% of world's population lives on less than $1 a day.
- 56% of world's population lives on less than $2 a day.
- The 4 richest people in the world are richer than the 40 poorest countries in the world.
- If the world population were shrunk in a village of 100 people, 6 would possess 59% of the entire world's wealth; all 6 would be Americans.
- The average per capita income in the USA is $36,000; in Uganda it is $350; Afghanistan: $320 (No doubt statistics such as these do hide the deep inequalities that exist within America or any other country). A Congressional Budget Office Study indicated that in 1988 the top 5% of American families received almost as much income as the bottom 60%. The top 10% receives roughly the same as the bottom 70%; 1% at the top had more money than the 40% at the bottom.
- Larry King (of CNN) is paid close to 7 million (base salary); 56 million including stock options (*News and Observer*, Monday, January 21, 2002).
- Over the last 10 years the average life span in the USA has risen to 77 (2001 estimate: 74 men; 80 women). Over the same period, the life span in many developing countries has plummeted. In Afghanistan it currently stands at 46 (men), 45 (women); Uganda: 42.59 men, 44.17 women. (Estimates indicate that in many African countries it will continue to fall to an average of 33 by the year 2021).
- In 1990 the GDP (Gross Domestic Product) of Zaire, for instance, (thanks in great part to Mobutu and the American CIA support that brought him to and kept him in power for over 25 years) was less than the daily intake of the giant American retailer, Wal-Mart.

- Over the last Christmas season, the wrapping paper industry alone registered over $3 billion of revenue from sales.

- In many parts of the Third World, families travel an average of 0.5 mile to find water (really a substance that barely looks like water). The cost of digging a well for a village of 120 people is roughly $5,000.

- In the war against terrorism currently going on in Afghanistan, one cruise missile costs close to $1 million.

- President Bush has asked Congress for 48 billion dollars for increased defense spending in the coming year to fight global terrorism. The justification: the need for more smart bombs, space-sensors, and smart tanks. Of course, given the USA GDP (9.9 trillion) 48 billion may sound like small change, but that is more than the GDP of Uganda (26.2 billion) and Afghanistan (21 billion) combined!

Locating September 11th against the background of these and similar facts is not intended to provide any "explanation" for the terrorist attacks. Nevertheless, doing so illuminates a number of things.

First, given these distressing facts, it is clear that while there has been much confidence about the "global economy" and the "American way of life" which liberal capitalism makes possible, the same global economic forces are responsible for trapping millions in a life of desperate and hopeless existence. It is therefore not an exaggeration to say that in many parts of the so-called Third World, death itself is increasingly becoming a way of life.[5]

Secondly, once such distressing facts are brought into the picture, it becomes possible to see the terrorist attacks as a kind of symbolic warfare in which it is not really America and Americans who are under attack. For, as Tom Brokaw and others have noted, the towers were not just any buildings, they were "symbols of American capitalism."[6] If this is the case, then one might begin to see in the attacks on New York and Washington as somehow an attack on the imagination that shapes the economic and military institutions of our world. This does not mean that the attacks are therefore justified. But against the background of the statistics above, one might see the attacks as the desperate cry of a people who want a different world than the world represented by the current global economic systems.

Thirdly, against this background, one begins to realize that it is not only a fringe of Islamic extremists who want a different world than the current world shaped by global capitalism. It is not just people in the Third World who want a different world. Millions of Americans and Europeans want a different world. The many protests and demonstrations against different forums and meetings for globalization bear witness to this fact. Mass demonstrations and protest were held in Seattle (World Trade Organization: November 30–December 3, 2000); in Genoa, Italy (G8: July 2001); in New York (World Economic Council: January 31–February 4, 2002); in Porto Alegre, Brazil (World Social Forum: January 2001 and January 2002); in Santiago, Chile (People's Forum: 1998); and again in Quebec City in 2001. In essence all, these protests and demonstrations seem to be a cry—a desperate, but defiant cry against a runaway global economic system, and a call for a different world: a different economic imagination.

Fourthly, that is why what is at stake here cannot be adequately characterized as "hate"[7]—a hatred of America or of "our values." Rather, what is required is to take more seriously the global connections of human solidarity, and to explore both the ethical and theological challenges of globalization. To be more concrete: September 11th is not just an attack on economic globalization, it shows the full effect of globalization. For within the world that globalization makes possible, *Coca-Cola*, *McDonald's*, and the Internet have become as much a Third World reality as they are American products. Similarly, the hopelessness, despair, and frustration that marks the lives of many in the so-called Third World can no longer be seen as "their problem."

The same globalizing forces that make *Coca-Cola* a Third World reality inevitably make "*their* many ways of dying" our own, too. But this is what makes the ethical challenge, to use the language of Job, one of realizing that a flourishing "American way of life" cannot be lived in isolation from the life and fate of numerous mountain goats. More importantly, this leads to the realization that the relationship between the American way of life and the life of everyone else is far more complex than the language of "our interests" and "hatred" suggests.[8] That is why, if we have to face the ethical and theological challenges in the wake of terrorism, then we must learn to recognize and resist clear but unhelpful recommendations for a way forward, as those, for instance, provided by President George W. Bush. Let me explain.

EITHER YOU ARE WITH US OR WITH THE TERRORISTS

In responding to the September 11th attacks, President George W. Bush declared an American-led "war on terrorism." In doing so, he offered the world a very clear choice: "either you are with us, or with the terrorists." While it is true that the world needs to weigh in on an effort to fight (in fact to prevent) terrorism, it is the stark option that I find disturbing. I am worried that "terrorism" will now become the primary or perhaps the only prism through which the world will be viewed. This means that just like Communism in the last century, terrorism will easily become the dominant form of social imagination through which America's view of the world is shaped but even more importantly, through which America's passions and involvement in the world will be mobilized. I am particularly concerned that the stark choice ("either with us or against us") will lead to a view of the world that is neatly divided up between those who are for us, and those who are against us: between those who "love us" and those who "hate us."

Moreover, with these stark options, it means that the rest of the world does not have any agenda of its own, except to support or work against America. Frankly, I am not sure why my mother should understand her life from these narrowly conceived alternatives. And yet I am afraid that this is what it is going to come to. For since the "war on terrorism" was declared, countries, particularly poor ones, have been tripping over themselves in a desperate attempt to appear to be on America's side. In Uganda, the leading papers have devoted large sections of the national news covering the war on terrorism—never mind that what appears in Uganda's *New Vision* for instance, is mostly a reproduction of the *Washington Post* or *New York Times* stories: "America Under Attach"—"America Fights Back"—or "The March to Kandahar."

It is also amazing to see the speed with which Uganda's Parliament, usually known for its sluggishness and inefficiency in debating and passing bills, is rapidly and effectively passing a number of anti-terrorist bills—all in a desperate attempt to appear to be on America's side. This seems to be no problem, except that, with poor countries all too keen to be on America's side, I am worried—and with reason—that my mother's concerns are in the process of being completely edited out of vision. Like many Africans, she has no safe, clean water; no health care system; no electricity.

That is why, from the point of view of the Third World, the war on terrorism and its stark choices bring back memories of the Cold War. During this time of America's war on Communism, the first question asked of any Third World leader was which side he was on: pro-East or pro-West? I cannot but also think of the number of African dictators that were sustained in power—Mobutu easily comes to mind—by the support of America and the West generally, just on the one merit that they were "allies" in the war on Communism.

Again as part of its "war on Communism," America openly supported such rebel groups like UNITA (against the MPLA in Angola) and RENAMO (in Mozambique) just because they were perceived to be fighting against Communist regimes. Many of these groups even openly employed "terrorist" methods, including the use of land mines to target civilians. The same case can be made about the American support for the Contras in Nicaragua and the Mujahedin in Afghanistan. All through this time, official America never saw the suffering of the Afghanistan people; or the people of Angola, or Mozambique, or Nicaragua: they were "collateral damage" in its war against Communism.[9] My fear is that today as well, in its war on terrorism, America may fail to see the lives of the Afghanistan people, or Iraqi people, or Angolan people, or even Pakistani people. They might just become collateral damage in whatever its current war happens to be.

It is therefore clear that the war on terrorism, as well as George W. Bush's so-called international coalition, does not represent a genuinely global response to terrorism, but merely the internationalization of America's foreign policy objectives. In fact, the war on terrorism may easily become America's new way of not seeing the real concerns and issues in the world. Even more pointedly, the war on terrorism threatens to leave the American people in the throngs of one dominant imagination of the world: namely, one shaped by the State Department, and one whose chief and perhaps only goal is to advance America's interests and power.

ON "GOING BACK TO SHOPPING"

That is why President Bush's call to the Americans to defy terrorism and "go back shopping" is even more dangerous than it appears to be on the surface. I am sure President Bush meant well to encourage American people to carry on with their lives in the aftermath of the terrorist attacks. It is the choice of "shopping" as an image for the

American way of life that is both unfortunate and yet telling. For while "shopping" might be good for the economy, it is not a practice that seems to encourage or foster the sort of global imagination that September 11th calls for. On the contrary, the invitation to "go back shopping" encourages people to become good consumers, which is to say, people without deep attachments or critical attentiveness to the wider events in the world. In other words, being good consumers encourages the sort of superficial, sensational, fragmented, and impersonal existence as depicted by Neil Postman. In *Amusing Ourselves to Death*, Postman describes a modern (postmodern?) world characterized by capitalistic sensibilities of the technological media and advanced capitalism—as a world of "trivial pursuit" and of an endless quest of satisfaction characterized by an "abundance of irrelevant information." It is a world that both distracts and entertains us; a kind of peek-a-boo world in which

> . . . *now this event, now that, pops into view for a moment, then vanishes again. It is a world without much coherence or sense; a world that does not ask us, indeed, does not permit us to do anything; a world that is like the child's game of peek-a-boo, entirely self-contained. But like peek-a-boo, it is also endlessly entertaining.*[10]

If Postman's description of our media-controlled world is true, as I suspect it is, then the invitation to "go back shopping" cannot but be a dangerous invitation for Americans to carry on "as usual" within this world. It is to encourage the same pre-September world in which the average American is uninformed and generally uninterested in the world beyond American borders. Within such an artificially insulated world, the State Department becomes the chief and perhaps only source of global imagination for most Americans. It defines for them what the world looks like, informs them who their friends and enemies are, and shapes and mobilizes their passions and pursuits in the world, all in a way that advances "American interests," which in this connection would be nothing but a promise for future uninterrupted shopping.

But this is what brings us right back to Job and his monologue. For with "shopping" as the most determinative aspect of the American way of life, we are thrown back into a "conversation" where it is all about "our economy," "our interests," and "our way of life." If we have to take the lesson of Job seriously, then the challenge is precisely to interrupt and move beyond the monologue of this illusory peek-a-boo world. And for this, we need a genuine conversation that will affirm the global connection between the well-being of Americans and the well-being of the mountain goats of our time.

CHRISTIANITY, CATHOLICITY, AND THE UNIVERSITY

I must proceed with caution, for I realize that the notion of "conversation" just as of "dialogue" can be very fashionable, and in our entertainment-centered world might simply lead to an "abundance of irrelevant information." That is why, for it not to be trivial, but ethically constructive, the conversation must be grounded in and sustained by concrete practices that both sustain and embody a substantive global imagination.

It is here that I locate the specific challenge and key role of institutions, especially those institutions that are founded on a Catholic ethos or imagination. I am particularly thinking of churches and Catholic universities. Since these institutions explicitly claim to be, and indeed are by their very mission "Catholic"—that is universal—then in the wake of September 11th the specific challenge is for these institutions to discover new ways and new practices of bearing and embodying this catholic (global) character.

I do not think that Christian churches in America, the Catholic Church in particular, have sufficiently realized what resources they have to interrupt the monologue of "Why do they hate us?" Part of the reason may be that churches have not understood their mission, existence, and way of life in terms of shaping alternative visions and imaginations of the world to those of the dominant culture. But this is exactly what Christian practice is meant to do. Take, for instance, a practice like prayer. The fact that Christians in Colorado and New York stand within the same imagination with Christians in Papua New Guinea, Honduras, Burundi, Chechnya, or Malube to pray to "Our Father in heaven . . ." does in itself already destabilize any neat or comfortable notions of "us" and "them." For with such a prayer it becomes clear that it is no longer mere geography, or race, or nationality that defines "us." In fact, praying to "Our Father" becomes both an invitation towards, and a commission to realize, a vision of community that is at once local and concrete, like the daily bread we need for our sustenance here and now; and at the same time to realize a community in which the "our" does not nicely correspond to the usual narrow vision of being American, African, or European.

The same is true for the Eucharist. The fact that Christians in all these places share the same cup and the one bread provides one of the greatest challenges to modern conceptions of individual consumption. It is also a concrete witness to a new sense of communion—*ecclesia*—at once local and global, that celebrates and is at the same time performed into existence by the one Body of Christ. It is therefore disappointing when, instead of becoming the site where this catholic imagination is exploded and lived out—into concrete commitments, partnerships and contacts between peoples, the practices of prayer and Eucharist—the churches simply become a party in the monologue that advances "our way of life." That is why, in a world where 23% of the members of the Body of Christ do not have basics like clean drinking water, I find the preoccupation with new carpets and new pews (or hitech baptismal fonts with thermostats to automatically regulate the temperature) of many Catholic churches in America to be quite disturbing, to say the least.

A similar challenge needs to be raised in relation to universities in general and Catholic universities in particular. For, on the whole, Catholic universities have not, in my opinion, provided much leadership in the cultivation of a global imagination in the wake of September 11th. If life stopped temporarily at many campuses on September 11th, many colleges are back to doing their American thing: competing for higher national and regional ranking; building up endowments; constructing bigger and more modern campuses; competing for the title of "most wired campus," and so on. Within this competition for excellence and profitability, subjects that might help in the cultivation of global awareness—such subjects like world geography, world history, and global concerns—increasingly lose out to more "productive" programs like business management and marketing. In this direction, we even witness a drive to recruit international students to these programs. The driving force behind this internationalization and globalization, however, is the "marketability and profitability" of "our programs." It is therefore not surprising that the admission office targets students in those places—China, Japan, and Europe—that can afford the costs of these programs.

The real challenge, however, is how to involve the so-called Third World within this conversation, or better: how to allow the Third World to challenge or interrupt this monologue of "American educa-

tion = profitability = marketability = success = more $$$." Given this
equation, the cultivation of gestures that can interrupt the monologue
is both crucial and necessary. Such gestures might include: a commit-
ment for scholarships for two students from Africa every year; estab-
lishing a rotating fellowship for a visiting scholar from the Third
World; providing funding to educate one or two students to go univer-
sity level in their own countries (and therefore costs less than a tenth
of what it takes to do so in America); or developing new partnerships
with colleges and universities in the so-called Third World and count-
less other creative possibilities. These are not gestures that make
money (in fact they lose money) for the university; they may not even
contribute to the marketability of the university and may not become
"profitable" in the long run. They are important and significant sim-
ply because they challenge us and train us to be a catholic university,
and thus a university outside the narrow confines of being an
"American" university.

To put the issue more positively, the challenge is one of reviving the
best values of both a liberal and Catholic education, especially as the
lead to the pursuit of happiness and fulfillment. I think it is in one of
your brochures that I saw this ad, which is meant to be a description of
what you are about here at Molloy. "What is a good life?" the ad ran.
"A better job, a stronger democracy, a more humane population, a
more aware society, a knowledge of the arts, a greater sense of moral-
ity. Liberal education leads to each of these. But none is its greatest
benefit. The ultimate reward of liberal education is understanding, and
its consequence: fulfillment."

I think by suggesting the search for fulfillment as one of your goals
already puts you on a very good start. For it should be the specific
challenge of any Catholic university to provide a richly textured con-
versation about the meaning of such elusive concepts as "happiness"
and "fulfillment." But even more importantly, in an education industry
that is so much driven by profitability and marketability, Catholic uni-
versities need to become spaces—wild spaces—where alternative
visions of fulfillment can be imagined and concretely lived out. In
doing so, these universities will not only be drawing on the deep roots
of their catholic ethos, they will seek to live out concretely what Job
realized—that true fulfillment is not a personal or parochial good that
assures my health, my job, or my security—but living with attentive-
ness to the global connection between God's creation and the provi-

dent Lordship of God, through which my well-being or suffering is connected to the well-being and plight of mountain goats and wild donkeys. This is fulfillment. It takes the cultivation of a global imagination to realize this, and even more importantly, to make it a reality. In the wake of September 11th, I find no more urgent, exciting, and challenging invitation than this.

Notes

[1] Public lecture hosted by the Center for Ethics and Society, Molloy College, Long Island, New York. February 11, 2002.

[2] *Newsweek*, December 31, 2001–January 7, 2002, pg. 92.

[3] See e.g., Patrick Ryan, "The Roots of Muslim Anger," (*America* November 26, 2001, p.14). Ryan traces Muslim fundamentalism to the frustration arising out of the historical failures of Islam—which is then exploited by powerful, but perverted leaders like Osama bin Laden.

[4] *Time* magazine has recently portrayed the terrorism as an indication a clash of civilizations: the West against Islam, liberalism against traditionalism (*Time*, December 10, 2001, p. 122).

[5] Zakes Mda's *Ways of Dying* (Oxford, 1995) is a novel, as the title suggests, about death as embodied in the story and lives of a professional mourner (Toloki), a nurse (whose duty is to narrate the last moments of a persons life and way of dying), and a coffin maker, Nefolovhodwe (who has recently become rich thanks to his new popular product, the collapsible coffin). The novel opens with a scene at the funeral Noria's son—a young boy who was killed by a rebel gang, purportedly fighting for the "liberation" of the community. "There are many ways of dying," the nurse shouts, "This little brother was our own child . . . . It is not the first time that we bury little children. We bury them everyday. But they are killed by the enemy . . . those we are fighting against. This little brother was killed by those who are fighting to free us." The way Mda tells the story, the question for this community is not a question of whether to live or die, but how to die. For as Toloki later tells Noria: "Death lives with us everyday. Indeed our ways of dying are our ways of living. Or should I say our ways of living are our ways of dying?" I am grateful to my friend Tinyiko Maluleke, who first drew my attention to Mda's book, and later sent me a copy. I am equally grateful to Maluleke's insightful comments on the events of September 11th in his, "Of Collapsible Coffins and Ways of Dying. The Search for Catholic Contextuality in African Perspective." (unpublished).

[6] www.nologo.org/article.pl.

[7] John Gray depicts it as a "deadly mixture of emotions"—a sense of injustice, cultural resentment, despair, and hopelessness. See John Gray, "Where There is No Common Power," *The New Statesman*, September 24, 2001. I am grateful to Mike Quirk for sharing this article with me, and for the many interesting exchanges with him on September 11th. As always, I find Mike Quirk's take on issues of global significance not only informative, but highly engaging. This may not be unconnected to his own biography as an Aristotelian philosopher, a computer programmer; and a parent (together with his late wife Eileen) of a talented Moldavian-born boy, Lim.

[8] One does not have to be an enthusiast of economic globalization to realize the fact of globalization, and how, as a matter of fact, globalization has destablized the notion and reality of the nation-state more than political theorists and technocrats have been willing to admit. That is why it is questionable when, even in the world marked by all forces of globalization, politicians theorists and technocrats keep hacking back to the notion of the nation-state and outmoded (i.e., seventeenth Century) appeals to national "sovereignty" and national "interests."

[9] What official America today calls collateral damage was not an unfortunate by product of war; it was the very point of terrorism that was adopted by many of these rebel groups. Perhaps this is not unrelated to the fact that America has now refused to sign the 1997 treaty banning the use, production, stockpiling, and transfer of anti-personnel land mines. There are over 100 million land mines in 64 countries.

[10] Niel Postman, *Amusing Ourselves to Death. Public Discourse in the Age of Show Business* (New York: Penguin Books, 1985), p. 77.

CHART 1: NET OFFICIAL DEVELOPMENT ASSISTANCE IN 2000

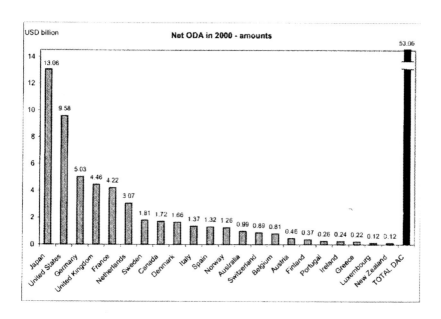

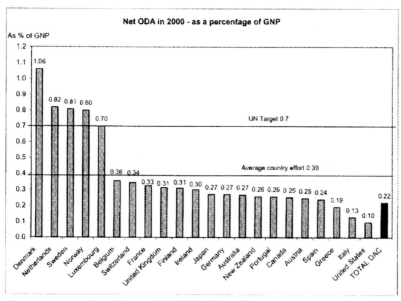

Source: www.oecd.org/dataoecd/50/37/191252.pdf

APPENDIX 2

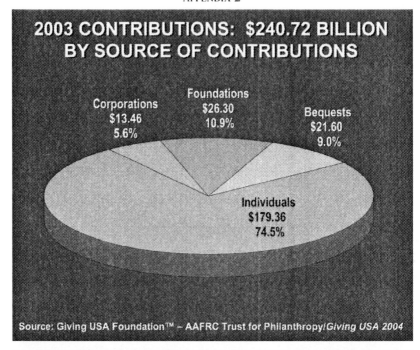

2003 CONTRIBUTIONS: $240.72 BILLION
BY SOURCE OF CONTRIBUTIONS

Corporations $13.46 5.6%

Foundations $26.30 10.9%

Bequests $21.60 9.0%

Individuals $179.36 74.5%

Source: Giving USA Foundation™ – AAFRC Trust for Philanthropy/*Giving USA 2004*

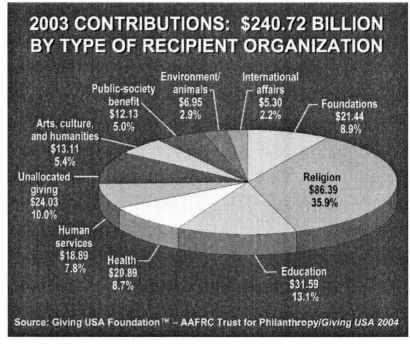

2003 CONTRIBUTIONS: $240.72 BILLION
BY TYPE OF RECIPIENT ORGANIZATION

Public-society benefit $12.13 5.0%

Environment/ animals $6.95 2.9%

International affairs $5.30 2.2%

Foundations $21.44 8.9%

Arts, culture, and humanities $13.11 5.4%

Unallocated giving $24.03 10.0%

Religion $86.39 35.9%

Human services $18.89 7.8%

Health $20.89 8.7%

Education $31.59 13.1%

Source: Giving USA Foundation™ – AAFRC Trust for Philanthropy/*Giving USA 2004*

SECTION TWO:

Performance

CHAPTER FOUR

POSTMODERN ILLUSIONS AND PERFORMANCES

As Marlow travels into the heart of what was the Belgian Congo, he begins to search for Mr. Kurtz, who was sent by the "gang of virtue," the Europeans who saw themselves as bringing Enlightenment and progress or Civilization to the Africans. Marlow believes that Kurtz will restore his faith in the vision of enlightened imperialism that is at odds with the pervasive evidence of corruption, lethargy, violence, and disease. As he reaches the interior, Marlow learns that Kurtz is dying. And meeting the dying Mr. Kurtz he discovers the ultimate corruption. At the bottom of the report which Kurtz has prepared to send back to the company in Belgium along with his shipment of ivory, he has scrawled the words which, were to be enacted repeatedly in the 20th Century: the final solution to the problem of difference— "exterminate all the brutes."

Carol Gilligan, *In a Different Voice*

I make reference to Conrad's 1902 classic novella in the epigram above in order to make clear from the very start the main argument of this essay. Present-day discourse on Africa is often premised on a certain postmodern optimism and spurious reference to the "new world order," the "global village," a "world economy," an "African Renaissance," and so forth. In spite of these various and honorific titles, there will be nothing radically new or liberating for many Africans in this "New Deal." Instead, many will find themselves still caught as the innocent and unsuspecting victims of Kurtz's chilling prescription, namely, "exterminate all the brutes." It is difficult to understand what might have motivated Kurtz to come to such an extreme "solution," except to see it within the context of his modernist revulsion to what he saw as the "barbaric and primitive" customs of the Congolese people.

In spite of its declared sensitivity to difference and otherness, post-modernism is still so much caught up in this modern predicament and failure or Western culture to accept and respect tastes, habits, and ways of life or rationalities which are different from her own way of life. In other words, in accord with Kurtz's enlightened modernism, whose history we are sadly aware of in Africa, postmodernism involves the same determination to destroy whatever is local or different. However, while Marlow *seems* to have come to the realization of (and be haunted by) "The horror! The horror" which lay at the heart of such human depravity undertaken in the name of progress and virtue, we in Africa may easily fail to notice the despair and even the terror that is part and parcel of our postmodern condition.[1] Instead, we may find ourselves as the all-too-willing victims of its enchanting machinations. In other words, it looks like a postmodernistic culture easily invents subtle ways to "exterminate the brutes," even as the latter continue to "acel-ebrate" their inception within the new world order.

In this essay, by focusing on three aspects (1) the postmodern celebration of difference, (2) the global economy, and (3) "condomiza-tion," I will show how there is something like a postmodern "reinvention" of Africa already underway.[2] Even more significantly, I hope to show that there is nothing radically new or liberating within this post-modern reinvention. Rather, it represents a heightened (modernist) determination in the destruction of whatever is local, particular, or different. The effect of this reinvention is nothing less than the creation of superficial characters and societies people—in other words, who have lost not just hope for a meaningful existence, but even the power to locate their lives and activities within any historically meaningful narrative. Accordingly, I see the greatest challenge facing the Christian churches in Africa in the twenty-first century in terms of whether they will be able to generate enough skills and resources to enable Christians to survive postmodernism, as well as allow African Christians to recapture a sense of hope and dignity. Such a task forms the wide context for African biblical hermeneutics in the twenty-first century.

I must confess, though, that it took me a long time to realize that African Christian theology might have a negative stake within post-modernism. In fact, on one occasion I had even suggested that post-modernism offered a unique possibility for us in Africa to develop local theologies—narrative theologies different from the totalizing master narratives against which we had up till now defined ourselves.[3]

Both Foucault's genealogical exposition of the power relations which lie behind the standard regimes of "knowledge," "truth," and "objectivity,"[4] as well Lyotard's announcement of the end of master narratives[5]—two authors I mostly associated with a postmodern trend—seemed to confirm these advantages. In fact, I saw the new directions being charted by hitherto excluded voices like African women theologians and African Independent Church theologies as confirming this optimism.[6] With a postmodern mood in place, I had thought that it was time to use the favored expression, "to drink from our own wells."[7] What better possibility to do so than in the space opened by the postmodern death of grand narratives and rehabilitation of difference?

Looking back, I realize that my naive enthusiasm was greatly due to the fact that I associated postmodernism almost exclusively with an intellectual style—one that casts suspicion on "classical notions of truth, reason, identity, and objectivity; of the idea of universal progress or emancipation, of single frameworks, grand narratives, or ultimate grounds of explanation."[8] Even though I still think there are decisive advantages in post-modernism as an intellectual style or set of moods, I have come to see that its cultural expressions are by far more determinative than its intellectual roots. I do not claim that one can neatly separate the two, but it is true that while very few of us would have heard of the name of Foucault, and even fewer of Lyotard, the most unlettered peasant in the Transkei or Amuria has to confront and negotiate her life around the media and market forces of late capitalism.[9] Thus, by focusing on three cultural expressions of postmodernism within Africa, I will show why and in what way a postmodern culture provides one of the greatest challenges for African Christian theology in general, and African biblical hermeneutics in particular.

AFRICA UNDER "THE GLOBAL GAZE": THE POSTMODERN CELEBRATION OF DIFFERENCE

It may not be immediately clear that postmodernism involves a determination to destroy whatever is particular and local. In fact, such a claim may sound surprising, since we are more used to associating postmodernism with a renewed interest in, and appreciation of, difference. This interest goes beyond the epistemological shift which, associated with such names as MacIntyre, Rorty, and Kuhn, has drawn attention to the historical nature of truth—and thus to the possibility of different rationalities and claims to truth—dependent rationalities and claims to truth. One also notices, from a Western cultural perspective, a renewed interest in African culture. This interest ranges from a tourist fascination with Africa's unique wildlife and "tribal" customs to an academic interest, which makes African Studies one of the favorite and competitive courses within the curriculum of a number of universities, particularly in the United States. Similarly, there is a growing number of cultural environmentalists fighting for the preservation of the unique cultural heritage of non-Western civilizations. Shouldn't we in Africa see this as a great opportunity for African culture and history, indeed for Africa's voice, to be recognized and accepted?

We must be careful not to come to this conclusion too easily. For there is something sinister about the postmodern celebration of difference, which at the same time renders differences ineffectual or inconsequential. In other words, the ability to recognize otherness and difference everywhere might just as well amount to an ironic shielding of oneself from listening or attending to the particular and historical claims of the "other." Looked at in this way, there is nothing radically new or liberating about this postmodern celebration of difference. Instead, the fascination seems to mask a heightened crisis in respect to the same old problem of difference. The point here can well be amplified by drawing attention to the particularly interesting work of Bernard McGrane.

In *Beyond Anthropology*, McGrane provides a history of different conceptions of "alien cultures" from roughly the sixteenth to the early twentieth century.[10] McGrane argues that four "general paradigms" have been used by Europeans and Westerners to interpret and "explain" non-European cultures and peoples: a theological, Enlightenment, sociological, and cultural paradigm, respectively.

1. Theological Paradigm. Up to and including the sixteenth century, the dominant cosmography represented the non-European "other" in terms of a theological horizon:

> . . . *the alienness of the non-European other was experienced and interpreted on the horizon of Christianity. It was Christianity which fundamentally came between the European and non-European other. Anthropology did not exist; there was, rather, demonology. It was in relation to the Fall and to the influence of Sin and Satan that the other took on his historically specific meaning.*[11]

As a manifestation of the "Prince of Darkness," the other "could never be anything but a 'pagan,' and hence (s)he inhabited a 'space' that was necessarily the inversion of the only real 'space'—the Christian 'space,' the 'space' of divine salvation. Christianity is the only religion, and those who did not profess it simply had no religion."[12] They dwelled entirely in the "hollow of absence," or as Mudimbe would say, in a *terra nullius*, whose only hope lay in being "discovered," "named," and "converted" by the organizing presence of Christians/ Europeans.[13]

2. Enlightenment Paradigm. In the Enlightenment, McGrane argues, this Christian theological paradigm was largely supplanted by an epistemological one. Such categories as "ignorance," "error," "untruth," and "superstition" were used to articulate the differences between the European and non-European "other." "For it was in man's relation to truth (light) at the same time as it was in the obscuring of that relation to truth . . . that the Enlightenment *located and accounted for difference*."[14] The "other" was labeled so precisely because (s)he belonged to a society that was "unenlightened." In an interesting manner, McGrane devotes a number of pages to the description of the trajectory that resulted in the radical transformation of the West's self-understanding: from regarding themselves primarily as "European-Christians" to the conception of themselves as "*civilized* Europeans."[15] What the trajectory amounts to, however, is that it is within the Enlightenment, "at this epistemological moment that the European becomes *civilized*," while the "other" typically comes to be regarded as "primitive." It is also within this Enlightenment space that "anthropology" emerges (and replaces "demonology") as the discursive practice whose systematic and administrative function is to maintain belief in and confirm the existence of exotic and aliens worlds, and to explain the "primitive mentality" of the aliens who dwell in these worlds.[16]

3. Sociological Paradigm. In the nineteenth century, McGrane argues, there was another paradigm shift as the preceding Enlightenment paradigm gave way to an evolutionary paradigm, in which time constitutes the difference between European and the non-European "other."

> . . . *There was a vast hemorrhage in time: geological time, developmental time lodged itself between the European and the non-European other. Anthropology, as practiced by, for*

example, E. B. Taylor, became the discipline which organ-
ized and administered the comparison between past and
present, between different "stages of development,"
between the prehistorically fossilized "primitive" and evo-
lutionary advancement of modern western science and civ-
ilization.[17]

Compared to its Enlightenment predecessor, nineteenth century anthropology comes therefore to be grounded in what McGrane calls a double transformation: "first, it transformed difference into *historical* difference, and then it transformed history into evolution (progressive evolution)."[18] As a result, the world, "which hitherto had been every-where contemporary with itself, became partitioned off into different times, different time epochs."[19] It is here, on the horizon of historical evolutionary development opened up by nineteenth century anthropology, that the notion of a "Third World" becomes meaningful, along with the different "theories of development" meant to expedite the former's "inevitable" evolution to a positive, modern, developed, "First World" status.

4. Cultural Paradigm. Finally, McGrane argues that in the early twentieth century the dominant paradigm for representing the difference between the European and non-European changed again. Now it was "culture" which accounted for this difference:

We think under the hegemony of the ethnological response
to the alienness of the Other; we are today contained with-
in an anthropological concept of the Other. Anthropology
has become our modern way of seeing the Other as, funda-
mentally and merely, culturally different.[20]

McGrane's work is helpful for a number of reasons—first, as an attempt at an "archeology of anthropology." It is able to uncover the crisis, "the perpetually present identity crisis," which underpins the successive characterization of "alien cultures." For the key to under-standing the various conceptions of alienness is to see that they are "constructed by a systematic thought-process of inversion." The alien "other" is everyone else except the European; but who, in his or her abnormal difference, specifies the European identity. This is the rea-son, McGrane concludes, that "the European's images of non-European man are not primarily, if at all, descriptions of real people, but rather projections of his own nostalgia and feeling of inadequacy." Consequently, the history of anthropology turns out to be little more than the "history of an identity crisis, and the history of the different identities we have existed."[21]

Secondly, and more significantly for our argument here, McGrane makes clear how the postmodern celebration of difference is but an aspect of the twentieth century paradigm of looking at the "other" as merely different. This means that with culture as the only all-defining lens, "difference" now becomes "democratized," such that the non-European "other" is no longer immured in the depths of some petrified past, but is reasserted into the present, "our" present, and is now "our" contemporary: "*the Other is not—inferior—but different,*[22] merely and only culturally different.

This of course may give the misleading impression that within the global project the West has become more sensitive to the historical and moral claims of other cultures. Not quite. For along with the "democratization" of difference (one's culture is just one among many), there is what McGrane calls a "paradoxical domestication and annihilation of difference."[23] If all cultures are relative, then in this respect, in this deep respect, none are different. They are only culturally, i.e., superficially different—*merely* different.

Moreover, with the advantages of travel, and with the simultaneous transposition of different cultures and cultural artifacts that the postliberal media puts before us for our "info-tainment," differences are easily stripped of their moral and historical claims, and become merely "aesthetic"—another aspect (commodity) for the postliberal individual to enjoy, especially if he lives in the rich countries of the North.[24] Economic globalization thus becomes an intricate and structural aspect of postmodernism, whose ideological effect is to obscure the deep social, historical, and economic inequalities between postliberal consumers of the rich North and the peasants in the South.[25] As a result, what is promoted is a very superficial celebration of particularity: what one might call a frivolous fascination with difference.[26] Seen from this perspective, the postmodern celebration of difference, just like its previous characterizations of difference, turns into nothing but a monologue *about* difference. As McGrane notes, "anthropology never *listened* to the voices of 'alien cultures,' it never *learned* from them—rather it studied them; in fact, studying them, making sense out of them, making a 'science' about them, has been the modern *method* of not listening, of avoiding listening to them."[27] With the postmodern

celebration of difference, we seem to be faced with the same monologue, where the postmodern liberal or cosmopolitan can always see
the "other" (from the comfort of his living room); he can even "speak
well of the other, but never to the other; and indeed cannot do otherwise because there really is no intractable other," since the "other" is
just or *merely* different.[28] Where Kurtz's enlightened imperialism
announced its "superiority" openly, and thus justified the conquest and
elimination of the "brutes," the postmodern monologue about difference sedately but ruthlessly domesticates and assimilates the
other—any other—in the name of difference.

This discussion, albeit long and involved, at least helps show why
a postmodern interest in African culture is not necessarily liberating. In
fact, I think that one of the greatest challenges facing us will be
whether we can mobilize enough intellectual and moral skills to resist
the postmodern celebration of Africa's cultural difference and uniqueness. African theology can unwittingly play up to this spectaculariza-
tion (say by a superficial "inculturation," which may just promote the
picture of a playing, singing, and dancing Africa). What is needed
instead is a more deeply entrenched theological practice which can
challenge the different histories and politics which tend to obscure the
actual historical struggles, conflicts, and aspirations of the African
peoples. An even more serious challenge facing us is how theology and
biblical scholarship in Africa can help Africa's voice—its distinctive
history and unique challenges—to be heard, instead of being reduced
to just another merely different, "neat," or "exotic" chorus in the endless cacophony of inconsequential differences.

AFRICA UNDER THE GLOBAL ECONOMY:
THE ENDLESS FUTILITY OF "LEAP-FROGGING"

The global market will perhaps remain one of the greatest cultural
expressions of a postmodern era. But as a few voices from the so-
called Third World have begun to point out, far from ushering an
"African Renaissance" and the expected eradication of poverty, this
institution is negatively affecting—indeed bringing impoverishment
to—the lives of millions of people in the so-called Third World.[29] This
is not just because of "unfair" trade balances between the rich North
and the poor South. Nor is it just because of the heavy debt owed to
the rich countries and international monetary institutions, which stifle
or cripple any chances for sustainable development. Even if the debt of

the poor nations would completely be written off—as I think it should—with the global economy in place, the poor nations would still be caught in a system that involves a systematic destruction of whatever is *locally* significant. In other words, what we are looking at here is a terribly sick system with the poor nations trapped at the bottom in an endless and futile exercise of "leap-frogging."

This metaphor of leap-frogging comes from an undergraduate student—an economics major at Washington and Lee University in Virginia. In a seminar organized by Professor Harlan Beckley of the Shepherd Poverty Program, I had pointed out how the market in many parts of Africa is at the service of highly superficial needs. I used the example of Microsoft Windows 98, and how the inauguration of this "latest" software program had been all over the news in Kampala. Both Radio Uganda and Uganda Television had hailed the advantages of Windows 98, especially the fact that it made "surfing the net so much easier." One would completely miss the irony if one did not realize that this occurred in a country where only a tiny fraction of the population, (about 2%) have ever seen, let alone used, a computer. Whereas Windows 98 might be a great event for some of us who fall within that select minority, I pointed out, what the greatest majority of people in many parts of Africa needed was perhaps not even a typewriter, but pens and paper, not to mention basic writing skills. "How can you celebrate Windows 98 when over 60% of the population does not even have access to clean and regular drinking water?" I remarked. It was then that the economics student pointed out that "Africa had no choice." She must "leap-frog" to "where we are" if she is not to be left behind.

It strikes me that this perceptive economics student's description of Africa's situation is indeed true; but that is precisely the problem, and not the solution. In fact, this is precisely what Africa has been doing since her colonial days—leap frogging through different theories and programs of "development" to Western patterns of life and consumption. But whereas within the nineteenth century evolutionary paradigm this "development" was mapped on a lineal evolutionary trajectory—and thus took a more predictable progression—the postmodern "where we are" has become decentered and highly unstable—an endless stream of "signifiers without a signified." Postmodern reality is thus based not on any lasting, stable, or predictable pattern, but is increasingly determined by what is "fashionable"—the novel, the "in thing." This really is what is going to make Africa's leap-frogging in the twenty-first century not just more erratic, but also tragically comic. One gets a sense of this comic leap-frogging when one notices how many leaders in Africa feel increasingly compelled to address themselves to the same "global" problems. Recently, the prime minister of one of the poorest African countries appeared on television advising the West to come up with a quick solution to the Y2K! I suspect that such a leader feels constrained to leap-frog to the same "global" problems every respectable leader must address. I am sure we are going to see even more tragic cases of leap-frogging on the part of African leaders. What many may perhaps not realize is that thanks to the destabilizing of time and space within the postmodern crave for novelty, the Western "where we are" is becoming increasingly a "virtual" reality of Windows 98 (or is that now 2000?!), the cellular phone, the Yahoo search engine, the Internet, and so forth.

Given the frantic and desperate leap-frogging that is required if one is to catch up with the operations of such "virtual" realities, it seems impossible, perhaps even out-of-step, to think about focusing on such "local" issues as cassava, millet, or goats—the lifeline of the man and woman in Malube or Umutata (their "actual," not their "virtual" reality). This is one reason, I suspect, that the language of globalization easily masks the true identity of that reality: a tantalizing form of tragic leap-frogging which effectively obscures from vision and attention issues that are just local and particular. As with the earlier language of "conversion," "civilization," and "development," leap-frogging bears the same assumption that the only real space to be is where the West is.[30]

What about the millions excluded from this space by the very nature of its internal logic? They are easily condemned to a "local" existence of precipitous and marginal survival, which easily degenerates into a form of what Jack Morris has called "rebel madness,"[31] i.e., the perpetuation of war and violence for its own sake. Is it not surprising, for instance, that in spite of Uganda's internationally acclaimed "economic miracle of recovery" it hosts one of the biggest concentrations of rebel groups on the African continent? All these rebel groups do not pose any serious threat to the government, and in any case none of them has any serious political agenda. On the contrary, with the exception of children forced into joining the rebels,[32] the rank and file of these groups is made up of young adults, who either have nowhere else to be or nothing meaningful to do. Participation in such rebel activities at least gives them a sense of purpose or goal in life, but also a voice which would otherwise never have received any attention from the leaders, whose focus and energy seems to be spent in an endless but futile exercise of leap-frogging. I suspect that with the global economy and the logic of leap-frogging at its center, we will see more of this sort of rebel madness. To be sure, this rebel madness might as well be an indication (an extreme indication) that the playful nihilism of postmodernism is already upon us ("killing as a game"). And so, perhaps we need to focus on another postmodern practice which encourages precisely this sort of posture within Africa.

"CONDOMIZATION" AS PLAYFUL NIHILISM

In an interesting work, George Ritzer describes modern capitalist society as a "McDonaldized" society.[33] The image is not only powerful, it rightly depicts the global spread of modern culture, which is characterized by the logic of standardization, efficiency, calculability, predictability, and control—for which the McDonald's hamburger is both a metaphor and the most popular symbol. Ritzer does not make a sharp distinction between modern and postmodern culture, and in fact understands (rightly in my opinion) the latter as but a heightened form of McDonaldization.[34] The fact that a great majority of Africans do not even know what a McDonald's hamburger is does not mean that they are strangers to the modern and postmodern culture. It just means that the latter culture has come to Africa through a different (back?) door. For example, the current process of condomization underway in many African countries seems to depict well the face postmodernism is taking in many African countries. In other words, not the *McDonald's* hamburger, but the condom is the symbol of postmodern culture in Africa.

If you ask any eleven-year-old child in Uganda, for instance, she will be able to tell you the names of at least five different brands of condoms. She may never have used one, but she certainly would have heard about their wonderful benefits on one of the many FM radio stations. A visitor immediately notices the clear signs of condomization in place: the endless commercials about condoms on radio and TV and billboards everywhere—in towns and along highways in the countryside. Condoms are readily available everywhere. They are sold in supermarkets, by hawkers on the street, and on makeshift candle stalls in the suburbs, where they are placed next to ready-to-go meals. In the countryside, the single-shelf kiosks may run out of sugar and paraffin, but not of their supply of condoms, clearly displayed.

The issue here is not whether condoms do or do not protect against the spread of AIDS, even though one may question the validity of some of the statistics that are often cited as a confirmation of the success of this condom-centered anti-AIDS drive. The issue is not even the narrow ethical concern of whether it is right or wrong to use a condom; and certainly not whether condom use is sanctioned by God, or a clear violation of God's will. The issue is to see that condomization is about the promotion of a certain culture—a postmodern culture.[35]

Disposability. One reason why the use of condoms is so popular, I suspect, is their disposability. Of course, one could see this as just an aspect of the same consumer culture of *Coca-Cola* cans, disposable diapers, and throwaway razors. Such disposability, however, fits quite well with the postmodern announcement of reality as an endless play of signifiers without any stable or permanent base, fueled by global capitalism's ever-accelerating need for growth. Disposability, not simply of goods, but of relationships and particular attachments of any kind, is the hallmark of consumption in the new economy.[36] Thus, condomization is not just about the convenience of disposable condoms, but more importantly, it is about the popularization of a certain form of sexual activity, i.e., one detached from any serious attachment or stable commitment, but which serves to promote a certain nihilistic playfulness of the unstable, decentered and postliberal self.

There is a certain ideological inversion of goals at play here. For "condomization" in Africa is often based on the assumption that Africans are naturally sexually promiscuous, and so the only way to curtail the spread of AIDS is through the promotion of condom use. But as Kanyandago rightly notes, such an assumption is just a myth.[37] What the assumption in fact does is to set up certain expectations, which ends up producing those very expectations (in this case, sexually promiscuous individuals or people incapable of any deep attachments). Such lack of attachment or stable relationships and commitments is often paraded within postmodernism as a high mark of flexibility and freedom.

Freedom. "Condomization" concerns itself with, and thus promotes, a certain view of *freedom*. This is the freedom of what the political theorist Michael Sandel portrayed as the "unencumbered self."[38] By this he meant the modern individual who assumes that one's commitments and responsibilities are not determined by any tradition, be it church or society, but by one's own *choices*. The *Straight Talk* programs which currently are in vogue in many African countries bombard their young audiences with exactly the same message; namely, that nobody has any right to tell them what to do or not do with their bodies. They have a right to decide if and when (or not) they have sex. The major and perhaps the only consideration in this choice is to make sure it is "safe" or protected. Behind such recommendations is the assumption that young people are naturally capable of making the right choices as long as they have the relevant facts (which *Straight Talk* is meant to provide). Of course, the real target of these recommendations are those familial, tribal, or church traditions which insist that freedom does not come naturally, but is a result of *training* into the relevant practices and habits or virtues. For it is not, of course, that these traditions discourage people from making choices. It is only that these traditions realize that whatever choices an individual makes are but a means of realizing one's potentialities as a member of the family, clan, church, or tribe. But now, by summarily dismissing their requirement for training as both archaic and authoritarian, *Straight Talk* encourages young people to believe that one can be free even without training in a particular tradition, as long as one is able to make the right (informed) choices. This not only helps to undermine the authority of the traditional institutions of the family, tribe, or church, but also creates free-floating individuals who easily become prey to their own whimsical needs and choices.

Feels Good. Much can also be said about the playfulness that "condomization" promotes. One clear observation has to do with the way the playfulness is constructed over and beyond everyday expectations and forms of life; the way it is detached from any meaningful form of material production. That is one reason why the most popular images associated with condom commercials are baggy jeans, *Coca-Cola*, rap music, and pale skin: not the images of an "ordinary" African life—but a certain "it feels good" culture more typical of American MTV. One wonders, however, whether we in Africa can afford the playfulness of such an "it feels good" culture, which in the West is not only made possible by the economic infrastructure of advanced capitalism, but also masks the deep frustration and nihilism within postmodernism.[39]

This, then, is what makes "condomization" an appropriate metaphor for the set of practices (call it a certain politics) whose goal is to transform Africans into postmodern individuals: free-floating *individuals*, incapable of any deep attachments, but who are character-ized by a certain superficial feeling and playfulness. To the extent that they become such individuals, they lose not only the possibility of locating themselves within any meaningful history, but more crucially they become increasingly prey to the manipulations and misrepresen-tations of the media and market forces. And as I noted earlier, it is not such a big step to move from this nihilistic playfulness to the violence of rebel madness. Accordingly, one of the greatest challenges for African Christian theology and biblical scholarship for the twenty-first century will be to confront realistically, and even to survive, such post-modern illusions.

I suggest that for African Christians the best hope for survival lies in the opposite direction of "condomization," i.e., in the ability to find appropriate relocation within some forms of community which are able to offer not only resistance, but an alternative to the nihilistic playfulness of postmodern culture. Since nihilism cannot be overcome merely by theory, the crucial issue is the possibility of communities whose way of life and practices embody a "prophetic vision of resist-ance and hope."[40] In this essay's final section, I will broadly portray the sort of self-understanding which makes it possible for the Christian churches in Africa to exist as such communities of resistance and hope.

THE CHURCH AS A COMMUNITY OF
RESISTANCE AND HOPE

Resistance Communities and New Forms of Fundamentalism

We have recently witnessed unprecedented growth in religious fundamentalism in Africa, giving rise to a number of new sects within both Islam and Christianity. While there might be many reasons to explain this fundamentalist religious outburst, I suspect that an implic-it motive of resistance inspires many of these Christian and Islamic sects. The latter call their adherents to a strict observance of the "revealed morality" (contained either in the Bible or the Koran) whose prescriptions are clearly at odds with forms of postmodern playfulness. They similarly encourage strong fellowship and solidarity among the "brothers and sisters"—a call for a return to some traditional form of community as a way to resist the "acids" of a postmodern culture. The one thing I find striking about these groups, then, is their sense of resistance as rooted in community. In other words, they bear witness to the fact that resistance is not just an individual thing, because individually it cannot be sustained. If it is to be sustained, such resistance must be grounded within and sustained by the life and practices of a given community. Without such a community, resistance will inevitably fail and may become just another heroic but narcissistic attempt by the postliberal individual to make it into the headlines.

While these fundamentalist groups may be communities of resistance, they are insufficiently tactical, inasmuch as they are characterized by a total rejection of the postmodern "culture of death." Such wholesale rejection fails to take seriously the ubiquitous nature of postmodern reality. For being postmodernistic is not a choice we have to make. Postmodernism and its cultural expressions are already upon us. The challenge for us is not to withdraw into some kind of "brethren" enclave, but to deal, critically and selectively, with postmodern culture. In other words, it is not enough for the church to be a community of resistance, it must be a tactical community of resistance.

Tactical Communities: The Survival of the Weak

Those familiar with Stanley Hauerwas' work will immediately recognize that I am drawing heavily on his understanding of the church as a community, particularly his reference to the church as a tactical community.[41] Against constant charges of "sectarianism" directed at his work by critics, Hauerwas shows that with the collapse of the Christian empire (Christendom), the church always finds herself on alien ground, totally surrounded by (post)modern culture, with no place that she could properly call her own—which means that there can be no enclave to which she can "withdraw." This not only makes any sectarian position untenable, it means also that the church must give up any pretensions of being a *strategy*, but must concern herself with being a *tactic*. Here Hauerwas draws upon Michel deCerteau's distinction between strategies and tactics.[42] By strategy deCerteau means any

> calculation (or manipulation) of power relationships that becomes possible, as a subject that will empower (a business, an army, a city, a scientific institution) can be isolated. It postulates a place that can be delimited as its own and serve as the base from which relations with an exteriority composed of targets or threats (customers or competitors, enemies, the country surrounding the city, objectives and

> *objects of research, etc.) can be managed. As in manage-*
> *ment, every "strategic" rationalization seeks first of all to*
> *distinguish its "own" place, that is, the place of its own*
> *power and will, from an "environment." A Cartesian atti-*
> *tude, if you wish: it is an effort to delimit one's own place*
> *in a world bewitched by the invisible powers of the Other. It*
> *is also the typical attitude of modern science, politics, and*
> *military strategy.*[43]

In sharp contrast to a strategy, a tactic, according to deCerteau, is

> *a calculated action determined by the absence of a proper*
> *locus. No delineation of exteriority, then, provides it with*
> *the condition necessary for autonomy. The space of a tactic*
> *is the space of the other. Thus it must play on and with the*
> *terrain imposed on it and organized by the law of a foreign*
> *power.*[44]

Tactic, in other words, does not have power to plan a general strat-egy or to view the adversary as a whole. It must operate in isolated actions, taking advantage of opportunities without a base where it can build up stockpiles for the next battle. It has mobility, but it gains mobility only by being willing to take advantage of the possibilities that offer themselves at given moments. As deCerteau notes, the tactic is the art of the weak.[45]

For Hauerwas this concretely means that, as a tactic, the church's primary reoccupation is not her own institutional existence, but that of providing her members with skills which will enable them to engage critically and selectively with the (post)modern culture in which they find themselves, and in which they live as "resident aliens." Such a posture is only possible to the extent that Christians find themselves members of a community whose story is powerful enough to sustain their tactical existence with hope.

Biblical Communities: The Bible as a Story of Hope

It is in the above context that Hauerwas underscores the moral authority of the Bible as a "story"—the story of a particular communi-ty who, given their unique experience of and with God, move on through history, through different challenges and trials as a communi-ty of resistance and hope.[46] This narrative character of scripture, how-ever, is often obscured in an attempt to objectify scripture as "Word of

God," which can be mined for individual tips for salvation or for some kind of "revealed morality." Whereas scripture no doubt offers such possibilities, Hauerwas' claim is to the effect that there is no way one can understand the full import of scripture if it is abstracted from the history of the community which produced it, and whose experience of and with God it reflects, and in turn shapes. That is to say, scripture is not only an account of a community's journey with God, it in turn creates a "community of memory"—people capable of reading and reliving the same story by placing themselves in the biblical tradition. This overall political context not only endows scripture with moral authority, it allows us to see that the reading of scripture is not just some pious exercise, but a political exercise, and even a subversive form of politics.

I have drawn attention to Hauerwas' understanding of church and scripture, for it is precisely such an understanding we need to recover if Christian churches in Africa are to help Christians survive postmodernism, but also meet with hope and dignity the challenges of the twenty-first century. I am certainly aware that historically Christianity and the Bible have played an ambivalent role in Africa.[47] The argument I am making, however, presupposes that Christianity will be able to exploit the theme of resistance which has somehow always been implicit within African Christianity and thus turn the Bible into a formidable weapon of struggle.[48] What such a recovery requires, however, is the ability to free the Bible from the liberal and individualistic notions of salvation, so that we allow its full potential as the story of a pilgrim community to inspire new forms of community which embody the same prophetic vision of resistance and hope. Such communities will not only critically challenge, but also embody much needed alternatives to the playful nihilism of a postmodern culture. In any case, given the sort of postmodernistic illusions which are already upon us, the formation of such churched communities who read and take the Bible seriously is not only a challenge—it is an urgent necessity for Africa in the twenty-first century.

Notes

[1] I use "seems," for it appears that even though Marlow himself was shocked by Kurtz's extremism, he adored the man and shared his mission. Accordingly, Marlow saw himself as "an emissary of light, something like a lower apostle: whose job included weaning those ignorant millions from their horrid ways: as his aunt had insisted" (Joseph Conrad, *Heart of Darkness* (New York: Dover Publications, 1990), p. 10).

Nevertheless, I am grateful to Keith Maiden, my co-guest professor at Molloy College, New York (Spring 1999), for helping me to see Marlow in a far less harsh manner by pointing out how, on returning to England (leaving the dead Kurtz buried in the Congo), Marlow was haunted by his ultimate realization of the depravity and despair ("The horror! The horror!") at the heart of the colonial project. It could just be that our differences reflect nothing but our biographical and literary differences. Maiden is British, and a professor of English literature at Lancaster, while I am Ugandan, and a professor of African Studies. However, even such biographical differences are crucial to the way in which one approaches such a compact and powerful book as Conrad's *Heart of Darkness*. For a more detailed discussion of this novel in a way that I find particularly instructive, see Edward Said, *Culture and Imperialism* (New York: Alfred Knopf, 1993), especially pp. 19–31.

2 I mean this in the sense in which Mudimbe talks about the "invention" of Africa. By using the work of Michel Foucault, Mudimbe shows how European conceptions of "reason" and "civilizations" were in need of, and succeeded in "constructing" an alter ego of a "savage" and "primitive" Africa. See V. Y. Mudimbe, *The Invention of Africa: Gnosis, Philosophy, and the Order of Knowledge* (Bloomington, IN: Indiana University Press, 1988). Here I argue that postmodern realities (especially the media and the market) are engaged in a similar "construction" of a new postmodern Africa. However, with the "age of Europe" giving way to "the age of America," a postmodern Africa will increasingly bear the stamp of an "Africa made in America."

3 Emmanuel Katongole, "African Christian Theology Today: On Being a Premodern Postmodernist." Unpublished paper read at the Graduate School of Theology, University of Natal, Pietermaritzburg, June 1998.

4 See particularly Michel Foucault, *The Archeology of Knowledge*, trans. A. M. Sheridan Smith, (London: Tavistock Press, 1972) and *Power/Knowledge: Selected Interviews and Other Writings, 1972–1977*, ed. C. Gordon (Brighton: Harvest Press, 1980).

5 J. F. Lyotard, *The Postmodern Condition. A Report on Knowledge*, trans. G. Bennington and B. Massumi (Minneapolis, MN: University of Minnesota Press, 1984).

6 See T. Maluleke, "Recent Developments in the Christian Theologies of Africa: Towards the Twenty-first Century," *Journal of Constructive Theology* 2/2 (1996), pp. 33–60.

7 Not unlike Mugambi and Bediako, I was anxious to get away from the theologies of inculturation and liberation which had dominated the African theological scene. For as Mugambi notes, even though the latter have been useful foundations within African theology, they have become inadequate to the requirements of the new world order. One reason why Mugambi feels these theologies are inadequate is "that they have tended to be merely reactive" to the physical and ideological misrepresentations of the old world order. Now that the old world order is gone, Mugambi proposes a theology of "reconstruction" which he hopes will relate more fully to the actual and ongoing Christian responses to the life experiences of Africans. See J. N. Mugambi, *From Liberation to Reconstruction: African Christian Theology After the Cold War* (Nairobi: East African Educational Publishers, 1995). For Kwame Bediako, too; "the era of African theological literature as reaction to Western representation is past. What lies ahead is a critical theological construction which will relate more fully to the widespread confidence in the Christian faith [and] to actual and ongoing Christian

responses to the life experiences of Africans." Kwame Bediako, "Understanding African Theology in the 20th Century," *Bulletin for Contextual Theology in Southern Africa and Africa 3/2* (1996), p. 6. Maluleke rightly notes the uncritical optimism that marks these suggestions, as well as the failure to question this so called "new world order" (Maluleke, p. 167). I am in fact arguing that the new (postmodern) world order presents forces that call for resistance and an even far more "reactive" stance than what was adopted in the older world order.

[8] Terry Eagleton, *The Illusions of Postmodernism* (Oxford: Basil Blackwell, 1996), p. viii.

[9] For the media and market as key postmodern institutions, see Fredric Jameson, *Postmodernism, or, The Cultural Logic of Late Capitalism* (Durham, NC: Duke University Press,1991).

[10] Bernard McGrane, *Beyond Anthropology: Society and the Other* (New York: Columbia University Press, 1989). I am grateful to Kenneth Surin's article, "Certain 'Politics of Speech': 'Religious Pluralism' in the Age of the McDonald's Hamburger," *Modern Theology 7/1* (1990), pp. 68–100, which drew my attention to the work of McGrane in the first place.

[11] McGrane, p. ix.

[12] Surin, p. 73.

[13] Non-Christians, Mudimbe notes, "have no rights to possess or negotiate any dominion in the then-existing international context, and thus their land is objectively a *terra nullius* (no man's land) that may be occupied and seized by Christians in order to exploit the richness meant by God to be shared by all humankind. Thus, these colonizing Christians will be helping the inferior 'brethren' to insert themselves in the real and true history of salvation." See Mudimbe, p. 30.

[14] McGrane, p. 56.

[15] *Ibid.*

[16] In this respect, McGrane rightly notes that there is great similarity between what we term modern "anthropological discourse" and "science fiction": For with the non-European Other as with the aliens from other planets, "what is significant is not whether such beings exist or not, but rather *the fact that they are conceivable.*" Thus, anthropology turns out to be, in this respect, "terrestrial science fiction, dealing with terrestrial aliens, as indeed, science fiction soon becomes extraterrestrial anthropology dealing with extraterrestrial aliens" (McGrane, p. 3). The possible being that could be encountered on earth and in the heavens were the same—the terrestrial "other" and the celestial "other"—were, of necessity, of the same order.

[17] Surin, p. 73.

[18] *Ibid.*, p. 93.

[19] *Ibid.*, p. 94.

[20] *Ibid.*, p. x.

[21] For the direct quotations in this paragraph see McGrane, pp. 1–6. The similarity and complementarity between McGrane and Mudimbe's work should be immediately obvious.

[22] *Ibid.*, p. 129.

[23] *Ibid.*, p. 117.

[24] As Bill Cavanaugh notes, "Global mapping produces the illusion of diversity by the juxtaposition of all the varied products of the world's traditions and cultures in one

space and time in the marketplace. Mexican food and tuna hotdish, mangoes, and mayonnaise all meet the gaze of the consumer. For the consumer with money, the illusion is created that all the world's peoples are contemporaries occupying the same space and time." William T. Cavanaugh, "The World in a Wafer: A Geography of the Eucharist as Resistance to Globalization," *Modern Theology* 15/2 (April, 1999), p.187.

[25] "So the conceit is advanced that my consumption contributes to your well-being through mutually beneficial global trade. The consumption of others' particularity absorbs them into a simulated catholicity while it simultaneously hides the way that space remains rigidly segmented between the [rich] Minnesotans who enjoy mangoes in the dead of winter and the [poor] Brazilian Indians who earn forty cents an hour picking them." Cavanaugh, pp. 187–188.

[26] McGrane calls it a "trivialization of the encounter with the Other" (p. 129), and Said warns against the "fetishization and relentless celebration of difference and otherness, which takes no account of the politics and particular histories which produce and reproduce the other." Edward Said, "Representing the Colonized: Anthropology's Interlocutors," *Critical Inquiry* 15 (1989), pp. 205–225. See also Jonathan Friedman, "Beyond Otherness," *Telos* 71 (1987), pp. 161–170.

[27] McGrane, p. 127, emphasis his.

[28] Surin, p. 77.

[29] For my own previous discussion of the global market, see "Globalization and Economic Fundamentalism in Africa"; "African Renaissance and Narrative Theology in Africa," *Journal of Theology for Southern Africa* 102 (1998), pp. 29–40; in *The Cries of the Poor in Africa: Questions and Responses for African Christianity.* ed. Peter Kanyandago (Kisubi: Marianum Publishing, 2002), pp. 57–78.

[30] This is what might be misleading about McGrane's history of the various conceptions of "otherness." It might give the impression that the different paradigms are neatly successive. This certainly is not the case, so that conceptualization of difference in the twentieth century involves fragments of the previous conceptions of "otherness."

[31] Jack Morris, "A Lesson from the Massacre of Foreign Tourists in Uganda," *America* 180/19 (May 1999), pp. 12–14.

[32] On the plight of children within the Lord's Resistance Army (LRA) in Northern Uganda, see *The Scars of Death: Children abducted by the Lord's Resistance Army in Uganda.* (Human Rights Watch, 1997). See also Els De Temmerman, *Aboke Girls: Children Abducted in Northern Uganda,* (Fountain Publishers: Kampala, 2001).

[33] George Ritzer, *The McDonaldization of Society: An Investigation into the Changing Character of Contemporary Social Life,* revised edition (Thousand Oaks, CA: Pine Forge Press, 1996).

[34] One reason I find Ritzer's small book so interesting is that he clearly points out that this heightened state of McDonaldization shows how modern society has already been thrust far into what Max Weber named "the iron cage of rationality," or what Ritzer calls the "irrationality of rationality." He argues for the need to resist or subvert the McDonaldization process through the cultivation of personal alternatives and/or individual patterns and attitudes of resistance. I find both Ritzer's analysis and argument interesting, even though I doubt whether such individual or personal nonrational niches of resistance are all that we need. In fact, the latter seem to be alternatives open only to "those who can afford it"—i.e., a leisured class of economic elite, the result of the same process of McDonaldization from which they are supposed to flee. I suggest that

more than personal or individual niches of resistance we need ecclesial communities of resistance and hope.

[35] The Catholic association Human Life International had this right: that condom use promotes a certain culture. However, by identifying all artificial methods of contraceptions alongside abortion and euthanasia, and rejecting everything under the rubric of "culture of death" (as opposed to the Gospel "culture of life)," they do not allow a more critical analysis of the historical and moral complexities involved in each of the practices.

[36] Cavanaugh, p. 188.

[37] The way facts about AIDS in Africa are presented, Kanyandago notes, "is inspired by the belief of the WHO and the Western medical establishment that Africans are sexually promiscuous. 'But apart from the fact that the first European-Christian missionaries in Africa held this belief, there is absolutely no scientific evidence for this view. On the contrary, Americans lead the world as far as changing sexual partners is concerned. They are followed by France, Australia, and Germany. South Africa, like Thailand, is well back in the middle of the sex league . . . . But there is of course a long Christian tradition of fantasizing about the supposedly licentious life of Africans.'" P. Kanyandago, "The Role of Culture in Poverty Eradication," in Deirdre Carabine and Martin O'Reilly, eds., *The Challenge of Eradicating Poverty in the World: An African Response* (Uganda: Martyrs University Press, 1998), p. 138. Citing C. Fiala, "Dirty Tricks: How the WHO Gets Its AIDS Figures," *New African* (April 1998), pp. 36–38.

[38] Michael Sandel, "The Procedural Republic and the Unencumbered Self," *Political Theory* 12/1 (1984), pp. 81–96.

[39] This frustration is certainly apparent in Rorty, one of the key voices who have helped to deconstruct modernity's quest for an independently-given notion of Truth and Objectivity. In the absence of any such foundation, Rorty suggests that an individual adopt, on the one hand, a certain attitude of suspicion (irony) to one's commitments and a pragmatic playfulness (light-minded pragmatism) on the other. It is as if Rorty is suggesting that with the postmodern condition we must learn not to take ourselves and our commitments too seriously. See Richard Rorty, *Contingency, Irony, and Solidarity* (Cambridge: Cambridge University Press, 1989), pp. xv, and passim.

[40] Gerald O. West, *Biblical Hermeneutics of Liberation: Modes of Reading the Bible in the South African Context* (Pietermaritzburg: Cluster Publications, 1991), p. 45. Theology, African theology in particular, Gerald West remarks, must necessarily be prophetic if it is to be meaningful. Citing from the famous 1985 *Kairos Document*, West surmises, "To be truly prophetic, our response would have to be, in the first place, solidly grounded in the Bible. Our KAIROS impels us to *return to the Bible* and to search the word of God for a message that is relevant to what we are experiencing. This will be no mere academic exercise. Prophetic theology differs from academic theology because, whereas academic theology deals with all biblical themes in a systematic manner and formulates general Christian principles and doctrines, prophetic theology concentrates on those aspects of the Word of God that have an immediate bearing upon the critical situation in which we find ourselves. The theology of the prophets does not pretend to be comprehensive and complete, it speaks to the particular circumstances of a particular time and place—the KAIROS" (West, p. 58).

[41] Stanley Hauerwas, *Against the Nations: War and Survival in a Liberal Society* (Nashville, TN: Abingdon Press, 1991), pp. 16–22. Hauerwas' influence in the position I develop in this essay, as well as in the overall evolution of my thinking, is far

beyond any explicit acknowledgment. The immediate motivation behind this article, for example, owes a great deal to Hauerwas', "The Christian Difference: Surviving Postmodernism," *Cultural Values* 3/2 (April, 1999), pp. 164–181.

[42] Michel deCerteau, *The Practice of Everyday Life* (Berkeley, CA: University of California Press, 1988), pp. 35–36. The chapter in question (III) is significantly entitled "Making Do: Uses and Tactics." In this chapter, deCerteau is concerned with the everyday relations or transactions between the strong and weak, and especially with the "actions" which remain possible for the latter. deCerteau argues that in spite of the disciplines, order, and constraints which dominating systems impose, by an art of "being in between" an individual can find "ways of using" and/ or composing "new stories" within those constraining orders.

[43] Hauerwas, *Against the Nations*, pp. 16–17.

[44] deCerteau, p. 37.

[45] Hauerwas, pp. 17–18, reference to deCerteau, pp. 36–37. *Tactic* is particularly the art of a guerrilla warfare, for as deCerteau notes, "it operates in isolated actions, blow by blow. It takes advantage of 'opportunities' and depends on them, being without any base where it could stockpile its winnings, build up its position, and then plan raids. What it wins it cannot keep . . . . It must vigilantly make use of the cracks that particular conjunctions open in the surveillance of the proprietary [strategic] powers. It poaches in them. It creates surprises in them, it can be where it is least expected. It is a guileful ruse." (deCerteau, p.37).

[46] See particularly, Hauerwas, *A Community of Character: Toward A Constructive Christian Social Ethics* (Notre Dame, IN: University of Notre Dame Press, 1981), pp. 53–71.

[47] The movement of black theology in South Africa, for example, is a response to this "historical dilemma," i.e., the fact that the Bible has been used as an instrument of social control and discrimination. See Takatso Mofokeng, "Black Christians, the Bible, and Liberation," *Journal of Black Theology in Southern Africa* 2/1 (1988), pp. 34–42.

[48] The recent work by the Comaroffs is perhaps the most comprehensive study to date of the relations between Christianity, power, and resistance within colonial Africa. See particularly John L. and Jean Comaroff, *Of Revelation and Revolution: Christianity, Colonialism, and Consciousness in South Africa*, Vol. 1 (Chicago, IL: University of Chicago Press, 1991).

CHAPTER FIVE

CHRISTIANITY, TRIBALISM, AND THE RWANDAN GENOCIDE

When Cardinal Etchegaray of the Pontifical Council for Justice and Peace visited Rwanda on behalf of the pope, he asked the assembled church leaders, "Are you saying that the blood of tribalism is deeper than the waters of baptism?" One leader present answered, "Yes it is."

-John Martin, Rwanda Why?

THE RWANDAN GENOCIDE AND THE "BLOOD OF TRIBALISM"

No event in recent history has challenged Christian ethical reflection in Africa more than the 1994 genocide in Rwanda. Within a period of less than one hundred days, more than 800,000 Rwandans were killed by fellow Rwandans, as the rest of the world stood by and watched. The fact that the majority of the killings were carried out by ordinary Rwandans against their neighbors, and moreover in a very close and intimate way, using machetes, sticks, and clubs with nails, makes the Rwandan genocide one of the most inexplicable tragedies of our time. What makes the Rwandan genocide a particularly chilling and challenging event for Christian reflection, however, is the fact that Rwanda has been, and perhaps remains, one of the most Christianized nations in Africa. It is estimated that as much as 90% of Rwandans in 1994 were Christians—62.6% Catholic; 18.8 % Protestant; 8.4% Seventh Day Adventist.[1] How then did the fact that the majority of Rwandans were Christians not make any significant difference when it came to the events of 1994? Where was the church? Did God just turn his back on Rwanda?

The more one probes these and similar questions, however, the more one faces the disturbing realization that in the 1994 Rwandan genocide, the church was not simply silent, but was intimately associated with the genocide. Not only did the majority of killings take place within or around churches, they involved Christians killing other

95

Christians. In fact, as Longman points out, the fact that the majority of Rwandans were Catholics meant that both the victims and their killers were quite familiar with each other and had even participated regularly in the same Eucharist celebrations, within the same church. He notes:

> *Church personnel and institutions were actively involved in the program of resistance to popular pressures for political reform that culminated in the 1994 genocide, and numerous priests, pastors, nuns, brothers, catechists, and Catholic and Protestant lay leaders supported, participated in, or helped to organize the killings . . . . In most communities members of a church parish killed their fellow parishioners and even, in a number of cases, their own pastor or priests.*[2]

In the wake of the genocide, there have been many attempts to "explain" this rather disturbing fact of a genocide taking place within a Christian country, and the mass participation by self-confessed Christians in the genocide. Among different explanations, some have noted the superficial nature of Rwandan Christianity.[3] Others have focused on the Church's failure to provide moral and spiritual guidance.[4] Other accounts have noted how the revival movement of the 1930s was narrowly "spiritual' and did not allow the church to integrate the gospel with all other aspects of life.[5] Other explanations, while focusing on the political dimension of the problem, have noted the naïve and uncritical view of authority that was encouraged by the church,[6] as well as the general lack of democracy and of respect for human dignity in Rwanda in the 1990s.[7] Although there is truth in each of these claims, the underlying problem behind the Rwandan genocide is one of tribalism. In this case, I feel that the question posed by Cardinal Etchegaray of the Pontifical Council for Justice and Peace, and the answer he received, needs to be seriously attended to. When he visited Rwanda on behalf of the pope, shortly following the genocide, he asked the assembled church leaders, "Are you saying that the blood of tribalism is deeper than the waters of baptism?" One leader present answered, "Yes it is."[8]

I am afraid that Cardinal Etchegaray's question was right on target and the response of the church leader even more so. The 1994 genocide in Rwanda had to do, in great part, with tribalism. I do, of course, realize that to admit that the 1994 genocide was a clear case of tribalism sounds like an easy and convenient explanation, which moreover seems to confirm Western impressions of Africa and Africans. For such an admission gives the impression that Africans are naturally tribal or that tribalism is a typically an "African thing"—a primitive mindset, or a cultural trait—which so-called advanced societies have thankfully managed to leave behind.

What, however, I would like to show in this essay is that tribalism is a distinctively modern problem, which has to do with the role of stories in the political imagination. This is to say that a tribal identity and the violence associated with tribalism are wired into the imaginative landscape of nation-state politics. In this case, the Rwandan genocide revealed the depth of the tribalism operating not only within nation-state politics in Africa, but also within the imagination of Western so-called "democratic" nations. More importantly, I would like to suggest that since tribalism is connected with the issue of political imagination, the urgent Christian challenge of responding to tribalism is one of political re-imagination. Such a task, I show, is possible to the extent that the church is able to conceive of itself as a "wild space" within which alternative forms of social existence can be engendered. In the last section of the essay I show that the Eucharist not only constitutes this wild space, it gives rise to a new politics, which lives with and through stories that form different political identities in the world.

TRIBALISM AND POLITICAL IMAGINATION IN AFRICA: THE POWER OF STORIES

The way in which the story of Rwanda is often told tends to suggest that the genocide was a natural outcome of what tribes with fundamentally different and clashing origins, cultures, and self-interests inevitably do to each other. The story often proceeds along these lines: when the missionaries and colonialists came to Rwanda at the end of the nineteenth century, they found three tribes living in the area: the Twa, the Hutu, and the Tutsi. Even though the Tutsi formed a minority (about 15% of the population), they dominated all political, economic, and social life. Both colonial politics and the church were unable to reverse the dominance of the minority Tutsi over the other tribes (but instead promoted and exploited it to their advantage) until 1959, when a Hutu revolution overthrew the Tutsi government. Thousands of Tutsis were killed, and many more went into exile. Then in 1990, some of these Tutsis, who had been living in exile in Uganda, staged an armed return to Rwanda. It was this Tutsi invasion from Uganda that led to the escalation of tribal conflict, was exploited by Hutu extremists in the ruling MRND, and finally resulted in the mass genocide of the Tutsis and the Hutu moderates in 1994.

Such a narrative, however, suggests that the genocide was the outcome of cultural and biological differences that have existed for centuries between these two tribes: the Tutsi and the Hutu. But this is misleading. For as a number of scholars have now pointed out, before the colonial occupation of Rwanda, the Hutu and the Tutsi were not "clearly distinct and rigidly separated ethnic groups."[9] This, of course, is not to say that Hutu-Tutsi categories were simply cooked up by the Belgian colonialists. In a very helpful study, Muhamood Mamdani traces the distinctions between the Hutu and the Tutsi back to the precolonial state of Rwanda but notes that Hutu and Tutsi operated as fluid "transethnic identities," based on economic patterns (agricultural versus cattle grazing) and power relations.[10] Within this precolonial setting, Mamdani notes, these differences did not translate into Hutu and Tutsi as distinct "tribes." Rather, the people called Tutsi and those who came to be called Hutu formed "a single cultural community of Kinyarwanda speakers."[11] They shared a common geography and language, common customs and religious practices and beliefs, and a high degree of intermarriage. In other words, one could not find a more cohesive national unity than existed in precolonial Rwanda.[12]

Mamdani's work is therefore highly significant, for it shows that rather than assuming that "Hutu" and "Tutsi" are identities that reflect either biological or cultural differences, Mamdani argues that they should be seen as political identities that were formed first and foremost through the state.[13] Central to this formation was the role of colonial mythology, through which racially-obsessed nineteenth century Europeans came to view the Tutsi-Hutu differences operating in precolonial Rwanda as an essential *racial* difference; one that reflected ontological superiority and inferiority, and one that came to play out historically as the conflict between invaders and natives. Part of the European view of Africa as a dark continent, and of Africans as incapable of any civilization, the story was built on the mythic history of the Hamitic conquerors to designate the Tutsi as a "civilizing race" in the Great Lakes region of East Africa. John Hanning Speke, the famous Nile explorer, plays a key role in the construction of what was later to become the unquestioned scientific canon of anthropological explanation. In his influential *Journal of the Discovery of the Source of the Nile*,[14] he felt compelled to "explain" the apparently well-functioning and organized monarchical institutions that he encountered in the interlacustrine region of eastern Africa. Since these developments were too refined to be Negro in origin, Speke concluded, they must be associated with the past arrival of a "conquering superior race." These "carriers of a superior race," who were the ancestors of the Tutsi, Speke wrote, must be "Caucasians in black skin" who may have had their origins in the North: "It appears impossible to believe, judging from the physical appearance of the Wahuma, that they can be of any other race than the semi-Shem-Hamitic of Ethiopia . . . [as descendants of] Christians of the greatest antiquity."[15]

It is this Hamitic story—with the assumption that the Tutsi people were fundamentally a different race from the Hutu (foreign, genetically superior, a civilizing race; black Caucasians with origins in the north)—that became the unquestioned canon governing the decisions of German and later Belgian colonialists in the administration of Rwanda. The story played a particularly crucial role during the reforms of 1927–1936, through which Belgian colonial power turned the Hamitic racial supremacy into an institutional fact, by making it the basis for reforms and changes in political, social, and cultural relations. The reforms were capped with a census that classified every citizen as either Tutsi, Hutu, or Twa, and issued each group an identity card reflecting one's race. In this way, Rwandan society not only became racialized—the key institutions of Rwanda's social, cultural, religious, and political life came to be dominated by the Tutsi, who as the Hamitic assumption went, were "the natural born leaders."

Given this background, it is not difficult to see how the fluid and transnational Hutu-Tutsi relationships which existed in precolonial Rwanda came not just to be transformed, but "fixed" into stable racial identities of an "inferior-superior" type: identities that were reproduced within the history of the Rwandan state. Gourevitch sums up the situation very well when he notes:

> *Whatever Hutu and Tutsi identity may have stood for in the precolonial state no longer mattered; the Belgians had made "ethnicity" the defining feature of Rwandan existence. Most Hutus and Tutsis still maintained fairly cordial relations; intermarriages went ahead, and the fortunes of "petits Tutsis" in the hills remained quite indistinguishable*

from those of their Hutu neighbors. But with every school-
child reared in the doctrine of racial superiority and inferi-
ority, the idea of a collective national identity was steadily
laid to waste, and on either side of the Hutu-Tutsi divide
there developed mutually exclusionary discourses based on
the competing claims of entitlement and injury.[16]

Prunier notes the same effect in a way that helps to capture the explosive animosity that had now been permanently written within the
Hutu-Tutsi categories. It would only be a question of time before this
social bomb exploded:

The result of this heavy bombardment with highly value-
laden stereotypes of inferior-superior would, over time,
achieve the very effect of inflating the Tutsi cultural ego
inordinately and crushing Hutu feeling until they coalesced
into an aggressively resentful inferiority complex. If we
combine these subjective feelings with the objective politi-
cal and administrative decision of the colonial authorities
favoring one group over the other, we can begin to see how
a very dangerous social bomb was almost absent-mindedly
manufactured throughout the peaceful years of abazungu
domination.[17]

Prunier is of course right. But it is not only during the "peaceful"
years of white colonialism that the mythological roots of this explosive
social bomb were never questioned. They were simply never questioned throughout Rwanda's history, not even in the aftermath of the
1959 revolution. For although the revolution was able to turn upside
down the world designed by Belgian colonialists (thus transferring
power from a Tutsi to a Hutu elite), it neither questioned nor changed
the underlying imagination of the Hutu and the Tutsi as racially different people. This means that, for all its gains, the 1959 revolution did
not question, but rather built on these racial myths, thus helping to
"naturalize" the political identities created by colonialism.[18]
Accordingly, "despite the Hutu monopoly on power, the Hamitic myth
remained the basis of the state ideology. So a deep, almost mystical
sense of inferiority persisted among Rwanda's new Hutu elite."[19] This
continued to be the case within the Second Republic (1973–1994) of
Juvenal Habyerimana. No doubt, one of Habyerimana's key accom-
plishments was to redefine Hutu and Tutsi as ethnic rather than racial

identities.[20] This redefinition, however, only succeeded in recasting the Tutsi from being a foreign "race" to an indigenous "tribe." It did not question the underlying assumptions that Hutu and Tutsi—now baptized tribes—were essentially different and that they had *always* been at war with each other.

Mamdani's work is important, because it helps show why the hatred or tribalism between the Hutu and the Tutsi is neither grounded in natural differences nor naturally arises out of differences in their respective cultural histories. Rather, it is the effect of a particular history of state formation. Crucial in this process is the significance of myths, political assumptions, and stories. As the Hamitic story of separate origins was used to explain a people who originally "spoke the same language, lived on the same hills, and had more or less the same culture," it succeeded in forming a society (modern Rwanda) where the Tutsi and the Hutu actually *became* separate communities, united in their hatred of each other.[21]

What this conclusion confirms is the fact that what we are—our identities—is in great part a function of stories and assumptions operating within the politics of our societies. To the extent that a Hamitic vision of Hutu and Tutsi as fundamentally different people was the assumption behind Rwanda's social, political, and cultural institutions, Rwandans, in effect, became Hutu and Tutsi. Moreover, what the genocide of 1994 confirms is the fact that stories do, in fact, kill. For once a vision of Hutu and Tutsi as fundamentally different had become entrenched into the collective imagination of Rwandans, such a story could easily be called upon to carry out and justify the killing of Tutsis. Over a century and a half after Speke told the story of the Tutsi as foreigners from Ethiopia, Hutu extremists were calling on their Hutu compatriots to send the Tutsis back to Ethiopia via the river. Within weeks, the Akagera River was literally flooded with bodies of dead Tutsis!

From an African viewpoint, it is particularly chilling to realize that the story of Rwanda is not the exception, but just an extreme example of the type of political imagination at work in Africa. At the heart of this imagination is a story or set of stories—one that was initially told by the first colonial settlers and is now reproduced through the postcolonial state—namely, that Africans incorrigibly live in tribes that are always at war with each other. While such a story provided a ready justification for colonial presence in Africa (to pacify the tribes

by building modern nations), it also served to sustain the colonial policy of divide and rule.[22] But, to the extent that this was the underlying
assumption of colonial politics, it led to the formation of nations in
which the very assumptions of tribes, tribalism, and "constant warfare"
came to be reproduced and confirmed.[23]

In fact, when one looks at it from this point of view, it becomes
evident that what Mamdani argues about the 1959 revolution in
Rwanda can be said of the independence movement in the rest of
Africa. Independence, for many African countries, turned upside down
the world of the colonialists. While power was handed over to
Africans, the raising of the national flag or the singing of a new national anthem, did not mean that the underlying myths and assumptions
about "Africans" and their "tribes" were ever questioned or challenged. Instead, rather than challenging and pioneering a way beyond
tribally shaped identities and politics, the independence movement just
locked African nations within this imagination, thus helping to both
naturalize and confirm the tribal identities created by colonialism. The
effect has been that tribalism becomes an ever-present and volatile
aspect of African political and social life. That is why, to the extent that
Rwanda reveals the depth of tribalism, Mamdani is right to characterize Rwanda as "a metaphor for postcolonial political violence."[24]

A CRITICAL PAUSE: TRIBALISM
A UNIQUE AFRICAN PROBLEM?

I have found it necessary to narrate the history and assumptions
behind the "tribalization" of Rwanda because from an ethical and theological perspective, I find the readiness with which both theologians
and others commenting on Rwanda have simply assumed "tribe" and
"tribalism" as a natural condition in Africa—part of the way that
Africans have always lived—to be extremely frustrating. Such an
assumption of course does not allow one to get behind these so-called
"natural" identities to discover the stories through which they are
formed and reproduced within nation-state politics. If one were to do
so, however, one would discover that tribalism is a distinctly modern
problem which is not limited to Africa, but which is connected to the
history of modern nation-state politics. That is why, I think, there is
also something convenient about the way the West tends to project
tribalism as a uniquely African problem, which in effect hides the need

for Christians in the West to critically look at the underlying stories behind their so-called democratic and developed nations.

It is clear, for instance, that the story of capitalism, with its insistence on "economic interests" was one reason behind the Western lack of intervention in Rwanda to stop the genocide noted.[25] Even as eight thousand Rwandans on average were being killed every day, U.S. officials were unwilling to refer to the killings as "genocide," which, under UN statutes, would have compelled the U.S. and other Western powers to intervene. Thus, despite clear evidence of the genocide, the Clinton administration insisted that what was going on in Rwanda was just a "tribal" war—just "another flare-up" in a long history of "ethnic conflict."[26] The truth of the matter is that for the Clinton administration as well as for many Americans, Rwanda was of little or no strategic importance to American interests. The then Republican Senate Minority Leader, Bob Dole, expressed it well: "I do not think we have any national interests there . . . . The Americans are out, and as far as I am concerned, that ought to be the end of it."[27] Given the absence of American interests in Rwanda, it was easy to find excuses for U.S. inaction by appealing to convenient views of "African tribal violence."[28]

It may of course be that many American Christians, as Clinton later admitted, were not even aware that a genocide of such magnitude was under way in Rwanda.[29] But this assumed lack of knowledge itself reflects another story—the story of race—that neatly divides up the world between "us" and "them." For as Haynes points out:

> Perhaps the failure of Rwanda's tragedy to penetrate the Western mind has to do with geography and race as well. The mental maps of most Americans do not include East Africa. The crises there—even when they reach the threshold of media consciousness—seem far away, the historical and political contexts unfamiliar, the "tribes'"involved indistinguishable. Unless a conflict pits "white" against "black" as in South Africa or Zimbabwe, it does not hold our attention for long.[30]

If Haynes is right, as I suspect he is, then it is clear that the Western nations are characterized by a far more insidious form of tribalism grounded in the story of "race" and of "Western economic interests."[31] It is these stories that lull Western Christians into thinking that they have no stake in the world or events affecting Rwandan Christians, as long as Western interests are not threatened. I do not think that, at least from the Christian point of view, this sort of tribalism is any less problematic than the Hutu-Tutsi tribalism in Rwanda. On the contrary, the tribalism of economic interest is much more detrimental to the Catholicity of the church than "tribal warfare" ever could be. In fact, this economic tribalism sets the foundation for the type of disinterested and detached response shamefully explicated by Senator Bob Dole. Furthermore, it just shows that as long as Western Christians locate themselves neatly within the dominant imagination of their nations they cannot begin to imagine that there is much they share in common with Christians in the so-called Third World, except perhaps some vague notion of humanity. This might be one reason why "humanitarian assistance" was the only response that the Western nations were willing to consider in the wake of the Rwandan genocide. But the fact that humanitarian assistance becomes the only conceivable Christian response to Rwanda just goes to show the extent to which Christians, whether in the West or in Africa, have lost the will and imagination necessary to question the tribalism of nation-state politics, which neatly divides up the world between "us" and "them."[32]

That was precisely the problem for Christians in Rwanda—the fact that a dominant imagination based on the Hamitic story succeeded in creating a world for Rwandan Christians which was neatly divided between us and them. Over time, this rat-cat world of Hutu–Tutsi animosity came to be viewed not only as natural but inevitable. The failure of Christian social ethics in Rwanda has to do with the fact that all along Christianity failed to question these so-called natural identities (successively named races, tribes, ethnicities) or to provide an alternative conception and/or imagination to the tribalism within Rwanda.

That is why, even though Christian social ethics need to question the church's involvement in the events of 1994—what Christians and the church did or failed to do during the genocide—the far more serious failure relates to the church's inability to resist the dominant imagination of Rwanda grounded in the Hamitic story. For once that story was accepted, the 1994 violence, though extreme, was nevertheless a predictable conclusion. And so in order to provide any credible recommendations for a way forward, we need first to explore the form Christian social ethics took in Rwanda, and show why, within this history, the church in Rwanda did not question, let alone embody, any credible alternative to tribalism.

TRIBALISM AND CHRISTIAN
SOCIAL RESPONSIBILITY IN RWANDA

Dominant as Christianity was in Rwanda, the church never questioned nor offered any credible alternatives to the tribal imagination of
Rwanda society grounded on the Hamitic story. For, as has been noted,
even the 1959 revolution itself was unable to challenge this story. On
the contrary, despite the Hutu monopoly on power that emerged from
the revolution, the Hamitic story remained the basis of state ideology.
Gourevitch notes:

> *Nobody in Rwanda in the late 1950s had offered an alter-
> native to a tribal construction of politics. The colonial state
> and the colonial church had made that almost inconceiv-
> able, and although the Belgians switched sides on the eve
> of independence, the new order they prepared was merely
> the old order stood on its head.*[33]

Does this mean that all through this time there were no sufficient
Christian social ethics in Rwanda? On the contrary, the church was
both ominously present and socially active—only it did not understand
its mission in terms of political imagination, but in terms of providing
relevant contributions to the politics of the day. Accordingly, the
church never radically questioned or challenged the politics of the day,
but instead neatly located itself within the dominant imagination
shaped by the Hamitic story. The effect was that the church, the
Catholic Church in particular, not only became a dominant actor within Rwanda's social and political history, it also became the state's most
reliable partner in elaborating, advancing, and defending the Hamitic
story. Mamdani notes: "When it came to breathe institutional life into
the Hamitic hypothesis, the colonial church acted as both the brains
and hands of the colonial state. In this instance, at least, the church did
both the strategic thinking and the dirty work for the state."[34]

The Catholic Church continued to play the same social role after
the 1959 revolution, in the era of Hutu political control, which, as I
have noted, was grounded in the assumptions of the Hamitic story.
Prunier notes:

> *If there was a link between the two versions of the myth
> (first Tutsi, then Hutu leadership) it was the Catholic*

> *Church. It has admired the Tutsi and helped them rule, but now it admired the Hutu and helped them rule. In both cases, this was perceived (and abundantly explained) as being the work of divine providence and a great step forward in the building of a Christian society in Rwanda .[35]*

What needs to be noted, however, is that in this respect, the church in Rwanda was not an exception. It simply reflected back to the universal church its own version of Christianity. For, as Michael Budde notes:

> *Despite the decades of efforts to inculcate the gospel in Africa, Asia, and the Americas in ways that free the message from its European trappings, one aspect of the European Christian synthesis has remained unchallenged throughout mainstream Catholicism—namely, the Constantinian bargain that hamstrings the gospel with the "responsibilities" of statecraft.[36]*

In the case of Rwanda, what the requirement for Christian social responsibility succeeded in doing was to securely lock the self-understanding and mission of the church within the political imagination of a tribalized society. Accordingly, the need to examine the underlying assumptions and stories on which Rwandan politics were based never even arose within the discussions of Christian social ethics. In fact, throughout this time, the most focused discussions in Christian ethics were in relation to inculturation—an attempt to find relevant African cultural expressions for the faith. These efforts were, in my opinion, quite successful, as evidenced by the fact that even today the Kinyarwanda Mass boasts of some of the finest musical lyrics and lively expression. What is evident, however, is the fact that these efforts at inculturation did not and could not translate into a re-imagination of the Hutu and Tutsi tribal identities that were produced within this dominant political imagination.[37] The reason, as Linden helpfully notes, is that inculturation had meant the immersion of the church in the divisions of a divided and stratified society:

> *It had never meant any serious challenge to Hutu and Tutsi identity as an imagined identity which was potentially open to being reimagined in a new Christian form because ethnicity had always been taken as given. But ethnicity and*

nationality is not a given, rather something that is interac-
tively imagined and lived. Christianity had been adopted
both as a faith that was inculturated in exclusive identities
and as a set of ethics that in practice prescinded from these
identities leaving them unchanged.[38]

And so, far from providing a challenge and an alternative to a tribal imagination of politics, the quest for inculturation simply placed the Rwandan church more firmly within the dominant political imagination grounded in Hutu-Tutsi tribalism.

It is for this reason that I find a great deal of the prevailing theological ethical recommendations for a way forward in Rwanda to be limited. Whether the recommendations have focused on the need for "deeper evangelization,"[39] or on calls for forgiveness and reconciliation,[40] on the need for democracy, or the promotion of human dignity and human rights,[41] they all fall short of the challenge for political re-imagination. In other words, the recommendations are all located within the standard imagination of Rwanda in that they are all built upon the "realism" that accepts the existence of Hutu and Tutsi as natural identities. And even when the role of ideology in constructing these identities is noted,[42] the recommendations offered still fall short of the challenge for a political re-imagination of Rwandan politics in a way that does not reproduce these tribal identities. The claim I am making is not simply that these recommendations do not challenge tribalism. I am making a stronger claim that they cannot do so, unless they are somehow able to invoke the reality of a church whose social force is located outside or at the margins of the dominant political imagination of Rwanda.

In this respect, in contrast to the mass participation of Christians in the genocide, the case of the Muslim community is quite telling. Prunier notes:

The only community that was able to provide a bulwark
against barbarity for its adherents was Islam. There are
many testimonies to the protection that members of the
Muslim community gave each other, and their refusal to
divide themselves ethnically. This solidarity comes from the
fact that "being Muslim" in Rwanda, where Muslims are a
very small (0.2%) proportion of the population, is not sim-
ply a choice dictated by religion: it is a global identity
choice. Muslims are often marginal people and this rein-

forces a strong sense of community identification which
supersedes ethnic tags, something the majority Christians
have not been able to achieve.[43]

There are a number of aspects that make this case of the Muslim community a provocative one for Christian ethical reflection. Among them
is the clear observation that if the Muslim community was able to
resist the barbarity of tribalism in Rwanda, it is because in their marginal existence, they were able to discover within their own tradition
resources for concrete forms of social existence: resources that did not
assume the dominant story of Rwanda was grounded in the Hamitic
mythology. What the example of the Muslim community therefore
confirms is the fact that resisting tribalism is not only possible, but the
possibility comes in the form of concrete social alternatives at the margins of a dominant political imagination. Similarly, if the church, particularly the church in Africa, has to face the challenge of political re-
imagination, it needs to view its social mission not primarily in terms
of "social responsibility," but in terms of the need and formation of
Christian communities, which can be both a challenge and an alternative to the tribalism of nation-state politics.

To be sure, it is not exactly clear how such marginal existence can
be recovered by Christians in our time, especially when Christians find
themselves in predominantly Christian countries like Rwanda. I suggest that as a start it might be good for Christians to give up the impression that they have a stake in the development of a "Christian nation,"
and instead focus on allowing the church to become a "wild space"
within (or at the margins of) the dominant culture. I borrow this notion
of wild space from Sallie McFague's *Life Abundant*.[44] In the face of the
modern consumer-oriented economy and culture, McFague uses the
notion of wild space to signal to the sort of skills and attitudes individuals need to cultivate if they are to resist, survive, or creatively reshape
the draft of an all-too-powerful consumerist world view. A wild space,
according to McFague, is whatever does not fit the stereotypical
human being, or the definition of the good life as defined by conventional culture. It is significant, however, to note that for McFague, a
wild space is not the province of a self-sufficient way of life outside
Western capitalist and consumer society. Rather, wild spaces are created or discovered in the rifts of that very culture. She invites us to imagine conventional Western culture as a circle with one's world superim-
posed over it:

If you are [a] poor Hispanic lesbian, your world will not fit into the conventional Western one. It will overlap somewhat (you may be educated and able-bodied), but there will be a large crescent that will be outside. That is your wild space; it is the space that will allow—and encourage—you to think differently, to imagine alternative ways of living. It will not only give you problems, but possibilities.[45]

Barring the overly individualistic overtones which are apparent in McFague's use of the notion, I find the notion of wild space a promising way to characterize the existence and social posture of the church in modern times for at least two reasons. First, the notion of wild space avoids the impression that in order for the church to become a distinctive social imagination in our time, Christians must withdraw from participation in modern societies. Secondly, the notion of wild space allows Christian ethics to draw attention to concrete practices like worship, which allow—and encourage—Christians to think differently, to imagine and embody alternative ways of living. And so, in this last section I would like to point to some of the stories and practices that help constitute the church as such a wild space.

EUCHARISTIC ALTERNATIVES: CHRISTIAN WILD SPACES

The Eucharist is a good place to start in thinking about the church as a "wild space" within modern nation-states. For it is within and through such a practice like Eucharist that Christians might be able to open up cracks within—and thus interrupt—the story of nation-state politics. Such an interruption, however, is not so much an individual accomplishment, but is in fact possible to the extent that Christians are part of a community—*ecclesia*—that reflects and is grounded in a another story: a different imagination. This is to say that the wild space that Eucharist makes possible is not an imaginary space, but a concrete ecclesiological possibility, a distinctive social reality—one realized not through violence or coercion,[46] but performed through an offering of "five loaves and two fish."

When it was evening, the disciples came to him and said, "This is a deserted place, and the hour is now late; send the crowds away so that they may go into the villages and buy food for themselves." Jesus said to them, "They need not go

*away; you give them something to eat." They replied, "We
have nothing here but five loaves and two fish." And he
said, "Bring them here to me." Then he ordered the crowds
to sit down on the grass. Taking the five loaves and the two
fish, he looked up to heaven, and blessed and broke the
loaves, and gave them to the disciples, and the disciples
gave them to the crowds. And all ate and were filled; and
they took up what was left over of the broken pieces, twelve
baskets full. And those who ate were about five thousand
men, besides women and children* (Mt 14:15–21).

In looking at this text, I have always wondered why all the gospel
accounts of this story are careful to record what on the surface seems
like an insignificant detail—namely, Jesus' command for everybody to
sit on the grass (Mt 14:19; Mk 6:39; Lk 9:16; Jn 6:10). When one looks
at it from the context of our discussion here, however, it becomes clear
the command to sit on the grass is not, as is commonly perceived, a
way to establish some order in an otherwise chaotic multitude, but an
attempt to counteract a temptation that is clearly evident from the attitude and suggestion of the disciples. The temptation amounts to nothing less than accepting the realism of situation. The disciples seem to
be overwhelmed by the situation and are apparently helpless. They
realize they are in a "deserted place, and the hour is now late."
Moreover, they "have nothing here but five loaves and two fish,"
which is not sufficient for their own needs, let alone for a crowd of five
thousand men, not counting women and children. That is why they
suggest, rather realistically, that the people should be sent off (to the
towns and villages) to buy food for themselves.

It is precisely this realism that Jesus challenges and counteracts
with a new imagination: there is no need to send the people to the
towns and villages—let everyone sit down on the grass. It is here at the
margins of the dominant political and economic imagination of Jesus'
day that the multitudes are gathered into an assembly (*ecclesia*) of five
loaves and two fish—a witness to the new community made possible
through a Eucharistic imagination. In other words, the command to sit
on the grass indicates the form and location that Christian social imagination takes. Christian social imagination takes place not within the
power centers—Kigali, Kampala, London, or Washington—but right
here (on the grass) where the disciples happen to find themselves on
the fringes of the dominant political imagination (here represented by

the "towns and villages"). Moreover, it is realized not so much as a set of ideas, recommendations, and insights (to advance democracy, justice, peace, or human rights) but as the performance of concrete local ecclesial communities.

Not unlike the disciples, the greatest challenge facing Christians today is how to resist the realism that assumes tribalism as our natural condition. If our discussion to this point has made clear that tribalism is the effect of stories operating with the modern political imagination, we are now suggesting that within a Eucharistic practice and the concrete ecclesiological wild space that such a practice opens for us, Christians are able to attend to stories that reflect a completely different vision of social existence. For instance, as they read and listen to the Scriptures within this Eucharistic context, they are able to hear another account of differences than the one provided by the Hamitic story or the story of modern economics:

> The cup of blessing that we bless, is it not sharing in the blood of Christ? The bread that we break, is it not a sharing in the body of Christ? Because there is one bread, we who are many are one body, for we all partake of the one bread . . . . For just as the body is one and has many members, and all the members of the body, though many, are one body, so it is with Christ. For in the one Spirit we were all baptized into one body—Jews or Greeks, slaves or free— and we were all made to drink of one Spirit (1 Cor 10:16–17; 12:12–13).

To be sure, Christians may have heard this story before. What becomes new however, is that only by not assuming an overarching "neutral" politics are Christians able to see the hitherto unexplored political potential of Paul's words in a way that explodes into concrete forms of social existence. For now they are able to realize that in talking about the Body of Christ, Paul is not just suggesting a metaphor for Christian life. Neither is Paul talking of a spiritual or mystical body, but about a concrete, real body politic: a visible community. And, in fact, what Paul is doing in the passage above is to challenge the Christians of Corinth to realize that the Eucharist is nothing but the visible performance of this story, which in turn forms the community into being the very Body of Christ that is celebrated.

Only a community that understands itself as a wild space is able to realize the full political potential of Paul's words. For such a community would have recognized within this story an account of differences far more basic (and more accurate) than any stories of modern anthropology or Darwinian science. And because they do, the story begins to take form in their lives as a new identity, one that does not simply build on, but challenges, resists, and reimagines our standard ways of being in the world as Hutu, Tutsi, African, American or any other contrived nationalistic or ethnic identity. This is to say that as Christians begin to view the world through such a story, they begin to see themselves accordingly. What perhaps needs to be stressed is that such "seeing" is not theoretical, but is connected to concrete stories and practices in which being Hutu or Tutsi, African or American begins to make little or no sense. Critically, therefore, it is by being drawn into a form of wild space existence that Christians are able to see the fully destructive power of the tribalism that forms us into a divided Body of Christ, willing to slaughter one another in the name of being a Hutu, Tutsi, Ugandan, or Congolese, and so forth. As this becomes possible, the Eucharist then becomes the very sign, sacrament, and practice of God's act of remembering the divided body of Christ.

Only a community so remembered or so constituted by a practice such as the Eucharist can stand as a witness and an alternative to the politics that would have us live as tribes, each set against the other. There is no doubt, however, that such a community may have no choice but to become a church of martyrs, as the example of the teenage school girls in Gisenyi and Kibuye. At both schools during the genocide, the militias ordered the girls to separate themselves—Hutus from Tutsis. At both schools the girls refused, saying they were simply Rwandans. They were beaten and shot indiscriminately.[47] The example of the young seminarians at Buta in Burundi exemplifies the same courage and witness:

> *There were 250 children ages 11 to 19 . . . . On April 30, 1997, around 5.30, we hear shots. In several minutes, the assailing rebels had become masters of the seminary. The soldiers charged with protecting us had fled. A troop of rebels had taken over the dormitories. The little ones on the first floor dormitory were able to free by the windows, but not the older students on the second. The assailants gathered us in the middle room and demanded that we separate*

into Hutus and Tutsi. The students refused. They were unit-
ed. Then the leader of the group, an enraged woman,
ordered their killing. There were 70 students. The assailants
fired the grenades. When the rebels left the seminary, I
counted 40 bodies.[48]

It is only by being a community formed by a story more determinative
than the Hamitic one that these young girls and seminarians were able
to resist the tribalism of Hutu-Tutsi. A courage and martyrdom like
theirs, however, does not make sense, and in fact cannot even be conceived unless it is informed by, or is the result of, sustained formation
in the politics of the Body of Christ. But for the church to be capable
of such witness, the story of the Body of Christ must already have
become the primary way of seeing the world and thus of shaping
everyday attitudes and expectations.

The recommendation here is not simply for more frequent celebration of Eucharist. It is for the realization of *ordinary*, real, and genuine
communities—communities that have come to view the whole of their
daily activities as nothing but the extension of the politics of the
Eucharist, which is to say the building up of the Body of Christ. Fr.
Sibomana's account of his pastoral ministry following the genocide is
a powerful reference to the sense of ordinary we have in mind:

We had to rebuild everything including minds and bodies,
public buildings, houses, families . . . . The houses were for
survivors who had lost everything. The workmen were Hutu
and Tutsi. At first, the Hutu and Tutsi would not speak to
each other. But this communal work helped to rebuild
bridges. At the inauguration of the first 200 houses on 21
August 1995, Hutu and Tutsi drank banana beer from the
same jug.[49]

Accordingly, within a Eucharistic assembly, the more Christians drink
from the one cup and attend to the stories of God within scripture, a
new social performance of local (grassroots) politics becomes possible
and concretely visible. For as the Eucharist becomes the primary way
in which Christians view and respond to the challenges of the world, it
shapes a world in which there are no Hutus or Tutsis (or as St. Paul
would put it, "no more Jew or Greek, Samaritan or Gentile, male or
female"). It is then that a new social imagination, in the form of concrete ecclesial communities, irrupts within the cracks and margins of

the dominant story of tribalism. It is such ecclesial communities which are an alternative to the tribalism of the world, and can therefore offer a visible hope that the waters of baptism can be, and in fact are, much deeper than the blood of tribalism. With witnesses such as the teenage girls of Gisenyi and Kibuye and the young seminarians of Buta beckoning us, Christians have no excuse for not seeking to live out such a hopeful future.

Notes

[1] Timothy Longman, "Christian Churches and Genocide in Rwanda," in *In God's Name: Genocide and Religion in the 20th Century*. Omer Bartov and Phyllis Mack, eds. (New York: Berghahm Books, 2001), 149.

[2] Ibid., 140.

[3] Gary Scheer, "Rwanda: Where was the Church?" *Evangelical Missions Quarterly* 31 (1995), 324–326.

[4] Tharcisse Gatwa, "Victims or Guilty? Can the Rwandan Churches Repent and Bear the Burden of the Nation for the 1994 Tragedy," *International Review of Mission* 88 (1999), 347–363.

[5] J. Kritzinger, "The Rwandan Tragedy as Public Indictment of Christian Mission: Missiological Reflections of an Observer," *International Review of Mission* 88 (October, 1999), 347–363.

[6] Roger Bowen, "Rwanda—Missionary Reflections on a Catastrophe," *Anvil* (13/1) (1999), 17.

[7] Tharcisse Gatwa, "Resisting Democracy in Rwanda: Genocide and Reconciliation," *Reformed World* 48 (1998): 190–205, and Scheer, Gary, "Rwanda: Where was the Church?" *Evangelical Missions Quarterly* 31 (1995), 324–326, 328.

[8] Peter Hebblethwaite, "In Rwanda, 'Blood is Thicker than Water - Even the Waters of Baptism," National Catholic Reporter. June 3, 1994,

[9] Timothy Longman, "Christian Churches and Genocide in Rwanda," 145.

[10] Mamdani, Muhamood. *When Victims Become Killers: Colonialism, Nativism, and the Genocide in Rwanda*. (Princeton, NJ: Princeton University Press, 2001), 73–74.

[11] *Ibid.*, 72.

[12] Commenting on this pre-colonial setting, Gourevitch (1998:47) notes how there are few people in Europe among whom one would find these factors of national cohesion. "Hutus and Tutsis spoke the same language, followed the same religion, intermarried, and lived intermingled, without territorial distinctions, on the same hills, sharing the same social and political culture in small chiefdoms." Gourevitch, Philip. *We Wish to Inform You That Tomorrow We Will Be Killed with Our Families: Stories from Rwanda*. (New York: Farrar, Straus, and Giroux, 1998), 47.

[13] Mamdani describes three types of identities: economic identities (the consequence of the history of development of the markets), cultural identities (the consequence of the history of the development of communities that share a common language and meaning), and political identities. Whereas modern political theory has tended to view political identity as arising out of either culturally based or market-based identities,

Mamdani argues that political identities need to be seen as identities that exist in their own right—the direct consequence of the history of state formation and not of market or cultural formation. Within the modern state, political identities are inscribed in law; they are legally enforced. If the law recognizes you as a member of a specific ethnicity and if state institutions treat you as member of that ethnicity, then you become an ethnic being legally and institutionally. "If your inclusion or exclusion from a regime of rights or entitlements is based on your race or ethnicity, as defined by law, then this becomes a central defining fact for you, the individual, and your group. From this point of view, both race and ethnicity [and I should add tribe] need to be understood as political—and not cultural, or even biological—identities." (Mamdani, 22).

[14] John Hanning Speke, *Journal of the Discovery of the Source of the Nile*. (New York: Harper and Brothers, 1864).

[15] *Ibid.*, 240–243, as cited by Gerard Prunier. *The Rwandan Crisis: History of a Genocide*. (New York: Columbia University Press, 1995), 7.

[16] Gourevitch, 57–58.

[17] Gerard Prunier. *The Rwandan Crisis: History of a Genocide*. (New York: Columbia University Press, 1995), 9.

[18] Mamdani, 36.

[19] Gourevitch, 66.

[20] Mamdani, 138ff.

[21] *Ibid.*, 52.

[22] Davidson, Basil. *The Black Man's Burden: Africa Under the Curse of the Nation-State*. (Oxford: James Currey, 1992), 99–117.

[23] Thus the crucial question now is not whether tribalism is real or not, but the sort of reality that tribalism is and how it has become such a permanent feature of African politics. The challenge is to understand the process and assumptions through which African society is tribalized, and in the process produces the very tribal identities that are assumed. See my forthcoming *The Sacrifice of Africa: The Church, Politics and Social Imagination in Africa*.

[24] Mamdani, xi.

[25] See Linda Melvern, *A People Betrayed: The role of the West in Rwanda Genocide*. (New York: Martins Press, 2000); Power, Samantha, "Bystanders to Genocide," *Atlantic Monthly*, (September 2001); and Stephen Haynes, "Never Again: Perpetrators and Bystanders in Rwanda," *Christian Century* (February 27 - March 6, 2002), 30–35.

[26] Samantha Power, "Bystanders to Genocide," *Atlantic Monthly*, (September 2001), 92.

[27] *Ibid.*, 93.

[28] The Assistant Secretary of State (director of the task force that managed the Rwandan evacuation of American nationals) said it best: "I felt very strongly that my first obligation was to the Americans . . . . I was sorry about the Rwandans, of course, but my job was to get our folks out . . . . Then again, people didn't know that it was a genocide. What I was told was 'Look Pru, these people do this from time to time.'" (Power, 93).

[29] Clinton's apology was offered in March 1998 on his visit to Rwanda: "It may seem strange to you here, especially the many of you who lost members of your family, but all over the world there were people like me sitting in offices, day after day, who did

not fully appreciate the depth and speed with which you were being engulfed by this unimaginable terror" (Power, 86).

[30] Stephen Haynes, "Never again: Perpetrators and Bystanders in Rwanda," *Christian Century* (February 27 - March 6, 2002), 33–34.

[31] The story of tribalism in Rwanda that we have told indicates that the formation of 'hutu' and 'tutsi' identities based on the Hamitic thesis is at the basis a story of European racism played out in Africa through the practices of European colonialism and the enlightened classification of peoples according to a racial hierarchy. Thus, a straight and very short line connects the stories of 'race,' 'Western interests' and 'tribalism.'

[32] Even when heroic, humanitarian assistance does very little to change or question the basic structure of powers in the world. In fact, as David Reiff has noted in his ruthlessly lucid book *A Bed for the Night: Humanitarianism in Crisis* (Simon & Schuster), humanitarianism can very often serve as a fig leaf, a moral cover for not wanting to change the basic structure of the world. For this reason, humanitarianism, far from representing a bulwark against evil, may in fact become one of its appendages. This is certainly true in the case of Africa, where humanitarian intervention often goes hand in hand with, or is simply the flip side of, an underlying Afro-pessimism as reflected in the Economist, 13–19 May 2000: "The Hopeless Continent" and in such accounts as Keith Richburg, *Out of Africa: A Black Man Confronts Africa* (Harcourt Brace & Co.: New York, 1998).

[33] Gourevitch, 61.

[34] Mamdani, 98. On the church's crucial role in education, and how the missionary schools became the 'wombs of racial ideology' see particularly, *Gatwa*, 353–356.

[35] Prunier, 81.

[36] Michael Budde, "Pledging Allegiance: Reflections on Discipleship and the Church after Rwanda," in *The Church as Counterculture*, Michael L. Budde and Robert W. Brimlow, eds. (Albany, NY: State University Press of New York, 2000), 221.

[37] On the contrary we learn of such disturbing accounts of people who attended mass each day and then went out to kill. "In a number of cases, people apparently paused in the process of carrying out massacres to pray at the church altar. In Ngoma parish, a Tutsi priest who was hidden during the war in the sanctuary by his fellow Hutu priests told me, 'people came and demanded that my fellow priest reopen the church and hold mass. People came to mass each day to pray, and then they went out to kill.'" Timothy Longman, "Christian Churches and Genocide in Rwanda": in *In God's Name: Genocide and Religion in the 20th Century*. eds. Omer Bartov and Phyllis Mack, (New York: Berghahn Books, 2001), 157.

[38] Ian Linden, "The Church and Genocide: Lessons from the Rwandan Tragedy," in *The Reconciliation of Peoples*. (Geneva: WCC Publications, 1997), 261–262.

[39] Mario Agular, *The Genocide in Rwanda and the Call to Deepen Christianity* (Eldoret: Gaba Publications, 1998).

[40] See Emmanuel Kolini, "Toward Reconciliation in Rwanda," *Transformation* 12/2 (1995), 12–14; and Paul Nzachayo, "Religion and Violence: Outbreak and Overcoming" in *Religion as a Source of Violence?* ed. Beuken Wimand Karl-Josef Kushel, (Maryknoll, NY: Orbis Books, 1997), 11–22.

[41] See Tharcisse Gatwa, "Resisting Democracy in Rwanda: Genocide and Reconciliation," *Reformed World* 48 (1998), 190–205; and Max Ngabirano, "National

Justice: A Challenge to the Great Lakes Region of Africa," *Afer* 43/4–5 (2001), 229–251.

[42] Emmanuel Kolini, "Toward Reconciliation in Rwanda," *Transformation* 12/2 (1995), 12–14.

[43] Prunier, 253.

[44] Sallie McFague, *Life Abundant: Rethinking Theology and Economy for a Planet in Peril.* (Minneapolis, MN: Fortress Press, 2001).

[45] Ibid., 48.

[46] This is precisely what Bishop Misago of Gikongolo fails to see. Questioned about his involvement in the genocide, particularly his inability to prevent the murder of eighty-two school children at a mission school in Kibeho, Bishop Misago pointed to his own helpless situation. 'What could I do?' he said. 'When men become like devils, and you don't have an army, what can you do?' (Gourevitch, 139). Whereas Bishop Misago's deference to the army reflects a form of realism, it bellies the habituated assumption that outside the dominant imagination which the nation-state (army) names and controls, Christianity has no resources or alternatives for peaceful social existence. What Bishop Misago does not realize is the fact that it is precisely this story that makes genocide possible. For once it has been assumed that there can be no other order or social existence other than that proffered by a threat of violence (army), then the machetes (of the genocide) simply became a logical consequence of the same story of violence.

[47] Gourevitch, 353.

[48] *National Catholic Reporter* 22, (2002), 11.

[49] Andre Sibomana, *Hope for Rwanda: Conversations with Laure Guibert and Harve Deguine.* Carina Tertsakian, trans. (London: Pluto Press, 1997).

CHAPTER SIX

KANNUNGU AND THE MOVEMENT FOR THE RESTORATION OF THE TEN COMMANDMENTS OF GOD IN UGANDA

*The night of March 15th, the members consumed the beef
and Coke they had purchased and celebrated the building
of the new church. The next night, the 16th, they spent most
of the night praying and then met in the new church early
the next morning. A little before 10 A.M. they were seen leaving the new church to enter the old church which was now
being used as a dining hall. The windows were boarded up
from the outside and the doors were locked. Authorities told
Mayer that it was impossible to tell whether the windows
were boarded from the inside or outside, but contrary to
media reports, the door had not been nailed shut. At 10:30
A.M., an explosion was heard by nearby villagers, and a fire
quickly consumed the building and all those inside.[1]*

INTRODUCTION: A DANGEROUS CULT

On March 17, 2000, an estimated 338 members of the
Movement for the Restoration of the Ten Commandments of
God (hereafter referred to as MRTCG) died near the village of
Kannungu in southwestern Uganda in what appeared to be mass suicide. However, the subsequent discovery of mass graves in various
other locations associated with the MRTCG not only raised the death
toll to more than 800, it also raised doubts about whether the inferno
at Kannungu was mass suicide or homicide perpetrated by the leaders
of the MRTCG. Perhaps we shall never know exactly what happened
at Kannungu and other centers associated with the MRTCG, especially because none of the principal participants of the MRTCG seem to
have survived.

Part of the frustration in understanding an event like Kannungu
derives from the fact that little is known about the MRTCG prior to

March 17th.2 In fact, both media and government reports do not seem overly interested in this comprehensive background, but instead are focused narrowly on trying to "figure out" the events of March 17th. But lacking any comprehensive context in which to evaluate the MRTCG, the reports of the deaths at Kannungu and other locations have tended to appeal to the usual "explanations," which, in essence, are meant to warn people against the dangers of cults and cult leaders. One such explanation has been to depict Kannungu as the result of a failed prophecy of the end of the world. According to this explanation, Kibwetere and the other leaders of the MRTCG had prophesied that the world would end on December 31, 1999. When this prediction failed to pass, followers began to request that the property they had surrendered in preparation for the end of the world be returned. In response, the leaders set out in a systematic elimination of these followers, first killing a few members and then finally the entire group, before taking off with all the money from the property.3

Even though this "explanation" is fairly standard, it is, however, very misleading, especially because it overlooks the evidence from the group's main theological text, *A Timely Message from Heaven*, which clearly states that the new Earth will begin after the year 2000 is completed.4 Moreover, by narrowly focusing on the time between December 1999 and March 17, 2000, the failed prophecy hypothesis does not throw light on the way in which the group operated and organized its day-to-day activities and interactions before the year 2000. But even within its own time framework, the failed prophecy hypothesis cannot account for the events immediately preceding March 17th, especially the mood of celebration and prayer by the members. Why, for instance, did the members hold on March 16th "a big celebration at the camp, with a very copious meal, which became their 'Last Supper'?"5

Even more misleading are the reports by which Joseph Kibwetere and Credonia Mwerinde, the group's key leaders, have been consistently dubbed "the Preacher and the Prostitute"—the latter a reference to Mwerinde's questionable way of life before her claimed vision of the Virgin Mary. In a similar manner, Kibwetere has been portrayed as an unstable, frustrated, and "manic depressive [individual] who had stopped treatment at a mental hospital."6 To be sure, these and similar reports are exaggerated: for there are other (and at least in this regard more credible) indications that suggest that Kibwetere was "known among many Ugandans for his piety, prayer, and good works." He founded a Catholic school and became the supervisor of other schools in the region. He was also apparently a person of some means as he donated land on which two other Catholic schools were built.[7]

Given such evidence, which seems to be intentionally overlooked, it is clear that the aim behind much of the media and government reports is to portray the MRTCG as a "cult" or "sect" whose leaders preyed on unsuspecting poor people, duped them out of their possessions, and led them to a tragic death. This also explains why, following the inferno, the Ugandan government issued warrants of arrest for Mwerinde, Kibwetere, and Father Kataribabo, even though it is highly unlikely they survived the fires at Kannungu on March 17, 2000.

But that these media and government "explanations" have neither been questioned nor challenged by any alternative explanation is itself telling. For it seems to confirm how difficult it has become for anyone to imagine that the members of the MRTCG or anyone else for that matter could take their religious convictions so seriously, to the point of voluntary suicide. Thus, the only explanation available is one that portrays the group as "victims" of the cult's leaders, who used "religion" as a means to attain their own selfish and wicked ends. At any rate, there is an impression that nothing positive can be learned from groups such as the MRTCG, except to use them as a warning to all against the dangers of fanatical religion, which in modern-day terms we have come to identify with sects and cults.

But this is what I find particularly misleading. For the "explanations" assume that the danger that Kannungu represents lies outside our usual, peaceful forms of social existence. I would, however, like to suggest that far from representing a form of danger "out there" (embodied only within certain clearly identifiable cults or sects), Kannungu is a parody of the violence and hopelessness that unfortunately are all too apparent within both the state and the church in Africa today. In fact, I would like to make an even stronger claim that, in many respects, the MRTCG was itself an attempt—a tragically failed attempt to be sure—to counter this hopelessness by embodying an alternative, more hopeful form of social existence.

This is a point that is missed by "explanations" for Kannungu. By portraying Kannungu as exclusively a design of the leaders, the explanations not only fail to take seriously the agency of the members of the MRTCG, they also ignore what one would call its subaltern or "popular" character. For instance, it is now clear that MRTCG had been in existence since 1989, and that during the ten or so years of its existence it had come to attract a following of more than 5,000 members and established "centers of evangelization" in various parts of the country. The crucial question, therefore, is in understanding how the MRTCG was able to attract so many people over so short a time. What kind of appeal or promise did it offer to its members? The appeal, I would like to suggest, had to do with the type of community the MRTCG aspired to be, and how such a social existence offered both a challenge, and at least initially, a promising and "attractive" alternative to available forms of social existence that, as our study has suggested, are caught up in a frustrating circle of hopelessness and mere "survival."

By making this claim I do not wish to condone the violence with which the MRTCG became increasingly enamored and which culminated in the fires of Kannungu on the morning of March 17, 2000. On the contrary, the claim I am making renders the violence of Kannungu even more tragic, given the MRTCG's explicit desire for a hopeful and peaceful existence through the restoration of the Ten Commandments of God. The claim I am making implies that the tragic end of the MRTCG cannot itself make sense except against the background of a social history in which nation-state politics have succeeded only in underwriting, for the majority of Africans, lives of despair and the violent frustration of unfulfilled individual aspirations.

In the final analysis, the MRTCG itself failed to provide any credible alternative to this history, but instead reproduced the despair and violence on a grand scale, thereby confirming the extent to which Christianity in Africa has come to be marked by the same habits of hopelessness and violence. That this is the case may of course be due to the churches having tended to uncritically assume and even mimic the same patterns of power (lordship and privilege) as those at home within nation-state politics in Africa. At any rate, the tragic story of Kannungu shows how any constructive and sustainable Christian imagination in Africa must involve an explicit determination to unlearn the patterns of power and privilege we have come to take for granted. At the same time, this imagination must undertake a creative "re-visioning" of the Church's practices and traditions in light of its attempt to be a credible social alternative of hope and peaceful existence.

That is why the MRTCG as well as the tragic story of Kannungu provide a serious challenge to Christian social imagination in Africa, both constructively and critically. And so, before we turn to these crit-

ical considerations that rendered the MRTCG a failure of social imagination, we need to display the sense in which the MRTCG might have
offered, at least initially, a serious social alternative by providing not
simply a hopeful *telos*, but also the social setting and disciplined practices through which this *telos* could come to be concretely embodied
in everyday activities.

THE MRTCG AND KANNUNGU AS SOCIAL IMAGINATION

1. An Alternative to Despair

In an editorial on April 4, 2000, a Ugandan newspaper, the *Monitor*,
noted, "The people of Uganda are desperate. Unless their conditions
change, we will see more Kannungu." The *Monitor* was, of course,
talking only about the desperate *material* conditions that include
poverty, malnourishment, and the widening spread of AIDS. To be
sure, many have noted a connection between the distressing material
conditions and the many apocalyptic sects and movements that spring
up every year in Africa's religious ferment.[8] Just a few days before the
Monitor editorial, Dr. Florence Baingana, a psychiatrist in the
Ugandan Ministry of Health, had noted how "fears of what is going to
happen in the year 2000 and grinding poverty had fueled the religious
sect movements in Uganda . . . . Our history has made us more vulner-
able because life has been very hard."[9] However, what the editorial of
the *Monitor* did not capture, but what our discussion has sought to narrate up till now, is that even more than material despair, the far more
serious form of despair that marks the lives of many Africans is the
lack of any meaningful purpose or *telos* to make everyday struggles
both valuable and bearable.

It is against this background of what we have alternatively characterized as "exhaustion" and "deflation" that one can appreciate the
alternative that the MRTCG embodied by a clear sense of mission and
purpose to its members. Moreover, theirs was an invitation to participate not in any adventurous undertaking, but in the "restoration of the
Ten Commandments of God." As one of the group's leaders observed,
"Ours is not a religion, but a *movement* that endeavors to make the
people aware of the fact that the Commandments of God have been
abandoned, and gives what should be done for their observance."[10] If
the MRTCG was able to present its mission in clear and precise terms,

it also showed it was serious about its goal by demanding extreme sacrifice of its members: prayer, silence, and celibacy.

That is why, even without interpreting the MRTCG in a strictly religious manner, one can see that, in providing an ambitious goal such as the restoration of the Ten Commandments, it offered its followers not only a *mythos*—an ideal beyond their small, individual aspirations—but also a worthwhile adventure in which they could participate and become agents. As our earlier discussion shows, it is precisely this sense of *mythos* and adventurous participation in a cause beyond mere "survival" that nationalist politics had gradually succeeded in editing out of people's lives. This alone might explain why the MRTCG was able to appeal to a cross section of the population—not just Catholics and the materially poor. Regarding the membership of the MRTCG, the Report from the Religious Department of Makerere University (MUK Report) notes, "Contrary to what some sections of the media reported, not all these were simple peasants. It emerged that there were many people who were educated and had a number of skills. There were teachers, carpenters, masons, businessmen, and ex–servicemen (police and army), ex-catechists, not to talk of the leaders who included at least three priests."[11]

There are a number of other important aspects of the social vision through which the MRTCG sought to embody its goal of restoring the Ten Commandments. These aspects provide an indication of the extent to which the MRTCG was able to challenge the prevailing atmosphere of helplessness and are central to the sort of social imagination that is called for in Africa.

2. A Disciplined Community

For the MRTCG the "restoration" of the Ten Commandments was, in the final analysis, about structuring an individual's way of life. Thus, the MRTCG seems to have realized that the commandments are not just safeguards for the salvation of individual Christians, but also that their restoration required and called into existence a community in which the commandments could be socially and visibly embodied. And so, as far back as 1992, Kibwetere and the members of the MRTCG moved to Kannungu, where "several hundred lived in a communal setting and practiced an austere life style. They built homes, a church, an office, and a school."[12]

Whatever else might be said about the community that the MRTCG aspired to be, their communal existence both required and inspired new ideals of sharing. As *A Timely Message* (XVI: 11) so clearly indicates: "If it is time to collect money, those who have should pay, those without should sell part of their property, and those with a calling [should] abandon the earthly life to go and preach like the 12 apostles of Jesus."[13]

Another noteworthy aspect that characterized the communal life of the MRTCG was the quasi-monastic existence that bears witness to the type of disciplined existence at Kannungu. The MUK Report[14] notes that the members would wake up at around 3 A.M. for a period of prayer called the "way of the cross." Following this, the members

> *would go back to sleep waking up again at 7:00 A.M., and would say morning prayers till 8:00 A.M. After this they would go to different kinds of work up to 1:00 P.M., followed by another prayer till 2:00 P.M. From 3:00 P.M. was their free time. Thereafter they would do other types of activities including their morning work schedules. Supper was around 8:00 P.M. followed by night prayers till around 11:00 P.M. when they went to sleep.*[15]

Such a monastic lifestyle may strike many of us as not only excessive but oppressive and a form of mass control. My aim in drawing attention to it is to highlight the discipline that underlies or sustains it. In a situation where "deflation" tends to generate forms of violence and nihilistic playfulness, discipline must not only be a part of but also be central to the task of any social imagination.[16] In this respect, the MRTCG was revolutionary in the type of disciplined social existence it required of its members and by which it sought to inspire and challenge the wider Christian community. This is perhaps why, in 1991, the members of the movement already were "planning to build a school and to make it a model for discipline."[17] But notice also how *A Timely Message* devotes a whole section to messages directed to different categories of people—medical doctors, schoolteachers, the judiciary, the police, public-health officers, drivers—in which the theme of discipline and commitment is central.[18] That there is even constant reference to "drunkenness" and a call for drivers to stop speeding shows how much the MRTCG had come to appreciate—rightly, in our opinion—that a life of discipline and commitment is indispensable to any attempt for social reconstruction, particularly in Africa.

3. A Thriving Community

Perhaps it should not be surprising that, given the clear sense of teleological purpose as well as the disciplined existence of the members, the MRTCG would soon come to grow into a self-sufficient and materially prosperous community. By 1995, reports indicate that the community of Kannungu had become a thriving community:

> Members lived communally on land bought by pooling the profits from their property, which they sold when they joined the cult. The church buildings were set in plantations of pineapples and bananas. Cows grazed on the hilly land. The followers had their own primary school, as well as dormitories where they slept together on simple rush mats. They had recently completed a new church and decorated it with colored bunting.[19]

Even the MUK Report, which on the whole is negative and dismissive of the MRTCG phenomenon, describes the existence of a

> large compound with a cemetery in the middle of the site . . . a number of fields where potatoes, bananas, pineapples, and sugar canes were grown; a dairy farm which became a model farm of about 30 Fresian cows; a poultry project. . . . Group members themselves carried out all the developments mentioned in the camp with little outside help or interference.[20]

The MRTCG seems to have been so materially secure and self–sufficient that "during periods of drought, the movement supplied food to the surrounding local people."[21] Perhaps it was on the basis of such signs of visible material hope that Kannungu came to be referred to by the members of the MRTCG as "Ishayuuriro rya Maria" or "the place where Mary removes her people from where they are stuck."[22]

4. On Taking Religion Seriously

What the preceding indications suggest is that the MRTCG had come to appreciate that the challenge of restoring the commandments

was in essence not just about "beliefs" or a mere set of ethical guidelines to be followed, but a concrete way of life. If they understood the
requirement of this way of life to be both rigid and demanding, they
were equally aware that as a way of life it involved not only the sort of
prayers one said and how one said those prayers, and not only the way
one received Holy Communion, but also the way one talked (and
refrained from talking), cultivated one's cabbages, and raised one's
chickens. In this way, the MRTCG aspired to move beyond the fairly
"modern" conceptions of religion in which the distinction between the
spiritual and material and souls and bodies is at home. This is perhaps
one of the reasons for which, in a statement already quoted, one of the
members of the group insisted, "Ours is not a religion, but a movement."[23] The latter simply meant that it aspired to an embodied existence in which the distinction between secular and religious and
between religion and politics had become superfluous. As a movement, the MRTCG would aspire not only to be all-inclusive (open to
all irrespective of religion), but all-encompassing as well.

But it is precisely such a "mixture" of religion with all other aspects
of one's life that strikes many as "fanatical" and dangerous. For it is
assumed that, in our day and age, no persons in their right mind can
take their religious vision seriously enough to allow those convictions
to structure their entire existence—unless of course such persons are
duped by "unscrupulous individuals who use religion for their proper
ends" or they themselves are willing "to follow them due to such reasons as poverty, diseases, and even ignorance."[24] In any case, the
impression seems to be that the problem of Kannungu was due to the
members of the MRTCG taking their religious vision seriously, and the
results were predictably tragic.

And so, in the days after March 17th the name of "Kannungu" was
used as a veiled warning to anyone who was perceived to be taking his
or her faith seriously. Thus, there were a number of instances when
groups of unemployed youths, especially around the taxi parks in
Kampala, would shout "Kannungu" at any nun dressed in a religious
habit. These youths might have seen the wearing of religious habits by
nuns, many of them fairly young and beautiful, and their determination
to remain celibate in a culture that prizes sex and procreation, as a clear
example of taking religion too seriously. By warning them with the
reminder of "Kannungu," they probably hoped to save the nuns from
the fanaticism that required such a sacrifice of them.

The youths were, of course, right to see in the nuns an example of taking one's religious vision and convictions seriously. They were also right in suspecting that members of the MRTCG had taken their religious convictions seriously. They were wrong, however, to assume that taking one's religious convictions seriously inevitably leads to Kannungu, or that it was this aspect of the MRTCG that led to the violence of March 17th. The problem of Kannungu is not that people died because they sought a social and material embodiment of their religious vision, but that their religious vision became unfortunately entangled in an increasing cycle of hopelessness and violence, in response to which March 17th might have seemed the only way out.

But this alone cannot count as evidence against taking a religious vision seriously or against the task of Christian social imagination as such. On the contrary, it shows that we need to take more seriously and translate into capital for social imagination the fact that has been noted by many: namely, that in Africa "the church is the most widely spread and most sustainable social institution, especially in the rural areas."[25] What the case of the MRTCG shows is that, if church communities are daring and imaginative enough to move beyond the security of the religious and spiritual realm, they can become social alternatives of a concrete, peaceful, and hopeful material existence.

This is what makes Kannungu an even more tragic and more troubling phenomenon to comprehend. How could a community like the MRTCG, which showed signs of being a hopeful and disciplined alternative to the prevailing forms of despair and violence, have ended up unleashing the worst form of violence and hopelessness? If we can shed light on the limitations and contradictions that constrained, frustrated, and eventually subverted the MRTCG's social vision, we might begin to see how Kannungu could not only have been avoided, but how it rendered the MRTCG one of the most tragic and failed experiments in social imagination. Accordingly, by looking at some of the limitations and contradictions within the MRTCG's vision that led to March 17th, we will be able to display the sort of Christian skills that must be in place if a community is to become a credible social alternative of a hopeful and peaceful existence.

TOWARD A MORE ADEQUATE
CHRISTIAN SOCIAL IMAGINATION

At least three major limitations and contradictions seem to have frustrated the MRTCG's efforts at social imagination: (1) a tendency toward isolation, (2) a failure to reimagine the nature of Christian leadership, and (3) a lack of hope. Focusing on these three shortcomings within the MRTCG's vision allows me to build a wider argument about the requirements of a truthful social imagination. Accordingly, I argue that for any community to embody the sort of imagination that would qualify for the label "Christian" such a community must, among other requirements: (1) be open to the stranger, (2) be willing to understand itself as a servant community, and (3) be a Eucharistic community of forgiveness and hope.

1. Openness to the Stranger

It is not clear, and perhaps it is not even that significant, why the MRTCG chose Kannungu as their headquarters. Whatever reasons might have influenced this decision, Kannungu remains, from a geographical point of view,

> a very isolated and generally quiet [place] and the only way of knowing what was taking place there was to actually visit the place. Located about two to three [kilometers] from Kannungu Trading Center, it was only accessible by a narrow road which was constructed by the movement members once they settled at the site. The road crosses a valley and there is a small bridge made of timber and rocks![26]

This geographical isolation would ensure not only that the MRTCG could carry out its activities free from public interference, but also that both the group's convictions and lifestyle would remain shielded from public view and scrutiny.

However, even more than geography, the isolation of the community of Kannungu was to a great extent the effect of the theology according to which members of the MRTCG understood themselves as the "elect"—those who were destined to go to heaven because they had come to accept and live according to the demands of the Ten Commandments. In fact, the more the group perceived themselves to be the elect, the more the group demanded of its followers a lifestyle that has been traditionally perceived, at least within popular Catholicism, as a mark of holiness. This included celibacy, meditation, monastic silence, strict obedience, the wearing of religious habits, and other demands.

From this point of view, one can see the lifestyle of the members of the MRTCG as a radicalization (and democratization?) of the "holiness" often associated with people in special ministry and status, such as bishops, priests, and religious leaders. What the Catholic Church demanded of only some of its members, the MRTCG demanded of everyone. The claim to special messages and apparitions from the Virgin Mary and Jesus did nothing to undermine this sense of special status, but instead bolstered and confirmed the group's vision of itself as a "holy" and privileged community. The more the group saw itself as a holy elect, the more they perceived the outside world as either still stuck in their sinful ways, or as "enemies"—agents of Satan—determined to oppose and finally destroy God's holy ones.

This was particularly the case following the numerous attempts by the local Catholic hierarchy to stop the MRTCG from claiming visions and messages from the Virgin Mary and, failing this, a final threat to excommunicate the entire group. But one can also detect a growing tension and impatience toward the outside world in the wake of the showdown with government officials when the group's school license was withdrawn in 1998. These external "threats," together with the approach of the year 2000, would push the MRTCG into further isolation, and at the same time, bend their theology into a tragic apocalyptic direction. For example, as a response to these perceived threats, the MRTCG required its members to cut off or reduce to a strict minimum contact with non-movement members, including family and friends. As the MUK Report notes:

> members would not leave camp unless necessary (those engaged in the two shops of the movement at Kannungu and those who went for "evangelization" purposes) . . . occasional visitors to the camp were welcomed though these were restricted to the visitors' area and were not allowed to tour the camp.[27]

The unfortunate consequence of this isolation, so it appears, was that, unable to meet the "threat" of the outside world, the MRTCG turned the violence on its own members, and thus became more intolerant of any divergent interpretations within its own ranks. Such a response was quite predictable, because a society that is unable to deal with external threats to its integrity tends to become more totalitarian in dealing with its own members. Accordingly, the mass graves at various sites connected with the movement might be a testimony to the fate of those within the group who were perceived as "dissidents" because they either questioned their leaders or held views different from those of the mainstream leadership.

However, even before the MRTCG felt the need to resort to these extreme ways of silencing divergent opinions of its members, it had already found subtle ways of stifling individual opinions. For instance, the strict rule of silence and the requirement that members use signs if and when they had to communicate (ostensibly to avoid breaking the Eighth Commandment) ensured that members remained isolated from one another. In the end, Kannungu and the MRTCG became a dangerous ghetto precisely because the members remained isolated from one another, from the outside world, and from the wider church.

What the MRTCG failed to generate—and this failure contributed to its tragic end—is sufficient latitude and openness to allow a conversation among its members and those outside itself concerning its own cherished convictions and way of life. In this way, the MRTCG was to fail a key requirement for a truthful social imagination: a constant willingness to reexamine, assess, and shape a community's vision in the face of changing historical situations and requirements. This simply means that the *telos* of any given community is not a fixed, stable, and static vision. But the conversation itself is part of what it means to be a community.

This does not require an "anything goes" sort of liberalism. Nothing, in fact, in the notion of "conversation" denies the presence and role of sacred texts such as the Bible, canons, and even explicit dogmas within a community's tradition. On the contrary, the existence of such texts is essential to provide the boundaries or guidelines through which a community's conversation is shaped, checked, and advanced. But what must be resisted is the temptation to assume that any such texts or dogmas contain a blueprint for social existence that can be read off and implemented anytime, anywhere. Rather, the task of social imagination is at the same time a hermeneutical exercise that involves and even requires a certain amount of creative tension, as one that is generated from alternative interpretations concerning the best way to read the meaning of the sacred texts themselves. Accordingly, you know a community is in deep trouble when it stifles any alternative readings of the tradition among its members in the name of holiness, orthodoxy, or obedience.

Similarly, the need for other communities in the search and clarification of a community's own vision cannot be underestimated. It is through interaction with other communities that a community comes to a deeper understanding of its own convictions, as the community confronts or is tested by those embodying different sets of convictions. It often takes the presence of a stranger for us to know who we are or what we stand for. Thus, an indispensable requirement for any constructive social imagination is the presence of other communities who help us to discover ourselves, precisely because they are different from us. Moreover, there is always much to learn from the time-tested skills of other communities. In this respect, the MRTCG's isolation from the wider Catholic community was perhaps one of its most tragic mistakes, which left the MRTCG without a wider horizon and scope to validate and realize the wider implications of their convictions. Take, for example, the claims regarding various visions and messages from Mary and Jesus. The Catholic Church has always believed in visions of God, Jesus, and the Virgin Mary, some of which relate to the end of the world, and in the course of time has developed a whole range of criteria and guidelines through which these visions and messages are read, interpreted, and understood. By isolating the visions of Jesus and Mary from the wider community of the Catholic Church and its time-tested skills of metaphorical interpretation, the MRTCG took the visions literally and acted on them.

In conclusion, we need to note, therefore, that even though our call for social imagination involves a valorization of "local" communities, there is nothing at all in that claim that suggests a sectarian withdrawal of the members of that community into a sort of sectarian enclave or ghetto. On the contrary, it is clear that the only way to remain a truly viable local community is through the cultivation of a key virtue of openness, through which the community can allow, confront, and peacefully negotiate differences of opinions—both internal and external. One criterion for truthful social imagination is openness to the stranger, which is, in the final analysis, a question of whether a community can find peaceful ways through which to handle alternative interpretations and contrary visions as they are embodied by individuals and other communities who are different. Because Kannungu failed to fulfill this requirement, it offered its members a dangerous form of ghetto existence in which a resort to violence seemed the only way to vindicate the truth of its convictions.

2. The Practice of Authority in the Life of a Servant Community

Another key constraint on the MRTCG's social imagination and threat to the existence of the community itself was the failure to reimagine the exercise of power and authority in a genuinely Christian manner: that is, in a manner different from those currently available within the nation-state. This claim itself sounds surprising because at least in its formal elements, the MRTCG's power structure, and its internal organization, resembled, in great part, that of the Catholic Church. The members of the MRTCG were hierarchically organized in three groups: the novices, comprised of the newest members who wore black; those who "had seen the commandments" and wore green; and the fully professed members, who were "those who were willing to die in the ark" and who wore green and white. Overseeing the entire organization were twelve apostles, or "Entumwa," led by Kibwetere, who filled the position of the head apostle on Kashaku's death.[28] At least on the outside, the organizational model seems Catholic in its hierarchical inspiration, and in some instances even shows itself to be more inclusive than the Catholic model. For instance, because the group believed that both Jesus and the Virgin Mary would return in the Second Coming, six women and six men were chosen to make up the group of twelve apostles.

If, in terms of external formalities, the MRTCG organization looked religious in its structure, in its specific exercise and role of authority it operated in a manner that was extremely authoritarian and dictatorial. Not only did the twelve apostles control all aspects of the life and activities of the group, but they also commanded and expected total obedience from members in all matters, including aspects of daily life. Moreover, the appropriation of the title "apostle" by the leaders provided them with a legitimacy that made it difficult, if not heretical, for anyone to question their authority and pronouncements. This, together with obligatory and unqualified obedience from members, meant that the exercise of power and authority within the MRTCG, rather than being a service to the truth, served either to silence the group into submission or to frighten them sufficiently to deter them from raising questions.

While the MRTCG might have emulated the external formalities of the Catholic hierarchical structure, its inner dynamic had less in common with the Catholic model of authority than with the military, whose top-down and one-way command structure it duplicated. This was an unfortunate consequence, but one that helps to explain why a movement, which had been perceived as an energizing alternative by many individuals who had been rendered powerless by the prevailing politics, ended up rendering these individuals even more powerless in the face of the group's own requirement for unqualified obedience. And if the interdiction of owning private property included the surrender of personal names, titles, clothes, academic papers—anything that could be called a "person's own"[29]—then it is clear that the requirement for absolute obedience was just another way of reducing the members into anonymous followers with little or no personal identity.

Thus, within the MRTCG's exercise of authority we see a reduplication and radicalization of the politics of disempowerment as we have narrated within the nation-state in Africa. And just as in the case of nationalist politics, the MRTCG came to be characterized by the same violent suppression of individual ideals, a ruthless deflation of energy, and a constant disappearance of bodies—a trend that came to a frighteningly dramatic and bizarre finale in the fires of March 17th. But perhaps even more frightening than this dramatic end is that Kannungu represents a latent potential in many churches in Africa, a result of their having assumed "the soul of a nation"—the African nation-state in this case. If the pattern and exercise of authority within the African nation-state has been characterized by both violence and exploitation, the Christian churches have not been able to provide any serious challenge to this conception of power, by failing to reimagine or embody an alternative pattern and practice of power. Instead, the Christian churches have themselves been gradually *learning* the same pattern and practice of power.

One can point to a number of disturbing indications in this trend. The first step seems to be one in which, having lived under various regimes in which the use of power is tantamount to violence, the churches learn to live with, and even begin to expect, a certain amount of violence as part of the "normal" way of life in Africa. Paul Gifford, for instance, notes how this is exactly what happened during Idi Amin's Uganda in the 1970s, where the churches seem to have done so little when the security forces harassed the people and threatened their civil liberties.[30] The reason, Gifford suggests (following Pirout), is that "it was easy to take for granted a certain amount of violence because it was part of the pattern of life in Uganda. The churches become so 'preoccupied with trying to maintain their position and privileges without realizing that the wider threat should also concern them.'"[31]

It is not a large step from a preoccupation with institutional security, survival, and privileges to a situation in which the churches themselves begin to mirror the patterns and skills for "survival" of nation-state politics. This stage has been reached when churches come to resemble mini-nation-states, characterized by the same violent struggle for power, by "tribalism" and by the same "politics of the belly." The leadership struggles that characterized a number of churches in Uganda in the 1990s must be placed within this context. In the Catholic diocese of Kabale in southwest Uganda, for instance, more than half of the priests and Christians rebelled against a bishop whom they accused of tribalism, mismanagement, and embezzling of diocesan funds. The bishop used his close links with security forces to harass his priest opponents and even had some of them arrested. He could not enter a number of his parishes without threat of serious violence against him.[32]

Similarly, for more than eight years, the Protestant diocese of Jinja was embroiled in an acrimonious, violent struggle to remove its bishop, Cyprian Bamwoze. The conflict has received enormous publicity and sucked in all relevant organs of church and state, including the high court. The dramatic clarity of this case makes it a prime example of the extent to which the Church can become a mini-nation-state in its view of, use of, and struggle for power. It is therefore important to cite Gifford's description of one day within this power struggle:

> On 13 July the four bishops comprising the investigating committee published their report. In this they listed all the reasons advanced for or against removing the bishop, and tried to arrange them in some sort of order. This report seemed to support the bishop, but its recommendations seemed to acknowledge the basic justice in the rebel's cause. The first of these recommended that the diocese be split into three new dioceses, and the second that Bamwoze remain as a diocesan bishop if requested to do so by any of the three new dioceses, or take early retirement within one year of the acceptance of the report. This report, however,

> solved nothing, because when Archbishop Okoth on 10
> August visited the diocese to communicate the recommen-
> dations of the committee, the anti-Bamwoze faction refused
> to meet him in a hotel and assembled at the cathedral
> instead. The archbishop refused to speak to the crowd
> assembled inside on the technicality that he could not enter
> a cathedral in his province without the consent of the local
> bishop, and offered to address the crowd outside the cathe-
> dral. The "mammoth gathering which had now turned into
> a mob" insisted that he address them inside the cathedral,
> and began dragging him there. It was only with consider-
> able difficulty that the archbishop reached his car, and
> managed to drive off, the "rear window smashed by stones
> thrown by the wild crowd." On 27 August (bishop)
> Bamwoze himself was subjected to similar physical vio-
> lence at Batambogwe.[33]

The preceding story helps to confirm my suspicion that it is just a short and straight line that runs through and connects the violence within Idi Amin's military regime to the violent protests in the Kabale Catholic Diocese—to the violent confrontation involving Bishop Bamwoze—to the tragic and violent end of the MRTCG. One can see these events as moments or stages in the process of the Ugandan church's learning a particular vision and discipline of authority. In other words, in its failure to re-imagine the notions of power and authority, Kannungu is not an isolated case, but part of a pattern in which the Christian churches have been learning to mimic the same "politics of the belly."[34] The magnitude and thoroughness of Kannungu just show how successful the learning process has been. Moreover, placing the Catholic diocese of Kabale in the same narrative as the Anglican diocese of Busoga and the MRTCG is meant to show that this is a lesson that cuts across all denominational confines.

In this case, Kannungu serves well as a wake-up call. Unless the Christian churches are willing to reimagine and embody an alternative conception and discipline of authority, they will not be able to serious-ly challenge or put a stop to the many Kannungus, secular and reli-gious, just waiting to explode in many parts of Africa. Instead, the churches themselves will increasingly become mini-nation-states, in which the threat and reality of violence will permanently lurk under the surface.

The challenge of social imagination is, therefore, at the same time one of unlearning the dominant vision and practice of authority as lordship, and of learning to embody an alternative practice of authority. We need, however, to stress the critical (unlearning) aspect of this process to register that the discipline of leadership required of us as Christians is radically different from, and therefore sits uneasily with, the practice of authority that came to hold sway within the MRTCG. We also need to stress the unlearning aspect to highlight that, given the extent to which this particular form of authority has captured our imagination, overcoming it must be a conscious and deliberate exercise. This is what makes social imagination a serious and demanding task. Fortunately, Christians are not without resources with which to engage this task.

The New Testament, for instance, provides a number of narratives that depict this challenge concretely by inviting the disciples into an imagination of authority different from dominant conceptions of authority as power and dominion. If we attend to one such passage, Mark 10:35–40 for example, we can begin to appreciate the new imagination of power and authority that Jesus' life and mission entails and how the invitation to be his followers is at the same time an invitation to embody a different conception of authority—to belong to a different kind of community.

Mark 10:35–40 is the familiar story involving the request by James and John, the sons of Zebedee, to be granted places of honor ("one to sit at your right hand, and one at your left, in your glory"). This request, as well as the indignation of the other disciples, shows how the disciples themselves are still captives of the standard imagination of authority as privilege and lordship.[35] In fact, in the Gospel of Mark, the request by the sons of Zebedee for places of honor arises from another incident when the disciples are engaged in a heated argument as to who was the greatest (Mark 9:33–37). Following this discussion, Jesus takes a little child, sets the child in their midst, and warns them, "If anyone wants to be first, he must make himself last of all and servant of all." This example of the little child was meant to open their minds to a new and radically different imagination of greatness. And so, in a series of related lessons, Jesus warns the disciples of the danger of simply mimicking the world and its image of greatness (Mark 9:33–37), its legal complacency (Mark 10:1–11), its endless desire for riches (Mark 10:22–27), and its vision of authority.

In these passages, Jesus calls to the disciples to become conscious-ly aware of and to explicitly resist the temptation in which the practice of authority forms part of the equation *authority = greatness = status = glory = self-aggrandizement*. He calls on the disciples to embody a completely different imagination and discipline of authority: namely, as servant leadership, to which the child and Jesus' own life and min-istry are the model:

> When the other ten had heard this they began to feel indig-nant with James and John, so Jesus called them to him and said to them, "You know that among the Gentiles those they call their rulers lord it over them, and their great men make their authority felt. Among you this is not to happen. Now; anyone who wants to become great among you must be your servant, and anyone who wants to be first among you must be slave to all. For the Son of Man himself came not to be served but to serve, and to give his life as a ransom for many." (Mark 10:41–45)

What is particularly significant in this passage is that here Jesus is offering not just another style of authority, or a set of impressive ethi-cal guidelines that Christians need to think about and take seriously. The new imagination of authority is not only concretely embodied by Jesus' own life and ministry, but it is also a vision that cannot be iso-lated from the life of the community that has been formed by the min-istry and death of Jesus. In other words, to appreciate this vision of authority is to begin to appreciate the type of community that Jesus' life and ministry gathers together, and how such a community must be marked by a different *telos* than it embodied "among the Gentiles." Thus, Jesus' invitation to the disciples to embody a different vision of authority is in essence a call for the imagination of a community whose *telos* is essentially one of service. Such a community is neither called into existence for the pursuit of individual ideals like honor, glory, or even one's own salvation, nor sustained through a discipline of ordered obedience. It is a community called into existence through service, self-sacrifice, and forgiveness. For this reason, while James and John request places of honor (at Jesus' right and left), the Gospels tell us that those places were reserved for two crucified thieves, one of whom was, through forgiveness, remembered into Jesus' kingdom that day.

I am, of course, aware that "servanthood" is not a popular notion, particularly in a modern setting, where it is often associated with weakness and powerlessness. But this is the liberating story that denies the self-serving practices of *la politique du ventre* that drives the nation-state in Africa and opens us to God as the *telos* of the church. It is such a *telos* that, according to Augustine, underwrites not domination and exploitation, but an alternative of peace, equality, and service. It is this alternative that the MRTCG was unable to offer its members, but instead, just mimicked a command and lordship structure of leadership operative within the nation-state generally. That it did so shows a failure to critically engage a humble and honest introspection regarding the type of community that Christians are called to be.

3. A Community of Eucharistic Hope

Another key aspect that undermined MRTCG attempts at social imagination and thus contributed to the tragic events at Kannungu was the group's failure to live as a Eucharistic community of hope. This may indeed sound surprising, given the stress on the frequent reception of the Eucharist by the members of the MRTCG. In fact, the Eucharist seems to have been so central to the message and life of the MRTCG that a key aspect of the restoration of the Ten Commandments involved a restoration of the "proper" reception of the Holy Communion. As *A Timely Message*[36] clearly states, "Our Lord says that the Church should no longer allow his Body to continue being held in the hands by the faithful; anybody who is not anointed should forthwith stop holding his Body in the hands. And the reception of the Holy Communion should be as it was in the past, the people should kneel down and receive Him on the tongue."

The problem, therefore, was not a lack of sufficient regard for Eucharist by the MRTCG, but the sense in which the practice of Eucharist amounted to nothing more than what William Cavanaugh calls a "cult of the host."[37] Among other things, this means that the Eucharist came to be viewed primarily as an "object" at the service of a certain "spirituality" of personal purity and holiness. To be sure, the MRTCG cult of the host seems to have drawn greatly from a long-standing Catholic tradition that limits the reception of Communion to Christians who are "worthy." This practice has had negative consequences in Africa, where many Catholics, who for various reasons think they are not "pure" or find themselves "in sinful situations," are effectively excluded from the Eucharistic table. In some cases, Eucharistic ministers literally pull those suspected of being "unworthy" out of Communion lines to ensure, as was once explained to me by a zealous catechist, that "children's food is not thrown to the dogs"!

It is therefore not difficult to see how, given such practice, the Eucharist becomes a kind of reward or privilege that "deserving" Christians (made deserving through their personal holiness, faithfulness, or obedience to the Church's teaching) receive, while the undeserving ones are reduced to envious spectators, so to speak. It is this sense of Eucharist that the MRTCG radicalized by its insistence on receiving Communion on the tongue while kneeling. The posture becomes the ultimate sign of holiness, obedience, and surrender. However, underlying such preoccupation with personal holiness and "reverence for a holy object," one detects the same politics of power, privilege, and personal aggrandizement at work as was noted in relation to the MRTCG's leadership. The only difference is that in relation to Eucharist, the politics of power and privilege now assume a "spiritualized" and more generalized form. The unfortunate effect of this development, however, is that the Eucharist ceases to be regarded as a practice that institutes and disciplines Christian hope, and simply becomes an object of purity, power, and privilege.

That is why the "cult of the host," as Cavanaugh notes, is "not necessarily an advance for Eucharistic practice."[38] In fact, by locating the rise of the cult of the host within the developments of the late medieval period (the feast of Corpus Christi began in the thirteenth century), Cavanaugh shows that one negative effect of this development was the gap it created between the clergy and the laity and the individualization of Eucharistic piety. As Cavanaugh notes, "Increasing clerical power was linked to the priest's power to produce the host . . . . lay people were increasingly left to silent contemplation [and reception] of the awesome spectacle, and this corresponded to a diminishing of the communal nature of the Eucharist and an individualizing of Eucharistic piety."[39]

The most serious consequence of the cult of the host, however, is that it renders the Eucharist into an object, thereby obscuring its more original meaning as an *action*. As Cavanaugh notes:

> *Modern Christians often speak of "hearing" or "attending" the Eucharist; priests "say" the mass. The ancient church by contrast tended to speak of "doing" the*

*Eucharist (*eucharistian facere*) or "performing" the mys-
teries (*mysteria telein*). The word* anamnesis *had the effect
not so much of a memorial, as one would say kind words
about the dead, but rather of a performance. The emphasis
is on the entire rite of the Eucharist as action, and not simply on the consecration of the elements.*[40]

It is important to underscore this sense of the Eucharist as action
because it is precisely this sense of Eucharistic performance that is
missing in many churches in Africa and that was squelched by the cult
of the host within the MRTCG. It is, however, difficult to see how and
in what sense the Church can be a social imagination without recovering this sense of the Eucharist as action. Perhaps a better way of putting it might be to say that if the Church is a social imagination, that
imagination is realized and displayed most concretely within the
Eucharist. In this sense, the Eucharist becomes the most determinative
form the Church's imagination takes; indeed it becomes the very social
imagination of the Church. Because this dynamic connection between
the Church, the Eucharist, and imagination has been well demonstrat-
ed by Cavanaugh in his treatment of the Church as the true Body of
Christ, we need not spend much time developing the connection.
Where Cavanaugh's work becomes significant for the particular argument of this essay is the way in which he shows that this dynamic connection becomes real only when the Eucharist is understood primarily
in terms of action and performance.[41]

To understand the Eucharist as action is to understand the paradox
within this performance. For on the surface, it looks like the Eucharist
is action performed by the church every time she gathers to "Do this in
remembrance of me." From this point of view the Eucharist is a reality constituted by such concrete acts of a worshiping community, which
"does" or performs the Eucharist. However—and here we touch the
paradox and the deeper level in which the Eucharist becomes performance—the Church is not an independently existing community that
then comes together to celebrate the Eucharist, because it is through
this very Eucharistic action that Christians are constituted into the
Church, the Body of Christ. As Jean Marc Éla notes,

*In saying "Do this as a remembrance of me," Jesus not
only inaugurates a rite, he invites his faithful, the people of
God, to do what he has done—that is, to break themselves,*

> *to be willing to die to themselves, and to share themselves*
> *in thanksgiving to God . . . as the indispensable condition*
> *of becoming the body of Christ in the Eucharist.* [42]

What Éla suggests here is that the performance in which the Eucharist takes place is the very act of gathering the people and the "transformation of a divided people into the oneness of Christ." Cavanaugh puts it even more succinctly:

> *The Eucharist is an* anamnesis *of the past; Jesus commands*
> *his followers, "Do this in remembrance of me"* (Lk 22: 19).
> *If we understand this command properly, however, the*
> *Eucharist is much more than a ritual repetition of the past.*
> *It is rather a literal remembering of Christ's body, a knitting*
> *together of the body of Christ by the participation of many*
> *in His sacrifice.*[43]

If we accept what both Éla and Cavanaugh are saying, then *anamnesis* is not simply any action, but a specific form of action: namely, a social imagination in which *remembering* performs or constitutes a particular community—a visible body of believers, who now become the true Body of Christ. What is significant here is to realize that it is God himself who through these actions remembers a people scattered by sin, gender, greed, despair, sickness, and even death into the one body of Christ. That is why it is significant that as part of the Eucharistic prayer Christians invoke God to:

> *Remember your people . . . ;*
> *Remember those gathered here . . . ;*
>
> *Remember your children scattered*
>   *all over the world . . . ;*
> *Remember the dead—those who have gone before us*
>   *marked with a sign of faith . . .*
> *And all those whose faith is known to you alone . . . .*

It is not that through such prayers Christians are prompting God's flagging memory, but acknowledging that it is his action through which we are made into the Body of Christ. The gathering of this particular community in prayer at this particular time and place thus becomes a confirmation, as well as the anticipation, of that final consummation of God's remembering action, when Christ will be one in all, and all will be one in Christ. Accordingly, the community so constituted can therefore already sing a song of triumph, realizing that:

> *Through Him,*
> *With Him,*
> *In Him. . . all Glory and Power. . . .*
> *For thine is the Kingdom, the Power and Glory. . . .*

The Eucharist thus becomes a real presence, a sacrament precisely because it makes visible the community as the Body of Christ. This is not to deny the real presence of Christ in the elements. But it is to realize, as Cavanaugh puts it, that the "Eucharistic realism" (of elements) is at the service of a far more primary "ecclesial realism" that "sees Christ's real presence in the elements as a *dynamic*, working toward the edification of the church." It is in this sense that Eucharist is not primarily an object, but a performance—one in which the church is both the subject and object. The church does not just perform the Eucharist; the Eucharist performs the church.[44]

It is this sense of Eucharistic performance that became completely unavailable to the MRTCG, enthralled as they were by the cult of the host. As a result, they failed in at least two key requirements that the Eucharist as social imagination makes available: namely, the practices of forgiveness and hope. These practices are intimately connected, since both require discipline and a practice of "patience" and "waiting." Moreover, there is no better way to learn the discipline of "patience" than through forgiveness, which requires nothing less than learning to be sinners who are forgiven, and to see and live with other sinners who are similarly in need of forgiveness.

But this is precisely what members of the MRTCG failed to see. Instead, they aspired to be, and indeed saw themselves, as a church of the pure and holy elect, an illusion that the cult of the host simply confirmed. Accordingly, within their community there was no room for the weak and the sinner, which explains the near fanatical preoccupation with avoidance of sin, exemplified by the rule against talking for fear of breaking the Eighth Commandment or by the high degree of intolerance toward any failure or weakness by the members. Lydia Bagambe tells the incredible story involving her daughter, Mary Kyomugisha (who later left the movement and was the only one of Bagambe's five children who survived Kannungu). In 1994, sect members locked Kyomugisha in a room for a week and wrapped her legs in burning banana leaves as punishment for "talkativeness."[45]

We do riot wish to take back anything we have said about the need for discipline in the task of social imagination and the MRTCG's attempt at being a disciplined community. What we need to stress here is that discipline is not contrary to forgiveness, and in fact, true discipline is Eucharistic discipline. For unless discipline is schooled and infused by forgiveness and hope, such discipline becomes tyrannical. This seems to have been the case with the MRTCG, which was a disciplined community that failed to become a community of forgiveness. I am suggesting that this is a limitation that could have been avoided if the MRTCG had aspired to be a Eucharistic community I have outlined.

The social imagination that the Eucharist performs is not a church of the "pure" or holy, but one of forgiven sinners. For, central to the memory that the Eucharist performs is that "on the night before he was betrayed," Jesus shared a meal with those who were to betray or disown him. And so, whatever else can be said about this meal, it is not a reward for the faithful discipleship of the disciples. Neither is it meant as a safeguard against their future failing or betrayal. It is a meal given as a gift to unfaithful but forgiven friends, a realization that by itself disciplines the community of disciples into the humble discipleship of forgiven sinners.

For Christians, therefore, the Eucharist becomes the performance of our reconciliation with God and with one another. It is also a performance through which Christians learn to live with our sinful selves and the failures of others, without, however, settling into facile complacency. For the gift of forgiveness is at the same time a command; we must "do in remembrance of me." Understood from this perspective, "doing" the Eucharist becomes the very practice of Christian hope: which is to say, a way of learning to live in that "already but not yet" space of God's kingdom. In the Eucharist, God's kingdom of love and forgiveness is already present but under signs. It is the full and glorious realization of that kingdom that we have to patiently wait for "until he comes again." In the meantime, we must live as a community of forgiven and forgiving sinners.

Because within the MRTCG the Eucharist was extrapolated from this context of action and way of life and constructed in terms of purity, privilege, and holiness, it failed to discipline the members into the relevant virtues of forgiveness and hope. On the contrary, under the cult of the host, the Eucharist failed to provide any resources to help the members live with the imperfections, failures, and limitations of the world, as well as those relating to their discipleship. Lacking any such Eucharistic practices, the MRTCG would soon resort to simplistic schemes to explain the hardships and suffering of the present times. In this way, the AIDS pandemic, as well as all sorts of other forms of suffering, were explained as "curses" and punishments from God— signs of God's judgment to a sinful world.[46] Similarly, having failed to ground the project of restoring the commandments in a Eucharistic discipline of forgiveness and hope, the MRTCG would soon hark back to a dangerous eschatology in which "going to heaven" becomes the only motive for the Christian life. *A Timely Message from Heaven* contains many messages in which either Jesus or the Virgin Mary urges the Christians to "repent . . . run away from hell and strive to get to heaven" and promises that those who remain faithful "will surely go to heaven."[47]

There is, of course, nothing wrong or theologically heretical with the promise of "going to heaven." The problem is that once "going to heaven" has become the only form of Christian hope available to Christians, it transforms Christian eschatology into a realm of existence that is detached from, and can only be accessed after this earthly existence. In this case, Christian eschatology easily becomes an escape from the shortcomings and limitations that both earthly existence and Christian discipleship impose on our illusions for "purity" and holiness. This is the form of eschatology that Marx rightly feared turns religion into an opiate and a dangerous ideology. But such an eschatology also becomes dangerous to the extent that a community so focused on "going to heaven" may find that it cannot resist the temptation to resort to violence as a way of expediting such an end. As is now clear, it is on this dangerous and apocalyptic road that the MRTCG dragged its members and delivered them over to the fires of Kannungu.

Thus, contrary to all appearances, a preoccupation with "going to heaven" does in fact entail a certain failure or lack of hope, which is to say, a failure to be a Eucharistic community. Without such hope, the MRTCG, all positive aspects notwithstanding, ultimately failed to provide any sustainable form of social existence as an alternative to the hopelessness pervasive in many places in Africa. Instead, the MRTCG reproduced the same hopelessness, only under a quasi-religious and more radical form.

If the current forms of hopelessness are to be overcome, then we need communities in which hope has become a way of life. Such communities would be able to provide both a critical challenge and real alternatives to the many forms of deflated existence on the one hand, and nihilistic playfulness on the other, that prevail today. What I have attempted to do in this essay is to display how, for Christians, making hope a way of life is not different from aspiring to be a Eucharistic community. This is not simply an invitation for more frequent celebration or more regular reception of the Eucharist. My argument is even beyond (or makes irrelevant) the questions of whether the reception of Communion should be on the tongue or the hand, questions that assume the cult of the host. Rather, it is an invitation to rediscover the imaginative and full political potential of the Eucharist as a practice capable of performing into existence local communities, and disciplining those communities into a life of forgiveness and hope.

CONCLUSION

This has been a long discussion, but I hope that it has been interesting and that, in any case, it makes clear why Kannungu cannot just be dismissed as an oddity that lies outside our "normal" social and religious forms of (peaceful) existence. I have argued that Kannungu needs to be taken seriously precisely because it displays the hopelessness and violence embodied within the mainstream community. In this respect, Kannungu and the MRTCG serves as a critical challenge to the state and church alike, particularly for Africa—where nation-state politics have succeeded only in creating the life of many into an endless cycle of violence and the hopelessness of "mere survival." What Kannungu helps to display is that, by not questioning but simply assuming these politics, the Christian churches have themselves come to be increasingly marked by the same hopelessness and violence. Thus, the critical challenge arising out of Kannungu is to develop the sort of skills that must be in place if the Church in Africa is to resist such politics. The constructive challenge is even more daunting, because it requires a necessary but faithful revisioning of the church's own inherited tradition that will enable the church to become a community that embodies an alternative history and *practice* of hope and peace. That is why the challenge that Kannungu provides is not limited to Africa, for it presents us with the fundamental task of the

Christian social imagination, calling on us to rethink the relation between church and state and between religion and politics in a radically new way. While such a task is necessary for the church everywhere, Kannungu serves as a reminder that such a task has become extremely urgent for the church in Africa.

Notes

[1] Elizabeth Auten, "Movement for the Restoration of the Ten Commandments of God"; Religious Movements homepage, http://religiousmovements.lib.virginia.edu/nrms/mrtcg.html, 7/20/00.

[2] There is more than one account of the group's founding, which can be traced back roughly to 1989 surrounding claimed apparitions of the Blessed Virgin Mary to various people, including Joseph Kibwetere and Credonia Mwerinde, the group's key leaders. Although the movement drew membership from various churches, the majority of its members were former Catholics, including two priests, Father Dominic Kataribabo and Father Joseph Kasapulari. Kibwetere himself was a former lay Catholic worker. This Catholic connection is not only significant in understanding the group's composition, but also in how its perceived mission and identity was derived from beliefs, themes, and practices that would be familiar to many Catholics. See, for example, Introvigne Massimo, "Tragedy in Uganda: The Restoration of the Ten Commandments of God, a Post-Catholic Movement," Center for Studies of New Religions, http://www.cesnur.org/testi/ugamda_002.htrn (5 April 2000).

[3] Chris Tuhirirwe, Gerald Banura, and Joseph Begumanya, "Kannungu Research Team's Report," in *The Kannungu Cult-Saga: Suicide, Murder, or Salvation?* ed. Kabazzi-Kisirinya, Deus Nkuruziza, and Gerald Banura (Kampala: Department of Religious Studies, 2000), 40.

[4] "When the year 2000 is completed, the year that will follow will not be year two thousand and one. The year that will follow shall be called Year One in a generation that will follow the present generation." "The Movement for the Restoration of the Ten Commandments of God": in *A Timely Message from Heaven: The End of the Present Times* (Rukungiri, 1996), IV: 56.

[5] Tuhirirwe, 41; Auten, 4.

[6] Tuhirirwe, 18, Auten, 7.

[7] Auten, 3.

[8] For more on the ferment within the Catholic Church in Uganda, see, for example, Ronald Cassimir, "The Politics of Popular Catholicism in Uganda," in *East African Expressions of Christianity*, ed. Thomas Spear and Isaria N. Kimambo (Nairobi: East African Educational Publishers, 1999), 248–274.

[9] *The New Vision*, (1 April 2000).

[10] *A Timely Message from Heaven*, XVI:II.

[11] Tuhirirwe, 26.

[12] Auten, 3.

[13] A Timely Message from Heaven, XVI:I

[14] Tuhirirwe, 26–27.

[15] *Ibid.*

[16] For more on this, see Emmanuel Katongole, "Postmodern Illusions and Performances." This text, Chapter 4.

[17] *A Timely Message from Heaven,* XV:14.

[18] *Ibid.,* XV.

[19] Anna Borzell, "Horrific Discovery," *Citizens Voice* (20 March 2000): 41.

[20] Tuhirirwe, et al, 23.

[21] *Ibid.,* 31.

[22] Tuhirirwe, 24.

[23] *A Timely Message from Heaven,* XVI:II.

[24] Tuhirirwe, 46.

[25] Jessi Mugambi, *From Liberation to Reconstruction: African Christian Theology after the Cold War* (Nairobi: East African Publishers, 1995), 225; Emmanuel Katongole, "Theological Perspectives on Poverty," in *The Challenge of Eradication of Poverty in the World: An African Challenge,* ed. Deirdre Carabine and Martin O'Reilly (Nkozi: Uganda Martyrs University, 1998), 64.

[26] Tuhirirwe, 24.

[27] *Ibid.,* 30.

[28] Tuhirirwe, 29; Auten, 5.

[29] Gerald Banura, "A Critical Evaluation of the Kannungu Tragedy," in *The Kannungu Cult-Saga: Suicide, Murder, or Salvation?* Ed. Kabazzi-Kisirinya, Deus Nkuruziza, and Gerald Banura (Kampala: Department of Religious Studies, 2000), 51.

[30] Paul Gifford, *African Christianity: Its Public Role* (Bloomington: Indiana University Press, 1998), 118.

[31] *Ibid.*

[32] *Ibid.,* 123.

[33] *Ibid.,* 126–127.

[34] See also Gifford's excellent treatment of the Christian churches in Cameroon (253ff.), where the churches reflect the same deep and pervasive divisions as the country at large, thus, in many ways holding up a mirror to the nation. "The self-serving use of power or *la politique du ventre* constitutes the ethos or culture into which the churches are inserted; they tend to replicate that model of society, being corrupt and malfunctioning, even to the extent of protecting their own hegemony when they sense it is threatened by new churches."

[35] In Matthew's rendering of the story (Matt. 20:20–28) it is the mother of the two who makes the request.

[36] *A Timely Message from Heaven,* VII:1–2.

[37] William T. Cavanaugh, *Torture and Eucharist: Theology, Politics, and the Body of Christ* (Oxford: Blackwell Publishers, 1998), 213.

[38] *Ibid.,* 213.

[39] *Ibid.,* 214.

[40] *Ibid.,* 230.

[41] *Ibid.,* 206–252.

[42] Jean Marc Éla, *African Cry* (Maryknoll, N. Y.: Orbis Books, 1980), 1.

[43] Cavanaugh, 229.

[44] *Ibid.,* 212, 235.

[45] Craig Nelson and Tim Sullivan, "Cult Members Followed Deadly Dream in Uganda," *Associated Press* (22 March 2002). In light of this evidence, I suspect that many of the deaths before 17 March were the result of a systematic program of "weeding out" those who failed to live up to some of the high demands of sanctity set by the MRTCG.

[46] *A Timely Message from Heaven*, IV; Passim.

[47] *A Timely Message from Heaven*, vi, vii, 10, 14, 20, 33, 53, 60, 65, 98–99, 102–103, 105, 110, passim.

SECTION THREE:

Imagination

CHAPTER SEVEN

A DIFFERENT WORLD RIGHT HERE
THE CHURCH WITHIN
AFRICAN THEOLOGICAL IMAGINATION

We must rediscover the gospel as a decisive force In histo-
ry's march to the fore . . . wherever creation is on the road,
wherever the kingdom of God is the goal of a quest, when-
ever the new universe is under construction—not a new
world in the sense of a world beyond, but in the sense of a
different world right here, a world being gestated in the
deeds of the everyday.

Jean Marc Éla, *African Cry*

INTRODUCTION

This essay argues that the greatest ethical and theological challenge facing African Christians in the twenty-first century is
the social imagination of new forms of church communities
which will enable Christians not only to survive, but also provide credible alternatives to the reigning secular ideologies (the new world
order, globalization, etc.). In order to uncover this challenge, African
theological reflection must both be grounded in, and seek to shape, the
life and practice of concrete church communities. In this way, theological reflection will reflect the concerns, anxieties, aspirations, hopes,
and frustrations of ordinary African Christians in their everyday struggles in the world. Recent suggestions for a way forward in African theology have greatly overlooked this crucial methodological starting
point. As a result, the suggestions fail to provide a convincing way forward, and are instead characterized by a triumphalistic assessment of
the status of Christianity in Africa on the one hand, and by an uncritical optimism in the secular, nation-state inspired ideologies on the
other.

In this essay, I examine the proposals of two of the leading voices
in African theology, the Ghanaian, Kwame Bediako[1] and the Kenyan,
Jesse Mugambi,[2] as representative of these two dominant trends,

respectively. The burden of the essay will be to show that behind their methodological shortcomings lies a far more serious problem: namely, the failure to take the church seriously as the social and historical embodiment of the Christian way of life, which accordingly must be at the center of any theological reflection. But the argument I make is not simply for the recovery of the church within African theological reflection, but more specifically, the recovery of a particular type of church. Let me explain by way of caricature.

One can identify at least three biblically-inspired ecclesiological visions: the Pious (which we can also call the Spiritual), the Pastoral, and the Prophetic Church, respectively.[3] Working with a very clear distinction between the spiritual and material realms, the Pious Church feels that her own competence lies in the deep, internal, spiritual realm from which she provides motivation for the Christian in her struggle in the world. Simon of Cyrene (Mark 15:22; Matthew 27:32; Luke 23:26) best exemplifies the ethical posture of this Pious Church. When pressed into the service of the state to help carry the cross of Jesus, Simon never questions the nature of the service. He never demands to know why the condemned prisoner is condemned, or if the prisoner should be condemned. He simply goes along, helping the prisoner to carry the cross.

The Pastoral Church is the Church as healer and servant of the poor. In the Bible, we can identify this Church with Joseph of Arimathea (Mark 15:43; Matthew 27:57; Luke 23:50–53), a simple and sincere man who walked across tradition with compassion and quiet. He never sets out to question or change the system. And just like the legendary Veronica who steps out of the jeering and shocked crowd and wipes the face of Jesus, Joseph of Arimathea appears after both religion and government have done their damage to the body of Christ in order to tenderly treat its abuse. He exemplifies the pastoral work of the Church. Necessary as such work is to care for those marginalized or battered by the system, it rarely questions the system or attempts to rise beyond the system.

Finally, there is the Prophetic Church of Mary of Bethany (John 12:1–8)—the woman who made a fool of herself by publicly wiping the feet of Jesus with her hair and anointing them with oil.[4] In the risky endeavor of this prophetic action, she envisioned change; an alternative witness and a new social order made possible by the life and story of Jesus. She typifies the Prophetic Church—a Church that cares for the coming reign of God and its obligation to bring it about now. A marked sense of urgency inspires Mary's unconventional, nay, shocking action and alternative witness. Her church is a church of jars, oil, tears, hair, and feet—it is a church that is deeply material. It is, therefore, a church which rises above the spiritual and pious salvation of souls, and above the necessary but enabling service of the Pastoral Church, to the everyday struggles and concerns of a community struggling to remain faithful and to bear witness in a precipitous and uncertain world.

I argue that while a vision of the Pious and Pastoral Churches underlies Bediako and Mugambi's theological reflections respectively, what African Christians need if they are to face and survive the challenges confronting them in the twenty-first century is theological reflection and practice which can inspire and is at the same time sustained by a vision of the Prophetic Church.

In its critical thrust, my argument owes a great deal to innumerable and succinct reviews made by Tinyiko S. Maluleke[5] of the developments in African theology in general, and of the work of Bediako and Mugambi in particular. Overall, I not only find Maluleke's familiarity with the developments in African theology amazing, but his literary production is sustained by such verve and critical insight of a rare and exceptional kind. What I, however, still find lacking (even) in Maluleke's highly insightful, but till now predominantly critical imagination is a constructive proposal for the vision of the Church in Africa. This is what I try to do in this essay, by underscoring the need for social imagination in general and the imagination of prophetical ecclesial communities in particular. In the last section of the paper I show that it is precisely this sort of social imagination that is at stake in the work of Jean Marc Éla.

KWAME BEDIAKO AND THE QUEST FOR A TRULY CHRISTIAN AFRICAN IDENTITY

1. The Optimism

One key aspect that characterizes Kwame Bediako's wide-ranging scholarship and publication on African theology is his optimistic assessment of the prospects of African Christianity. He has noted:

> *If in our time there has been much allusion to the margin-*
> *alization of Africa, following the end of the Cold War*
> *era . . . in one particular aspect, Africa will not be margin-*
> *alized. That one area is the field of Christian theology end*
> *Christian religious scholarship generally.*[6]

In that one area, we witness what Bediako variously characterizes as an "incredible miracle" in the "phenomenal presence of Christianity on the African soil."[7] In fact, this "success story" is a clear indication that the "modern shift of the centre gravity of Christianity," predicated by Barrett, is already underway, making Africa "one of the heartlands of the Christian faith in our time."[8]

To be sure, Bediako is not alone in noting the prospects of Christianity in Africa.[9] We draw attention to Bediako's work because it provides a good example of the limitations as well as assumptions that sustain this certain type of "the future of the church is in Africa" optimism. Let me, however, make it clear from the start that I, for one, also hope that the future of Christianity is in Africa, but the crucial question that concerns me is the type of future, and the type of Christianity that will be associated with Africa. I suggest that for such a future to be qualitatively different from the present, it will have to be characterized not simply by the numerical growth[10] of the Christian population, nor merely by an abstract concern for African Christian identity, but also by such mundane concerns of how Africans Christians draw water, plant cabbages, dig pit latrines, raise babies, educate children, etc. However, in order for these concrete issues to be the focus and mark of Christianity in Africa, the notion and reality of the church has to be central to the theological project.

And to the extent that the reality of the church is obscured in theological reflection, such reflection cannot uncover the concrete challenges facing African Christians in the twenty-first century, let alone provide resources for confronting such challenges. Bediako's work provides a very good case study of this failure. But in order to understand how he concretely fails to face this challenge and even avoids it, we need to look at the narrative through which Bediako reads the prospects of African Christianity. At the heart of this narrative is a disembodied notion of African Christian identity.

2. The Success Story: The Vindication of Africa's Christian Identity

The Past. The "quest and demonstration of the true character of African Christian identity" is the central theme of Bediako's theological preoccupation. What Bediako tries to do in much of his work is to show that this quest for Christian identity is grounded not solely in a scriptural basis, but requires "an equally valid historical dimension."[11] This insight alone explains why a great deal of the early work in African theology was marked with a preoccupation with the African pre-Christian past in general—African traditional religions in particular. All this was "an endeavor to clarify the nature and meaning of African Christian identity" by affirming a historical continuity between the past and the present.[12] Accordingly, African theological reflection was to take, in this early crucial stage, a decisively "reactive" stance (apologia), precisely because it defined itself against the "Western impact," which tended to view the African pre-Christian past either as a "tabula rasa" or as a "problem" which had to be rejected or overcome (converted from) in the quest for a new, authentic Christian identity.

What the early work in African theology was able to achieve in this respect (a theme Bediako has returned to in his numerous discussions of John Mbiti, obviously his hero in this formative stage of African theology) was to raise awareness of the *preparatio evangelica* role played by the African pre-Christian past in general, the African primal religions in particular. To a great extent this status has been well vindicated, both historically and theologically. Historically, by the massive presence of Christianity in Africa (African traditional religions, Bediako notes, "are the single most important clue to the success of Christianity in Africa"), and theologically by the popularization of the different theologies of indigenization which portray Jesus as our "supreme ancestor."[13]

The Future. Whatever other lessons Bediako draws from Africa's theological past, the "success" or vindication of this early stage means that it is now time for African theological reflection to move away from the "reactive" preoccupations of indigenization and assume a new and positive idiom:

> *The era of African theological literature as reaction to Western misrepresentations is past. What lies ahead is a critical theological construction which will relate more fully the widespread African confidence in the Christian faith to the actual and ongoing Christian responses to the life-experiences of Africans.*[14]

Even though Bediako notes that this may well prove to be a more demanding task than vindicating the *preparatio evangelica* status of the African past, the task is grounded in an unmistakable optimism. We now live, Bediako notes, in the "age of Africa's faith and *confidence* in the Gospel of Jesus."[15] We have entered a new era . . . in which Christianity is here to stay.[16] No doubt for Bediako, the future of the Church is not only in Africa, that future is already here. This is the era of "African Christian *maturity*,[17] in which Africa has become not only the privileged arena for Christian and religious scholarship"[18] but also a "privileged area of Christian religious, cultural, social, and political engagement in the world."[19] In fact, this vindicated African Christianity, Bediako suggests, holds the promise not only for the "renewal" and "global transformation" of Christianity, but also for "how the West (itself) may be converted."[20] And finally, Christianity in Africa points to the way ahead, which may amount to nothing less than helping to "show how the church may live, worship, and witness in a post-Christendom, and a 'world-Christianity' era."[21]

3. A Critical Pause: Whence the Optimism?

We need to interrupt Bediako's narrative here with a critical pause. While much of what Bediako says about the prospects of African Christianity sound impressive, we are concerned about the issues that he fails to draw up in his narrative of African Christian identity. For instance, while Bediako spends a considerable amount of time reveling in the global significance of African Christianity as a "Benediction to the West"[22] he offers virtually no reflection on what this same Christianity can do for the African Christians themselves. Does (or will) this vindicated African Christianity offer African Christians any skills with which to make meaning of their lives? Will it provide them with meaningful possibilities of existence and witness in a "post-missionary era" which is also marked by a "post-Enlightenment critical outlook"? What does this "post-Enlightenment," "post-Christendom," "postmodern" world[23] look like? What sort of skills do African Christians require if they are to remain faithful within or even survive such a postmodern world?

True, Africa is a massively Christian continent. The issue is how to record and narrate this fact without, however, hiding the apparent contradiction that Africa is also "faced with a food deficit, [and] is the most hungry continent in the world."[24] Or the fact that it experiences widespread or recurrent situations of poverty, AIDS, political dictatorship, etc. Bediako's failure to include this "rough ground" in his narrative of Christianity in Africa is not only striking, it is surprising, especially since elsewhere Bediako suggests the need to pay attention to (as he calls it) the "living experience of African Christians," and to take seriously those elements of everyday spontaneous or implicit theology."[25] He even notes that an "interpretative depth" of African Christianity is not always found in official documents and standard narratives but ". . . in 'informal' ways, in which religious choices are made in situations which may not appear to be religious."[26]

With considerations such as these, one would have assumed that Bediako would provide some display of some of these "informal" ways, or at least of the concrete concerns and challenges facing African Christians in their daily life. Instead, he concludes that since African Christian identity has been well-vindicated by the past, the remaining challenge facing African Christianity is an *intellectual* one:

> . . . the 'Christianizing' of the pre-Christian tradition could also be seen as one of the most important achievements of African theology . . . . The residual question [the challenge that lies ahead?] now is this: will African Christianity be able to find viable intellectual grounds upon which to validate and secure its African credentials?[27]

This conclusion is indeed surprising, but what it reveals is the fact that the adoption of the notion of "African Christian identity" as the central focus of his theology allows Bediako to dwell on a smooth level of theoretical transportation, thus saving him from the need of looking at the rough and messy ground of tensions, contradictions, and challenges facing African Christians in their concrete existence.

But such a limitation could have easily been avoided if Bediako had invoked (instead of *identity*) the far more basic and substantive category of *church*. Such a move would have allowed him to see that the Christian life in general, the formation of Christian identity in particular, is socially and historically embodied, and that it is the concrete communities of church which provide such an embodiment or context. But this is the direction that Bediako tries to resist. A brief look at the central argument behind Bediako's *Christianity in Africa* will help to make this shortcoming clear.

4. Christianity as a "Foreign" Religion?

In spite of the highly optimistic prospects of African Christianity, Bediako notes that there is still one nagging concern ("burden") which has to be resolved for the true identity of African Christianity to be fully vindicated.

> For all its "massive and unavoidable presence in the African scene," Christianity in Africa continues to carry a burden, a "veritable incubus" which it has to come to terms with and, if possible, seek to overcome and lay to rest.[28]

The "veritable incubus" is nothing other than the challenge posed by "African" critics (Blyden, Mazrui, Okot p'Bitek, and Osofo Okomfu Kwabena Damuah with his Afrikania movement in Ghana). The critics share a lingering suspicion of Christianity as an essentially Western (foreign) religion, which, given its negative complicity in Africa's colonial past, will continue to have "an alienating effect on African life," and so will "never become an adequate frame of reference for the full expression of African ideals of life."[29]

The Gospel as Infinitely Translatable. In order to resolve the alleged "foreignness" of Christianity on which the challenge is based, Bediako invokes the distinction, drawn by Mbiti, between:

> Christianity which "results from the encounter of the Gospel with any given local society" and so is always indigenous and culture bound, on the one hand, and the Gospel, which is "God given, eternal and does not change" on the other . . . We can add nothing to the Gospel, for this is an eternal gift of God, but Christianity is always a beggar seeking food and drink.[30]

One reason Bediako finds this distinction helpful is because it "in effect 'exorcises' the 'Westernism' and 'foreignness' in the Western transmission of the Gospel, and internalizes whatever was of the Gospel."[31] For, if the Gospel is the "eternal gift of God," then it means that important as the missionary endeavor is (was), it is not central to the transmission of the gospel. The latter begins and is carried on by God Himself. Since "God, the Father of our Lord Jesus Christ is the same God who has been known and worshiped in various ways within the religious life of African peoples,"[32] the gospel preceded the missionaries to Africa. The missionaries might have brought Christianity to Africa, but not the Gospel. "They did not bring God; rather God brought them."[33]

Bediako also appeals to Lamin Sanneh's argument for translatability. It is not the missionary agency, Sanneh argues, which is the key factor in the transmission of the Gospel, but the "indigenous assimilation [of the Gospel] and African religious agency effected through the translation of Scriptures"[34] in African languages. What Sanneh's argument in fact comes to is that with the availability of scripture in the vernacular, "the central categories of Christian theology—God, creation, Jesus Christ, history—are transported into their local equivalent"[35] thus making it possible for local cultures to have direct access to the Gospel, in spite of missionary shortcomings:

> *Once we have subordinated Western missionary transmission to local assimilation under African agency, then we cannot continue to appropriate Christianity as an ideological theme and annex it as a subplot to the history of "Western Imperialism." If we wish to maintain the principle of translatability of the Christian religion as well as the proper religious perspective on the process of its transmission, then we must admit that Sanneh is right.*[36]

Accordingly, the claims about the alleged foreignness of Christianity rest on a false premise, a "serious misconception."[37] For it is not Christianity, but the gospel itself which is the object of mission. Whereas Western Christianity may have been marred by colonialism and imperialism, the gospel, thanks to the inbuilt logic of translation, is always able, as it were, to "slip through the fingers of missionaries into the bosoms of vernacular speakers,"[38] thus subverting any cultural possessiveness of the faith.

There is no doubt that Bediako's argument is quite fascinating, and even helpful in recovering the agency of African Christians within mission. The very idea of "indigenous assimilation" ensures that Africans are (were) not passive victims or recipients of missionary ideas and preaching, but active agents who received and shaped the message according their particular needs and experiences.

Overall, however, there is something misleading about his attempt to prove the non-foreignness of Christianity by setting up an infinitely translatable Gospel—not Christianity—as the crucial factor in missionary work. First, the language and logic of "translatability" which Bediako appeals to rests on an outdated premise of a foundational epistemology, which only serves the promotion of a putative universality.[39] Translation is never an innocent or ideologically neutral exercise, but as has been shown, can itself become one of the most effective weapons for "colonizing minds and spaces."[40]

Secondly, Maluleke is right. The alleged foreignness of Christianity cannot be resolved by mere logic, even when such logic is sophisticated. For, as Maluleke points out, Christianity will still remain alien and non-liberating if African Christians continue to experience its liturgical, doctrinal, and church structures as such,[41] and particularly if it fails to shape and transform their day to day life struggles. In other words, the only way Christianity can be shown not to be a "foreign" religion in Africa is to provide a narrative display of the agency of African Christians in their historical and social context. But this is exactly what Bediako fails to do by setting up, following Mbiti, the "gospel" as a category in its own right, distinct from "Christianity," and proposing it as the touchstone of both missionary and African agency.

What the distinction amounts to, however, is an attempt by Bediako (and Mbiti) to bypass the historical processes of Christianity in favor of a gospel that is ahistorically neutral and "infinitely translatable," precisely because the latter can (and/does) stand clear of any historical contagion, and thus remains shielded from the shortcomings of its missionary agents. What Bediako fails to realize, however, is that this attempt to unhinge Christianity from its past (even a colonial past) simply drives an unfortunate wedge between that gospel and history. In the end, the concrete practices of history where Christians find themselves, their historical and exemplary witness, and in fact, the church itself as the social and historical embodiment of the gospel are all rendered irrelevant and inconsequential to the future of the gospel, whose transmission must succeed regardless.

Another way to put the issue is to note how the Gospel and Christianity distinction not only minimizes historical transmission in favor of local assimilation, it trivializes the social, historical, and cultural embodiments of Christianity. This is what leaves the assimilation of the gospel not only an individual experience, but a deeply internal and spiritual experience—one that finds its foundation in the eternal Word of God that is infinitely translatable, and thus available to anybody, whatever their historical situation might be.

A "Spiritual" World: A disembodied "African Christian Identity." That this is the case, is clear from the way in which Bediako only rarely makes reference to church in his writings, and when he does, it is not so much the church in its dimension of social and material embodiment that is Bediako's primary interest, but the church as a spiritual communion of individuals. Thus, abstracted from its social and historical context, Bediako's version of African Christianity essentially operates within a "spiritual world." It is here on the "specifically religious plane"[42] that an African Christian identity is formed. Also, it is here that even before the coming of missionaries, Jesus "had shouldered his way into the African *religious* world, and could be discovered *there* through *faith* by all those who approach the *spiritual* world with requests for guidance and help in difficulties, even where these requests are formulated in traditional terms."[43]

It is this preoccupation with the "spiritual" world that, in the final analysis, leaves the African Christian without any resources with which to understand, let alone confront, the social-material challenges facing him or her. For even when Bediako comes to offering concrete proposals for a way forward, the recommendations are aimed at the "specifically religious plane." The challenge facing African theology in "the new age of Africa's faith and confidence," Bediako writes, ". . . is to make clear in the *religious* world which men and women inhabit and by whose *spiritual* realities they make sense of their existence, that Jesus Christ [is] the supreme Ancestor."[44]

To be sure, Bediako notes that this "spiritual" world is not "separable from the realm of regular human existence,"[45] but he does not tell us exactly how the two are related. One imagines that Bediako is envisaging something like a Weberian scenario, where the beliefs and pious processes within the spiritual realm might lead to far-reaching socio-political consequences.[46] But if this is the case, then all Bediako is hoping for is that African Christians will be able, just like Simon of Cyrene, to draw sufficient ethical and psychological motivation from the "universe of their religious ideas, forces and powers" to help them bear the requirements of material existence, whatever those might be.

It has been necessary to dwell on the shortcomings behind Bediako's version of African Christianity located on the "specifically religious plane" because it augurs quite well with the Pentecostal and Evangelical forms of Christianity prevalent on the African continent.[47] While not the only factor, the statistical projections from these traditions have contributed to the picture of Africa as a Christian continent, thus sustaining "the-future-of- Christianity-is-in- Africa" optimism. As I noted earlier, the crucial issue, it seems to me, is not so much whether the future of Christianity is in Africa, but the sort of Christianity which lies behind this "phenomenal Christian presence." What I find disturbing is the fact that even as Africa's social and material conditions seem to be worsening, there is a surge in forms of Christianity which are so narrowly focused on the "spiritual world" of the Africans. But as my extended analysis of Bediako's work has been able to show, such disembodied forms of Christianity may just succeed in providing a tantalizing illusion of "Africa's confidence in the Gospel," without however er helping us to understand our particular straits as African Christians. For, as African Christians, we live not only in "the universe of *religious ideas*, forces, powers, and *spiritual* agency,"[48] but in a social-material world in which corruption, political instability and violence, poverty, powerlessness, AIDS, etc. are an everyday reality.

The issue is how do such concrete social-material challenges impinge on the shaping of African Christian agency? How can these historical processes and events be drawn up into a meaningful narrative of African Christian identity? I suggest that for this to be possible, one will have to invoke some account of the church as the social historical and cultural embodiment of the Christian way of life. In other words, not the spiritual and infinitely translatable Gospel, but concretely existing communities of church that provide a far more promising point of reference in understanding the prospects of African Christian identity. In any case, without reference to the forms of existence we call the church, African theology can neither understand the sort of material challenges facing African Christians, nor help to shape their agency in a way that provides a constructive alternative to the prevailing ideologies.

By invoking the notion of *church*, Mugambi begins to uncover some of these challenges, and in this respect, represents a clear advance over Bediako. He (Mugambi) however, fails to provide a constructive way through them, because at the crucial moment he fails to see that the church and her embodied existence are capable of providing an alternative way of shaping and mobilizing even the material needs of African Christians. A brief look at his *From Liberation to Reconstruction*[49] will help to uncover this limitation.

JESSE MUGAMBI AND THE NEW WORLD ORDER: TOWARD A THEOLOGY OF RECONSTRUCTION

1. Introduction: Disturbing Observations

Like Kwame Bediako, Jesse Mugambi's theological reflections[50] are premised on a central conviction relating to the massive presence of Christianity in Africa. However, by invoking the *church*, Mugambi is able, in a way that Bediako is not, to uncover a key challenge facing African theology—namely, the apparent contradiction that contemporary Africa remains at once one of the most religious continents in the world and one of the most materially and socially distressed. In Africa, he notes, "the Church remains the most influential and most sustainable social institution especially in the rural areas."[51] But Mugambi also notes the disturbing fact that Africa:

> is faced with a food deficit; it is the most hungry continent in the world. It is faced with a debt crises; next to South America it is the most indebted continent. It has the highest level of illiteracy in the world, and half of the world's refugees are Africans. [52]

How can such a contradiction be explained? "Is this religiosity authentic and genuine, or is it superstition arising from despair?"[53] How could it be that the peoples who continue to call on God most reverently are the ones whom God seems to neglect most vehemently? Could it be that "the Gospel has reached many people in Africa as very bad news?"[54]

By raising such questions, Mugambi's work seems to represent, methodologically at least, a clear advance over Bediako's. For it is clear that no reflection can provide a genuine and constructive way forward without confronting the apparent success of African Christianity on the one hand, with the face of a distressed and distressing Africa on the other.[55] In fact, uncovering this paradox and seeking to provide a way forward through it is, in my opinion, the real burden: the "veritable incubus" of African Christianity.

The problem with Mugambi, however, lies with the fact that when it comes to offering recommendations for the future of African theology, he (Mugambi) shifts his reflection away from the church and her practices, and instead suggests a "theology of reconstruction" whose main protagonist and beneficiary is the African nation-state. In order to fully uncover this limitation we need to note the uncritical optimism Mugambi places in the ideology of the "new world order."

2. The New World Order: Towards a Theology of Reconstruction

The central argument of Mugambi's *From Liberation to Reconstruction* revolves around the conviction that the end of the Cold War, and with it the collapse of the "old world order" provides African theology with a unique opportunity to shift to a new creative stage. Hitherto, African theological refection has been dominated by the concerns of inculturation and liberation. Although these theologies have been useful "foundations" for theological refection in Africa, they have largely become either dysfunctional or inadequate to the requirements of the new world order. For one, these theologies have tended to be merely reactive to the theological, physical, and ideological misrepresentations of the old world order. Now that the Cold War with its ideological misrepresentations is over, the "stage is free" for more *proactive* theological models which will relate more fully to the creative challenges ahead. Accordingly, Mugambi proposes that we now adopt "reconstruction as a new paradigm for African Christian theology in the 'new world order.'"[56] This paradigm will not only afford African theology an original and positive starting point, it will usher in the much needed renewal and transformation of African societies:

> *African Christian theology in the twenty-first century will be characterized by these themes of social transformation and reconstruction. The shift from liberation to social transformation and reconstruction . . . involves discerning alternative social structures, symbols, rituals, myths, and interpretations of Africa's social reality by Africans them-*

*selves, irrespective of what others have to say about the
continent and its peoples.*[57]

I greatly share Mugambi's creative restlessness and commitment
to find what he calls "new visions," and an "alternative future" for
African theology in the face of the rapidly changing world and Africa's
place in that world. Accordingly, one couldn't agree more with his
prognosis: "New language will be needed for the 'New World Order'
. . . the 'New World Order' will require a new understanding of the
Church and a new corresponding *theology.*"[58] Moreover, there are elements within his proposal for a reconstructive theology which merit
serious consideration. For example, he suggests that it is not the Book
of Exodus (associated with Moses and the theme of liberation), but the
book of Nehemiah which will become "the central biblical text for
African theology in the twenty-first century."[59] He also notes that the
theology of reconstruction will have to be sustained in an ecumenical
spirit,[60] and that it will involve a selective and creative retrieval of the
positive values within African tradition in order to allow the "future to
reshape those values according to the specific demands of the future
contexts."[61]

A Critical Pause: Whose New World Order? The problem in
Mugambi's theology of reconstruction, does not lie with these highly
promising recommendations even though they call for further elaboration and development. The problem lies with Mugambi's failure to
question or provide any concrete insight in the workings of this so-
called new world order. Mugambi simply assumes that the end of the
Cold War creates *new*—and wonderful possibilities. Not only does the
end of the Cold War for Mugambi mean that the old "ideological enemies have become partners,"[62] but that we now witness the end of ideology as such. The "theatre is now free for another show, in the twenty-first century" to commence "in which all the peoples of the world
participate without being branded with either one ideological label or
the other."[63] For Africa in particular, this end of ideology affords an
opportunity for "the beginning of Africa's Renaissance and Reformation."[64]

It is this overly sanguine view—nay, celebration—of the new
world order within Mugambi's work that one finds disturbing.
Mugambi never even asks whether for many Africans there is anything
"new" within the new world order, or whether it is orderly at all, and

for whom, as Maluleke asks.[65] Accordingly, we are left with what sounds like a very promising description of our prospects: a new world order—one, however, whose real historical, ideological, and economic processes and effect on Africans remain completely hidden from sight. Perhaps if Mugambi had taken time to subject the notion of "new world order" to a more critical inspection, he might have discovered that at the base of this "order" is a postmodern philosophy which tends towards forms of playful nihilism and frivolous superficiality.[66] He might also have noticed that the dominant cultural manifestations of this new order, particularly its market and media monopolies, both impose and "reinvent" asymmetrical prescriptions and structures which threaten to plunge the majority of African peoples into worse forms of dependency and marginalization.[67]

Just Another Ideology. The issue we are raising is not limited to Mugambi's work, and certainly not to his optimism in the, by now, outdated ideology of the new world order. For while the specific label might be outdated, the philosophical, political, and economic realities and relations behind such a label haven't changed, except in terms of reinventing themselves under new labels. In fact, it looks like there is always, on the African scene, one nation-state inspired ideology after another—each promising to end Africa's suffering and marginalization. However, whether it is "civilization," "modernization," "industrialization," "development," "liberalization," or more recently, "globalization" or the "new deal"[68]—none of these ideologies seem to work in the best interests of their claimed beneficiaries. On the contrary, with each new ideology, the plight of ordinary Africans has become more precarious.

A key problem has been, so it seems to me, the uncritical optimism or naïvete with which we (in Africa) have embraced these various ideologies. Even theology has not helped us to unmask the reality, contradictions, and interests that tend to be covered up by such spurious titles as "development," "modernization," "new world order," "global economy," etc. On the contrary, theology has tended uncritically to assume and seek to build on these ideologies. Accordingly, the theological challenge has been to see what theological insights cohere with these ideologies, and to offer these insights as a way of contributing "relevantly" to Africa's "development" or social reconstruction.[69]

In his uncritical optimism for the new world order, Mugambi nicely portrays this tendency. However, Mugambi's failure to question the reigning ideology reflects a deeper problem concerning the nature and role of the church, which is rooted in a Constantinian history of church-state relations. At the center of this arrangement is a well-established (institutional) church, one, however, with no social-material agenda of its own, but whose task it is to provide legitimation and support for the empire, or in modern times, to the various ideologies of the nation-state. It is this arrangement that gives rise to the usual discussions of the relation between religion and politics. Behind such a discussion, however, is the failure to realize that the church's own existence and way of life can be a site from which Africa's social and material needs might be analyzed, mobilized, and shaped in a definite manner. Such a task, it is just assumed, belongs to the realm of *politics*, while the church's own competency lies elsewhere in the *religious* realm, even though she may offer guidelines for, assist in, and even influence this political process.

It is precisely this conception of church-state relationship that lies behind Mugambi's work, and explains his failure to question and, in fact, his uncritical optimism for the reigning ideology of the "new world order." The unfortunate effect is that given this deference to politics, he shifts his theological attention away from the church to the nation-state as the framer and primary agent for reconstruction. In this task, the church and theology are only assigned a marginal role.

3. The Church: A "Catalyst of Reconstruction"

I have already noted how, at least on the surface, Mugambi's theology of reconstruction seems to promise a new vision of the church in Africa. He suggests that "the new world order will require a new understanding of the Church and a new corresponding theology."[70] He also notes that "we ought to be more concerned with the Church of the future, than with the future of the Church";[71] and that such a "Church may have to change its outward character in order to maintain its essential identity."[72] But that is as far as it goes. For a close reading reveals that the church is assigned only a marginal role in the task of reconstruction. No doubt he says many things in different places concerning the role of the Christian theology in the social reconstruction of Africa, particularly how "Christian faith definitely has a positive function in this reawakening."[73] He also notes how the Churches "should be the catalysts of this process, as they were in Europe at the end of Medieval period."[74] And since in Africa the "Church remains

the most influential and the most sustainable social institution, especially in the rural areas,"[75] it has the "ingredient entry points and
opportunities for the process of social reconstruction in Africa."[76]

Underlying these recommendations is Mugambi's central concern
that the church ought to be relevant to Africa's needs, and therefore,
"ought to help Africans to regain their confidence and hope."[77]
However, once one critically examines the specific proposals by which
the Church is to be relevant to Africa's needs, it becomes clear that
even this "most influential and most sustainable social institution"
does not have any say in "defining" what reconstruction might mean,
or what a successful reconstruction might look like. Instead, she can
only "prepare the people for this immense task,"[78] and provide pastoral
amelioration to the victims of reconstruction. In the end, the much-
needed "structural adjustment" of the church which Mugambi called
for (see earlier) just seems like an attempt to make the church a more
effective pastoral agent, which rehabilitates individuals and groups
who will be marginalized by this project, as well by other natural and
social circumstances.[79]

What Mugambi does not realize (or fails to question) is the fact
that assigning such a "pastoral" role for the church, even though fairly standard, invests nation-state politics an unquestioned competency
and validity to determine the shape, direction, and goal of the social-
material processes (now under the rubric of reconstruction)—and to do
so using whatever new ideology is at hand. Of course, it is not clear
why Mugambi thinks that the African nation-state will carry out this
task of reconstruction effectively, since up until now it has been essentially an "agency for control and extraction."[80] In other words, what
Mugambi fails to confront is the critical realization that the source of
Africa's distressing social-material conditions has to do, in great part,
with the way nation-state politics has defined and shaped those social-
material processes. Thus, by operating from within this standard
"church-state" relationship, Mugambi's "theology of reconstruction"
leaves us in the same straits of an increasingly distressed and distressing Africa—with a majestic church that has been reduced to a pastoral
role (of Joseph of Arimathea), at once needed to repair the damage
wrought by the systems, and yet gradually slipping away into irrele-
vance and anachronism. But even worse, African Christians are left
without any meaningful alternatives by which to understand and
reshape the distressing vagaries of their social and material existence.

4. The Church as Social Imagination

The critical issue I am raising is not the *issue* of reconstruction, but reconstruction of *what*? As it stands, Mugambi's reflections seem to assume that what is at stake is the reconstruction of a space and practices that essentially lie outside the competency of the church. This is what shifts the burden of Mugambi's theology from the church to a secular ideology like the new world order. From this perspective, even though coming from different angles, both Mugambi and Bediako share a similar conception of Christianity as a religion whose competence does not lie with shaping social-material processes. Whereas Bediako locates Christianity's competency in the formation of an individual's *spiritual* identity, Mugambi locates it within the church's *pastoral* agency in the world governed by nation-state politics. Neither seeks to understand, let alone explore Christianity's essential *political* nature.

By "political nature of Christianity," I do not of course mean that Christianity has to align herself with one political group or the other, but that the church's own life and practices themselves are the site for understanding and transforming Africa's social-material distress into an alternative, more hopeful future. In other words, the church does not have to "wait" (so to say) for an ideology like new world order, development, or globalization to define what Africa's needs are, and how they are to be met; but that her own stories, life, and organization itself embodies a specific social-material vision and practice. However, for this vision to be realized, theological reflection has to move in a different direction both methodologically and constructively than the alternatives represented by Bediako and Mugambi respectively.

Methodologically, it means that it is not enough to make reference to church in one's theological discussions, but to make the church both the locus and object of theological reflection. Moreover, such a reflection will have to move both in a critical and constructive direction as it assesses the historical limitations and displays the latent possibilities of the church.

Constructively, such theological reflection must seek to move beyond the Pious and Pastoral ecclesiological models, exemplified by Bediako and Mugambi respectively, and seek to recover a Prophetic vision of the church, one that can engage the social-material sphere in her own right: that is, as if the nation-state did not exist. Of course, such a claim in and by itself might sound radical, and even appear like an attempt to replace nation-state with church government. However, what is at stake in the claim is nothing but the recovery of the church in its social-material dynamism, by allowing theological reflection to both grow out of, and seek to shape, the life of concrete church communities. For it is these concrete communities that become a new *social imagination* by being a concrete embodiment and exemplification of an alternative history in Africa. In his writings, the Cameroonian priest Jean Marc Éla provides a very good example of the type of theological refection grounded in, and directed to shaping the church's concrete practices. And so in the remaining part of the essay, I will sketch the outline of his theology as way of making explicit the methodological and constructive direction of a theology committed to the recovery of the church as a social imagination.

JEAN MARC ÉLA AND THE
TASK OF SOCIAL IMAGINATION

At the outset it must be pointed out that what makes Éla's work distinctive is the fact that he does not just make reference to church, but that the church is both the locus and object of his theological reflections. In fact, both *My Faith as an African* and *African Cry*[81] arise out of, and reflect Éla's own pastoral experience and ministry with the rural church communities in northern Cameroon. The essays thus belong to a distinctive genre of "shade tree theology"—a "theology that, far from the libraries and the offices, develops among brothers and sisters searching shoulder to shoulder with unlettered peasants for the sense of the word of God in situations in which this word touches them."[82] It is this concrete experience of church, in the face of distressing social-material conditions that explains both the necessity and urgency of Éla's call to "rethink the whole question of understanding and experiencing faith."[83] What the call to "rethink the Christian faith" amounts to, however, is a call for a new, different experience of church. We can make this conclusion clear by drawing attention to some key elements within Éla's theology. Even though Éla does not set out to write a systematic work of theology, one can still recognize the overriding concern which unifies his theological reflections:

> *Called to confess Jesus Christ in a continent which tends to become a veritable empire of hunger, perhaps we should rethink the whole question of understanding and experienc-*

ing faith. Our reflection must begin with the concrete prac-
tices and alternatives wherein the memory and resistance of
our people have been articulated.[84]

From this citation one can identity at least five key elements which help to explain the methodological and ecclesiological visions which sustain Éla's work.

1. The Paradox: "Called to Confess Jesus Christ in a Continent That Tends to Become a Veritable Empire of Hunger"

Just like Mugambi, the background of Éla's reflections is the disturbing social-material situation in Africa, which according to Éla constitutes the "shock of the Gospel in Africa." Éla's writing is therefore an attempt to understand what it means to live the Christian faith on a "continent which tends to become a veritable empire of hunger." At various places in his writing, Éla captures various angles of this "shock" as he describes the frustration, the apparently meaningless existence, the extreme and paralyzing poverty, the violation of basic rights, the colonial and neocolonial violence, multinational exploitation as well as hunger experienced by Christians in northern Cameroon. It is this "rough ground" which, according to Éla, provides the unique challenge for Christianity in Africa today; "our practice of Christian faith faces a major challenge from African men and women who agonize over where their next meal is coming from."[85]

2. The Search for a Different History

Éla is clearly aware that this is not an individual problem that can simply be addressed through a call for spiritual or moral motivation (*a la* Bediako). The problem, he notes, is one of a social system which "has not been restructured from the bottom up to respond to the social needs of the majority."[86] For instance, "food shortages result not so much from natural calamities as from the policies of an economic model that is wholly oriented toward the outside world and abandons the most important part of the population." In the same way, the health, medical, and educational systems, indeed the very nature of politics in Africa, is set in such a way that only a minority elite benefit.

Accordingly, the crucial challenge facing Africa is not simply one requiring new doctrines and/or more adequate methodologies and social strategies. It is the challenge of confronting the particular history in which Africa has been cast, and of seeking to overcome it through an alternative history. The practice of Christianity in Africa must itself be placed within this context of the search for "another history, another society, another humanity, another system of production, another style of living together."[87]

However, unlike Mugambi, for Éla the search for an alternative history is not initiated by, nor premised on, a secular ideology like the new world order, globalization, etc—to which the church can contribute through her social pronouncements or spiritual inspiration. The search for an alternative history takes place within the church's own concrete life and ministry, which is to say that for Éla, the church itself can be and must become that alternative history. And because the church has so often failed to embody this alternative, the task is one of "rethinking the whole question of understanding and experiencing faith." Such a task requires nothing less than an honest and critical look at the current models of church and Christian practice in Africa.

3. A Critical Look at the Church in Africa: Christianity Under Babylonian Captivity

At various places in his writing, Éla offers a scathing critique of the "moribund Constantinian Christianity" whose "false universality" has reduced the churches in Africa to a mere institutional and canonical rubble.[88] He also refers to this situation of the church in Africa as a sort of Babylonian captivity. Christianity in Africa, he writes,

> has been made captive by Roman structures that are weighted down by an ecclesiastical mentality, by the sociological burden of a religion of the other world; by forms of piety and devotion of Christianity in decay; by the disguised apolitical stance of Western missionaries; by the massive apathy, irresponsibility, and intolerable greed of certain members of the clergy; by the disembodied spirituality of some indigenous lay people; and by the lack of awareness or infantilism of African religious trained in a European fashion.[89]

It is clear from the above citation that the brunt of Éla's criticism (to which he returns regularly) is directed at the forms of disembodied spirituality which the Christian churches in Africa tend to promote by focusing their mission on the salvation of souls,[90] a situation he compares to the distribution of "visas to eternity."[91] Elsewhere he notes how, in an Africa "where domination, hunger, exploitation . . . form an integral part of the collective memory, one cannot shut Christianity up within the limits of a religion of the beyond."[92]

Behind such an observation is a deeper concern that Christianity in Africa has failed to become a way of life, but has remained captive to a particular Western history, in which the church remains either a spiritual enclave or an agency for pastoral care. But by failing to question and supplant this Western history of Christianity, the African church comes to be characterized by mimicry and smug conformism, a situation which means that even the "so-called young churches are born with symptoms of early senility."[93] Moreover, it is not only the lack of creativity and initiative that Éla bemoans about the African church. He is also concerned that unless the African churches are able to face their own history, and thus reinvent "new styles of presence and activity"—different from Western-inspired models of "disguised apolitical" and dematerialized spirituality—Christianity itself will become the "the locus of our daily alienation"[94] by reproducing the same structures of dependency as the other neocolonial institutions.

4. Social Imagination: Rethinking "The Whole Question of Understanding and Experiencing the Faith"

For Christians therefore, the search for an alternative history is at the same time a search for an alternative experience of Christianity, an alternative experience of the church:

> The history that has been forced upon us now obliges us to a self-rooting that will produce something very different from a resurrected past . . . in the churches of Africa, as Baba Simon, the barefoot missioner from Cameroon put it: The time has come to "reinvent Christianity, so as to live it with our African soul."[95]

And for this to happen, the church in African must dare to reinvent herself in a prophetic way. As Éla notes:

> *The church in Africa is faced with a serious choice. Swept*
> *up in the mutations of African society, it finds itself before*
> *two inexorable alternatives: slip away into anachronism*
> *and become a stranger to the real questions of today's*
> *Africa, or else become prophetic and daring, but at a price*
> *of a revision of all its language, all of its forms, and all of*
> *its institutions, in order to assume the African human*
> *face.*[96]

Concretely what does this mean? How does the church provide for, and itself become an alternative history? Even though Éla does not offer a blueprint, he provides indications, all of which point to a vision of the church that is radically embodied within everyday practices. First of all, Éla talks about the reinvention of African Christianity in terms of the "release" of the gospel as a power for the transformation of Africa:

> *We must allow ourselves to hear the challenge of the origi-*
> *nality of the gospel . . . the essential thing is to take up the*
> *gospel in everyday life. . . . Only at this price will the*
> *Christian message, instead of being hammered out in para-*
> *lyzing routines or shrivelled up in little enclaves, be an*
> *energy released for the transformation of Africa.*[97]

Elsewhere, he talks about "rediscovering" the gospel as "a decisive force in history's march to the fore."[98] What is at stake in both of these claims is Éla's attempt to recover the link between revelation and history, and to show that the church itself is this link. This is the argument that Éla particularly develops in his the essay on "An African Reading of the Exodus,"[99] where Éla shows how "the social and temporal reality is the locus of God's intervention and revelation." Within the Exodus, not only does God reveal himself in the midst of Israel's history of slavery, the revelation ("I am") discloses a new history or future for Israel. Thus, Éla argues, revelation is not so much a doctrine, but a promise which inevitably assumes a historical and social form. Ultimately, "revelation stirs up a community in exodus, whose mission is not only to live in expectation of the fulfillment of the promise, but also to promote the historical transformation of the world and of life."[100] In the end, there can be no way that the history and the truth of God's revelation can be known apart from the concrete community which God's revelation forms, and the extent to which such a community is able to exemplify, in ordinary ways, the promise of a new future.

5. The Kingdom of God:
"Gestated Within the Deeds of Everyday"

What the foregoing discussion means is that for Éla the task of re-inventing African Christianity is essentially a call for recovering the link between revelation and history, but more specifically for recognizing that it is the community of the church in her concrete history and practices that *is* the link. That is why the search for an alternative history is at the same time the search for a different experience of church, one through which Christians can begin to experience a new world —"not in the sense of a world beyond, but in the sense of a different world right here, a world being gestated in the deeds of the everyday."[101]

Thus, what is distinctive about Éla's theology is not only the significance of the church, but the recovery of the church in her essential material and social nature. For this reason, he notes that the quest is not for churches that are just spiritual enclaves or "mere administrative provinces of Rome, but *authentic* churches . . . [to the extent that they are] adequate to engage *every* value of humanity."[102] Elsewhere, he even notes that Christians of Africa are searching for a church that will rediscover its evangelical identity by seeking salvation not just within the spiritual realm, but "the salvation and *total* liberation of the person, society, and of the material universe."[103]

Concretely, what Éla envisions are church communities beyond the traditional spiritual-material distinction. It is such communities that bear witness to the truth of God's revelation, who through the Incarnation sets up his Kingdom in the midst of his people that "they might have life and have it more abundantly." Such abundant life is not merely "spiritual" but as material as the jars, feet, hair, and tears of Mary's *prophetic* witness. If the church is to be the embodiment of such a hope, then it must be "gestated in the deeds of everyday" in such a way that ordinary activities like ploughing, harvesting, pasturing, the cultivation of vegetables, as well as the digging of wells and of pit latrines is as much a matter of concern for Christian salvation as the reading of scriptures and the celebration of baptism.

It is precisely for the same reason that when Éla talks about the church, it is not so much the church in its institutional complexity, but local communities. For it is here within local congregations, caught within concrete demands of everyday life, that one is able to "deal with down-to-earth questions, and get back to ground level where the Kingdom of God is built day by day."[104]

CONCLUSION

We have thought it necessary to draw attention, even though in a very sketchy fashion, to the work of Jean Marc Éla in order to capture the significance of the church for theological reflection. What the foregoing discussion has shown is that by locating the church at the center of his reflections, Éla's theology offers decisive advantages both methodologically and constructively over Bediako's and Mugambi's respectively. Methodologically, for instance, by grounding his theological reflections in the life and experience of concrete church communities, Éla is able to discover and lay bare the complexities, contradictions, and key challenges facing African Christians, and even suggest a way forward through them. The challenges come down to one of history: the particular history of dependency and marginalization in which African communities have been cast. Moreover, Éla rightly realizes that, given such a history, any constructive way forward cannot be secured merely through personal spiritual renewal the ennobling pastoral care of the church, important as both of these are, but by the provision of an alternative history, by and of the church itself.

Thus, what Éla's theology helps to show is the fact that the church's ability to provide for and embody this alternative history is dependent on the recovery of the social and material nature of the church. No doubt, such insight is itself dependent on learning to overcome the assumption that there is something like an independent area of politics that assumes the task and responsibility over the social and material dimensions of life. In this connection, what Éla's theology helps to confirm is not just the fact that the church has a stake in the social-material activities of everyday life, but that she can only be church to the extent she is the Kingdom of God "gestated in the deeds of everyday life."

Accordingly, Éla's theology helps not only to underscore the significance of the church for theological reflection, it points to a concrete vision of the church as a way to ensure an alternative and more hopeful history for Africa. Thus, if African theological reflection can move in the manner and direction exemplified by Éla, it will be able to provide African Christians not just with another ethical theory, but an alternative and materially well-entrenched Christian praxis. Such ecclesial visions not only provide African Christianity with a new future—it may prove to be one of the most enduring gifts African Christianity can offer to the world. For if we are able to recover such social-material dynamism of Christianity, then we may be struck by the same realization as Dubois was in 1914: namely, that "there is always something new out Africa."[105] Only this time, what is new will not be cinnamon, tortoiseshell, ivory, a new mineral, or human power, but a new understanding and exemplification of church.

Notes

[1] Kwame Bediako is the director of the Akrofi-Christalier Memorial Centre for Mission Research and Applied Theology in Akropong-Akuapem, Ghana. He is also a visiting lecturer in African Theology at the Centre for the Study of Christianity in a Non-Western World, New College, University of Edinburgh—where he himself studied.

[2] Jesse Mugambi was for many years Dean of the Religious Department at the University of Nairobi where he still teaches. He has played a key role in World Council of Churches (WCC), and in such representative bodies as EATWOT (Ecumenical Association of Third World Theologians), AACC (the All African Conference of Churches); ESEAT (Ecumenical Association of East African Theologians).

[3] I am indebted to Joan Chittister for the original insight into these three visions of church, which I have liberally used and enlarged. See Chittister, Joan, "New World, New Church, Political, Pastoral or Prophetic," *Catholic Studies*, 1992: 1–11.

[4] In Luke's gospel this action is attributed to an unnamed woman (Luke 7:36–50). However, a long Christian tradition has often associated and at times even conflated this woman with Mary or Magdala, who bore the news of the Resurrection to the apostles (John 20:11–18). For informative and helpful literature on this mix-up, see Moltmann, Wendel, *The Women Around Jesus* (New York: Crossroads, 1987), p. 51–104; Schaberg, Jane, "How Mary Magdalene Became a Whore," *Biblical Review* 7 (October, 1992), 30–37; 50–52.

[5] Professor Tinyiko S. Maluleke is the Dean of the Faculty of Theology and Biblical Religions at the University of South Africa (Unisa). He taught in Unisa's Department of Missiology before becoming the dean and is also the General Secretary of the Southern African Missiological Society (SAMS).

[6] Kwame Bediako, "Cry Jesus: Christian Theology and Presence in Modern Africa," *Vox Evangelica*, 1993, 23:11.

[7] *Ibid.*

[8] David Barret, "AD 2000: 350 Million Christians in Africa," *International Review of Mission*, 1970, 50.

[9] In the recent Post-Synodal Exhortation *Ecclesia In Africa*, John Paul II (1996:232–238) himself notes 'the glory and splendor of the present period of Africa's

evangelization' and the 'tremendous growth' of the church in Africa. For my more extended reflections on *Ecclesia In Africa*, see Katongole 2001.

[10] Estimates of the last decade indicate 41% of Africa's 550 million people to be Christians, with sub-Saharan countries registering a much higher percentage, for instance, Uganda: 78% Christian; Ghana 60%; Cameroon 65%; and Zambia 75%, (Gifford 1995: 61, 119, 183, 251; Taylor 1990).

[11] Kwame Bediako, *Theology and Identity: The Impact of Culture upon Christian Thought in the Second Century and in Modern Africa* (Oxford: Regnum Books, 1992), ix.

[12] Kwame Bediako, "The Roots of African Theology," *International Bulletin of Missionary Research*, 1989, 13:59.

[13] Kwame Bediako, *Jesus in African Culture: A Ghanian Perspective* (Accra: Asempa Publishers, 1990) and *Christianity and Africa: The Renewal of a Non-Christian Religion* (Maryknoll, NY: Orbis, 1995), 83.

[14] Kwame Bediako, "Understanding the African Theology in the 20th Century," 1994, *Themelios* 20:17.

[15] Kwame Bediako, *Christianity and Africa: The Renewal of a Non-Christian Religion* (Maryknoll, NY: Orbis, 1995), 85.

[16] *Ibid.*, 3, 82.

[17] *Ibid.*, 263.

[18] *Ibid.*, 253ff.

[19] *Ibid.*, ix.

[20] *Ibid.*, 260.

[21] Kwame Bediako, "Five Theses Concerning the Significance of Modern African Christianity: A Manifesto," *Transformation*, 1996, 13:27.

[22] Kwame Bediako, *Christianity and Africa: The Renewal of a Non-Christian Religion*, 259ff.

[23] Kwame Bediako, "Five Theses Concerning the Significance of Modern African Christianity: A Manifesto," 28.

[24] Mugambi, J.N.K. *From Liberation to Reconstruction: African Christian Theology After the Cold War* (Nairobi: East African Education Publishers, 1995), 160.

[25] Kwame Bediako, "Five Theses Concerning the Significance of Modern African Christianity: A Manifesto," 21–23.

[26] Ibid.

[27] Kwame Bediako, *Christianity and Africa: The Renewal of a Non-Christian Religion,* 4.

[28] *Ibid.*, 4.

[29] *Ibid.*, 5, 14.

[30] *Ibid.*, 117.

[31] *Ibid.*, 118.

[32] *Ibid.*, 116.

[33] *Ibid.*, 118.

[34] The D. Willis James Professor of Missions and World Christianity at Yale, the Gambian-born Lamin Sanneh has written extensively on African Christianity. Even more than Bediako, Sanneh devotes a greater part of his theology building a defense against the widely-felt notion that Christian missions have been intricately associated

with colonialism, imperialism, and the slave trade. (See particularly Sanneh, *Translating the Message: The Missionary Impact on Culture* (New York: Orbis, 1989).
[35] Kwame Bediako, *Christianity in Africa*, 120.

[36] *Ibid.*, 121.

[37] *Ibid.*, 123.

[38] Tinyiko Maluleke, "Black and African Theologies in the New World Order: A Time to Drink from Our Own Wells," *Journal of Theology for Southern Africa*, 1996, 4.

[39] Emmanuel Katongole, *Beyond Universal Reason: The Relation between Ethics and Religion in the Work of Stanley Hauerwas* (Notre Dame, IN: Notre Dame University Press, 2000), pp. 185–189.

[40] Musa W. Duke, "Consuming a Colonial Time Bomb: Translating Badimo into 'Demons.'" In the Setswana Bible (Mt 8:23–34; 15:12; 10:8) *Journal of the Study of the New Testament*, 1999, 73:33–59.

[41] Tinyiko Maluleke, "Black and African Theologies in the New World Order: A Time to Drink from Our Own Wells,"8.

[42] Kwame Bediako, *Christianity and Africa: The Renewal of a Non-Christian Religion*, 111.

[43] Kwame Bediako, "Understanding the African Theology in the 20th Century," 17. emphasis mine.

[44] Kwame Bediako, *Christianity and Africa: The Renewal of a Non-Christian Religion*, 85.

[45] *Ibid.*, 101.

[46] Bediako, for example, makes the case that the spiritual process can lead to far reaching political consequences, more specifically the desacralization of power, thereby checking the dictatorial and absolutist claims that seems to be inherent within African politics. Bediako, Kwame, *Christianity in Africa: The Renewal of a Non-Western Religion* (Maryknoll: Orbis, 1995), pp. 243–249). Max Weber, *The Protestant Ethic and the Spirit of Capitalism*. (London: Routledge, 1992).

[47] Paul Gifford, "African Christianity: Its Public Role." (Bloomington, IN: Indiana University Press, 1998).

[48] Kwame Bediako, *Christianity and Africa: The Renewal of a Non-Christian Religion*, 85.

[49] Mugambi, J.N.K. *From Liberation to Reconstruction: African Christian Theology After the Cold War* (Nairobi: East African Education Publishers, 1995).

[50] All references to Mugambi are from his 1995 collection of essays, *From Liberation to Reconstruction.*

[51] Mugambi, J.N.K. *From Liberation to Reconstruction*, 225.

[52] *Ibid.*, 160.

[53] *Ibid.*, 160.

[54] *Ibid.*, 44.

[55] Tinyiko Maluleke, "Christianity in a Distressed Africa: A Time to Own and Own Up," (*Missionalia*, 1998), 26:324–340.

[56] Mugambi, J.N.K. *From Liberation to Reconstruction*, 2.

[57] *Ibid.*, 40.

[58] *Ibid.*, xv.

[59] *Ibid.*, 166.

60 *Ibid.*, 80.

61 *Ibid.*, 78.

62 *Ibid.*, xv.

63 *Ibid.*, xv.

64 *Ibid.*, 5.

65 Tinyiko Maluleke, "Recent Developments in the Christian Theologies of Africa: Towards the Twenty-first Century," *Journal of Constructive Theology*, 2(2): 43.

66 Emmanuel Katongole, "Post-Modern Illusions and the Challenges of African Theology: The Ecclesial Tactics of Resistance." This book, Chapter 7.

67 Emmanuel Katongole, "Globalization and Economic Fundamentalism in Africa: On why the Market Cannot Save Us" (forthcoming: ESEAT Publications, Nairobi).

68 Clinton's "New Deal" was a legislative package of trade measures and investment incentives meant to encourage the American business community to invest in the "New Africa." The high point of this "package" was Clinton's well-publicized 1998 visit to Africa, which was portrayed as a step to encourage Africa's tentative steps toward democracy and economic reforms, but also as a way to inaugurate the United States "New form of engagement with Africa—a partnership for the 21st century." (http://africanews.org/usafrica/stories/19980211_feat3.html). For my reflections on the same, see Katongole 1998c.

69 Elsewhere, I have referred to this attitude of uncritically riding on reigning ideologies as the Zacchaeus syndrome. In the Gospel story of Luke 19:1–10, even though Zacchaeus is a small man, everything around him seems to be happening in a big way. In an effort to fully grasp what is going on, he climbs a big sycamore tree. We realize this is a temptation when Jesus orders him to "come down" into the messy, disorderly crowds and stand on his own feet. See Katongole, "African Renaissance and Narrative Theology in Africa: Which Story? Whose Narrative?" *Journal of Theology for Southern Africa*, 102 (1998), pp. 34–35.

70 Mugambi, J.N.K. *From Liberation to Reconstruction*, xv.

71 *Ibid.*, 173.

72 *Ibid.*, 174.

73 *Ibid.*, 164.

74 *Ibid.*, xiv.

75 *Ibid.*, 225.

76 *Ibid.*, xiv.

77 *Ibid.*, 176.

78 *Ibid.*, 51.

79 *Ibid.*, 176.

80 Paul Gifford, *African Christianity*, 4–6.

81 I am limiting myself to only two publications by Éla: namely, *African Cry* (1988) and *My Faith as an African* (1995).

82 Jean Marc Éla, *African Cry* (Maryknoll, NY: Orbis, 1986), vi.

83 *Ibid.*, xvii.

84 *Ibid.*, xvi.

85 *Ibid.*, 87.

86 *Ibid.*, 71.

87 *Ibid.*, 84.

[88] Jean Marc Éla, *African Cry*, 111.

[89] Jean Marc Éla, *My Faith as an African*, 154.

[90] Jean Marc Éla, *African Cry*, 31.

[91] *Ibid.*, 7.

[92] *Ibid.*, 38.

[93] *Ibid.*, 108.

[94] *Ibid.*, 4.

[95] *Ibid.*, 120.

[96] *Ibid.*, 134

[97] *Ibid.*, 119.

[98] *Ibid.*, 53.

[99] *Ibid.*, 28, 38.

[100] *Ibid.*, 35.

[101] Jean Marc Éla, *African Cry*, p. 53.

[102] *Ibid.*, 111; emphasis added.

[103] Jean Marc Éla, *My Faith as an African*, 123.

[104] *Ibid.*, 146

[105] Josiah Young, *African Theology: A Critical Analysis and Annotated Bibliography*, (London: Greenwood Press, 1993), 41.

CHAPTER EIGHT

OF FACES OF JESUS
AND *THE POISONWOOD BIBLE*

AFRICAN CULTURE, NEAT CHRISTOLOGICAL
TRANSLATIONS, AND NARRATIVE GLIMPSES OF
THE CHURCH IN AFRICA

*When the great lord passes, the wise peasant bows deeply
and silently farts.*

— An Ethiopian Proverb

*Then there is batiza. Our Father's fixed passion. Batiza pro-
nounced with the tongue curled just so means "baptism."
Otherwise, it means "to terrify." Nelson spent part of an
afternoon demonstrating to me that fine linguistic difference while we scraped chicken manure from the nest boxes.
No one has yet explained it to the Reverend. He is not of a
mind to receive certain news. Perhaps he should clean more
chicken houses.*

— Barbara Kingsolver,
The Poisonwood Bible

INTRODUCTION

When I was asked to address the topic of inculturation and the faces of Jesus in Africa,[1] I knew I was in trouble. I was being asked to address not only a very important theological topic, but one that also has become increasingly popular in our time. Whereas I had no problem with the topic being important, I had problems with its popularity. Any topic that deals with faces of Jesus in Africa is important. Given the marked growth of the church in Africa, there's an urgent need to understand the status, vitality, and dynamism of African Christianity, as well as the hopes and challenges it provides to world Christianity. The discussion of the African faces of Jesus nevertheless seems to take the predictable form of an attempt to relate the world of the Gospel or Christianity, on the one hand, to the world of African culture on the other. To be sure, this trend of theological discussion, which in our time has come to be known by various names—inculturation, indigenization, contextualization, translation, vernacularization, etc.—has become so popular that it has become difficult to raise critical issue with it without appearing to be in bad faith.

Yet this is what I intend to do. For I think that, in becoming popular, the theological conversation of inculturation has come to embody a subtle temptation for those of us doing theology—though I suspect that this is not just true of inculturation theologies, but of theological notions and methodologies in general. Once they become trendy, they quite often lose their critical and thus, useful edge. In the case of inculturation theologies, however, the temptation lies in the fact that the discourse on faces of Jesus in Africa seems to accord African theologians an opportunity to provide their own coherent, respectable, and unique contribution to theology. What could be more affirming for African theologians than the hope that we too can now add our distinctive, unique voices and stamp to the conversation of theology? Yet I think such a theological conversation, to the extent that it is narrowly focused on Africans and their culture, tends to mask the richness as well as the tensions within African Christianity—particularly the complex ways in which African Christians understand, respond to, inhabit, negotiate, and survive the power of the Gospel in Africa. To be more direct: I do not think the notion of African culture allows enough complexity to offer a rich enough entry point into the conversation of how Christianity is concretely experienced and lived in Africa. Therefore, I suggest that in order to engage this complex world of African Christianity, we need to draw in and from narratives which bring attention to the murky reality of the Church in Africa and its many faces: which is to say, its promises and frustrations. In this task literature, and even the world of fiction can provide a very helpful starting point.

Before I get into this discussion, however, let me note that the popularity—and thus temptation—of inculturation theologies in Africa can be located in a number of related factors. Central to this development, I suspect, is the assumed success or vindication of African culture within African theological discussions. There was a time, not so long ago, when the relation between the Gospel and African culture was anything but a settled question. In fact, African theology as a distinctive discipline was itself born within this tension, occasioned by colonial condensation and the negative view of African culture shared by many missionary agents. A great many of the early contributions of African theology were defined by, and sought to respond to, this negative characterization and summary dismissal of African culture as pagan, primitive, satanic, or barbaric. The result was that a critical discussion emerged within this context, in which African theologians debated and many times disagreed about the meaning and nature of theology, the status and significance of African culture, and the proper relationship that ought to exist between Christianity and culture in general and African culture in particular.[2]

This does not seem to be the case any more, since we all now seem to have come to recognize not only the significance of culture for theological expression, but more specifically the many ways the positive elements within African culture not only anticipated, but served as a helpful preparation for the Gospel message. In fact, as Bediako would argue, the phenomenal growth of Christianity in Africa must be explained in terms of the continuity that Africans perceive between the world of the Gospel and the primal worldview of their African culture.[3]

My concern is that with this assumed vindication of African culture we seem to have arrived at a more or less settled expectation that what is left for African theologians to do is to display the various elements, traditions, and practices within African culture, and to show how these nicely cohere with the message of the Gospel. This is what gives rise to the neat and very systematic Christological formulations in the discussions of *Faces of Jesus in Africa*. That this is the case is clear from Robert Schreiter's *Faces of Jesus*.[4]

FACES OF JESUS IN AFRICA: NEAT TRANSLATIONS

In this dated (1998) but still popular collection, Schreiter brings together several essays by African theologians on the theme of Jesus Christ in Africa today. In his essay, Douglas Waruta provides a good statement of the impetus behind the development of an African Christology. He notes that Jesus' question to the disciples in Mark 8: 27: "Who do you say I am?" is the same question that is put to every Christian, one that must be answered by each in their own context and situation. An attempt to answer this question is "an attempt to develop a Christology; an interpretation as to who Jesus really is in every context and situation—Africans have every right to formulate their own Christology, their own response to who Jesus is to them."[5]

What is implied in Waruta's observation above, but becomes clear in the rest of his essay, as well as through the other contributions in the collection, is the fact that "every context and situation" is understood to mean everyone's *cultural* situation. And so in providing a summary of the methodologies which underlie the quest for an African answer to Jesus' question, Charles Nyamiti helpfully notes: "There are those who attempt to construct an African Christology by starting from the biblical teaching about Christ, and strive afterwards to find from the African *cultural* situation the relevant Christological themes. Secondly, there are those who take the African *cultural* background as their point of departure for Christological elaboration."[6]

It is against this background that, by noting how the stages and rites of initiation form a central place within the cultural heritage of many societies in Africa, Sanon proposes the image of "Jesus as Master of Initiation." Such an image, he argues, not only evokes the African experience of initiation as the ongoing process from childhood to ancestorhood that makes us progressively more human, it nicely resonates with such biblical passages as the image of the invisible God, the firstborn of all creation (Col 1:15–29). This means that in seeing "Jesus as Master of initiation," African Christians come to appreciate Jesus as a Savior—one "who has gone before us in the process and knows all that we must endure."[7]

In a similar vein, reflecting on the role and status of a chief in many African societies as source of unity and power, but also as judge, law giver, and head of the community, Kabasele proposes the title of "Jesus as Chief."[8] Even though the title of Jesus as chief might sound outdated and even evoke imperial overtones, Kabasele's aim is to show that all the positive attributes and prerogatives of a Bantu chief are fully realized by Jesus Christ. "Power belongs superlatively to Jesus Christ because he is a mighty hero, because he is the chief's son and the chief's emissary, because he is 'strong,' because he is generous, wise, and a reconciler of human beings."[9]

In another essay, reflecting on the role and status of the elder brother in many African societies, Kabasele suggests the image of "Jesus as Elder Brother."[10] As elder brother, Kabasele notes, Christ is thus not only the firstborn among many brethren who with Him form the Church, he is the founder of the Great Family, the Church, which embraces everyone irrespective of color, sex, or nation. For his part, Nyamiti (also Bujo, and Poebe) moves from what he understands to be the central role that ancestors play within African society to propose the image of "Jesus as brother-ancestor."[11] According to many African beliefs and practices, Nyamiti notes, a dynamic relationship exists between the Supreme Being and humanity on earth, as well as between the living and the dead.[12] Maintaining this dynamic relationship is the special preserve and task of ancestors, who gain this status by their many attributes and passage into the world of the living dead. Christ not only shares these attributes—kingship, superhuman status, exemplarity, mediation, and sacred communication—by his death He "merits to be looked upon as ancestor, the greatest of ancestors, who never ceases to be the 'living dead.'"[13]

No doubt, there is a lot that one finds interesting and even helpful in these and similar images of Jesus in Africa. For once, they confirm the fact that theology, all theology, develops within specific historically and culturally-based contexts, a realization that might help to draw Western theological reflection to its own historical specificity. It is the very interface that these Christologies establish between the world of the Gospel on the one hand and the African cultural experience on the other that one finds disturbing.[14] Not only does this easy translation obscure the social, political, and ideological aspects of Christianity in Africa, it has the danger of reducing the complex dynamics of mission to a problem of cultural encounter.[15] Such an assumption cannot but give the misleading impression that the major issue facing the transmission of the Gospel was one of cultural difference—the foreign culture within which the missionaries stood and thus the foreign cultural associations, language, and idioms through which the Gospel was presented to Africa. But now, since this cultural problem has been somewhat resolved, with Africans Christians having found a way to "translate" and express the Gospel message into their cultural idioms and images, the relationship between Christianity and Africa is a settled one.

But this is misleading, since the missionary contact between Christianity and Africa was not just a "cultural" contact, but a complex performance that was shaped and in turn formed cultural, economic, political, and social patterns and histories. Similarly, as many have pointed out, the African response to and within this encounter often took the form of a complex interaction or multilayered conversation, in which the interaction involved "hidden" as well as "public transcripts."[16] If this is the case, as I think it is, then in order to get a clearer picture of the processes within African Christianity, we need to invoke more complex narratives than the narrative of "African culture." Such narratives would provide a more adequate account of the encounter between Christianity and Africa, but would also be able to display the characters that are formed at the intersection of this complex encounter. It is here that a work of fiction like *The Poisonwood Bible* can generate an interesting and insightful theological conversation.

THE POISONWOOD BIBLE AND THE HIDDEN TRANSCRIPTS OF AFRICAN CHRISTIANITY

Barbara Kingsolver's *The Poisonwood Bible* is the story about Nathan Price, a fierce and unbending Southern Baptist missionary from Georgia (USA) who, along with his wife Orleanna and four daughters, sets out on a mission to the small village of Kilanga in the Congo. In their journey to the African mission, the Prices not only carry the Bible, but whatever else they believe they will need (and can fit within the plane's weight limitations) in Africa. But as they soon discover, none of these quite "fits" within the flow of life in Kilanga. But soon, all of it, from garden seeds to Scripture—their own lives included—is calamitously transformed on the African soil. In the end, his zeal and dedication to the salvation of Kilanga notwithstanding, Nathan fails to win a single convert for baptism; his standoff with the village chief (Tata Ndu) and the village customs lead to a heated confrontation. In one fine twist within this confrontation, the village applies the newly-introduced practice of democratic elections to call for a vote on whether or not to retain Jesus Christ in the office of personal God, Kilanga village.[17] Jesus loses eleven to fifty-six.[18] Soon after, Ruth May, the youngest Price daughter, dies of snakebite when an attempt by Tata Kivudundu to scare the Price family away from Kilanga goes tragically wrong. Following Ruth May's death, Orleanna abandons Nathan and leaves Kilanga with her three remaining daughters. Nathan stays behind, but ends up (years later) moving further into the jungle, where he is eventually suspected of witchcraft and burned to death.

The Poisonwood Bible seems to paint a picture of a tragically failed mission. And even though the story might be read as a stinging postcolonial critique of the assumptions and practices of mission, I think it provides a very good starting point for a conversation regarding the status of African Christianity today. In fact, I would like to suggest that the story of *The Poisonwood Bible* does not seem to cohere with the current picture of an apparently thriving Christianity on the African continent (over 90% of the population in the Democratic Republic of the Congo). Much of African Christianity arises out of a history of mission similar to the one depicted in *The Poisonwood Bible*. That is why a closer look at the main characters of *The Poisonwood Bible* might provide key insight into the reality of African Christianity today: its complexity, challenges, promises, and frustrations. Three characters stand out.

1. Nathan Price and the Complexity of Mission

First, the complexity of mission. What immediately becomes clear from reading *The Poisonwood Bible* is the fact that even though Nathan himself thinks of his mission—the salvation of Kilanga—in spiritual terms (saving souls of the natives), much more is at stake. Set in the year 1959, the story unfolds against the backdrop of political upheaval in the Congo. The upheaval was marked by Congo's transition from Belgium's colonialism to independence, the subsequent C.I.A. staged murder of Patrice Lumumba, the first democratically elected prime minister, and his replacement with Mobutu—who quickly became a corrupt and brutal dictator. In fact, it is this wider historical context that defines Nathan's mission beyond a narrow, spiritual understanding of salvation and reveals it to be part of a performance that involves the social, cultural, economic, and political history of the Congo. Nathan's failure to realize this fact, no doubt blinded by his evangelical zeal and simplistic faith, is the source of his problems in Kilanga, and finally leads to his fateful end. He is so busy looking to God and the mission he believes God has given him that he fails to see the concrete lives and history of the people that God has put before him. "My father," Leah would later remark, "was God with his back turned, hands clasped behind him and fierce eyes on the clouds. God has turned his back and was walking away."[19]

But Nathan is also a very violent man—a violence that is very difficult to separate from the assumptions of his own self-righteousness, as well as the assumptions of power that sustain his mission. On landing in the Congo he prays, "Father please make me a *powerful* instrument of thy perfect will here in the Belgian Congo."[20] His own self-righteousness however, blinds him to this violence as it unfolds in his relation with his family, as well as in his dealing with the people of Kilanga.[21] The violence is already evident in Nathan's first sermon in Kilanga.

Upon arriving in Kilanga, the Price family finds themselves swept immediately to the Church grounds, where, as a sign of welcome, the village people have prepared a feast of goat and *fufu* in their honor. Asked to "please offer with us a word of thanks for this feast," Nathan immediately launches into a diatribe on the sinful ignorance of those whose bounty he is about to receive. Fixing his eyes on a bare-breasted woman, who, oblivious to what is going on, innocently bounces her baby on her lap, Nathan prays:

> *The Lord rideth in the person of His angels of mercy, His emissaries of holiness into the cities on the plain, where Lot dwelled amongst the sinners . . . the emissaries of the Lord smote the sinners, who had come heedless to the sight of God, heedless in their nakedness . . . . Nakedness, Father repeated, and darkness of the soul! For we shall destroy this place where the loud clamor of the sinners is waxen great before the face of the Lord . . . . And Lot went out and spake unto those that were worthy. Up. Get ye out from this place of darkness! Arise and come forward into a brighter land! . . . Lord, grant that the worthy among us here shall rise above the wickedness and come out of the darkness into the wonderous light of our Holy Father. Amen.[22]*

From this scene's opening prayer, it becomes clear that even though Nathan's ambition and goal is the salvation of Kilanga, his message strikes his audience not necessarily as good news, but its opposite. Nathan, of course, does not realize this because he lacks the necessary humility and skills to do so. But Adah, more than any of the other Price children, observes this effect of Nathan's preaching, and thus helps to draw our attention to another key feature of African Christianity— namely, that in looking at African Christianity one needs to pay attention to both the public and hidden transcripts.

2. Adah: Learning to See the Hidden Transcripts

Adah Price is the younger of the Price twins. She has been handicapped from birth and written off by most of her family members as strange and slow. Not unlike Africa, little is expected of her and little attention is paid to her. "Last of all came Adah the monster, Quasimodo, dragging her right side behind her left in her body's permanent stepsong sing: left . . . behind, left . . . behind."[23] The reader soon realizes, however, that Adah is a highly intelligent and perceptive girl. She is quite often readily able to see through appearances and understand the underlying motivations and connections between things. One reason for her acute sensibilities is the fact that, because little attention is paid to her, she can stop, and does often stop, to pay attention to the details of what is going on. Moreover, because she is able to watch the world from behind, she is able to see details that others, in their rush, fail to notice. She also likes to read, but since they have a limited supply of books in Kilanga, she has read the same books over and over again, each time discovering new details and insights. But what is most amazing about Adah is that she has discovered how to read between the lines and even how to read backwards, and so to discover fresh connections and meanings in a book. "*Ti morf sgniht wen nrael nac uoy dna tnorf ot kcab koob tnereffid a si ti*"[24]—It is a different book from back to front and you can learn new things from it, she has discovered.

Given Adah's skills of attentiveness, she is able decipher the nuances, silences, and hidden transcripts of Nathan's preaching, and to recognize that the challenge facing her father is not simply one of translation. For she notices that even when translation is assured, there is a lot that can slip through and between the words, which can make a whole world of difference in terms of meaning. Adah has, for instance, observed that in the Kikongo language one word can mean more than one thing, much depending on how one says it:

> In Kilanga the word *nzolo* is used in three different was, at least. It means "most dearly beloved." Or it is a thick yellow grub highly prized for fish bait. Or it is a type of tiny potato that turns up in the market now and then, always sold in bunches that clump along the roots like knots on a string. And so we sing at the top of our lungs in church: "Tata Nzolo!" To whom are we calling?[25]

That is why Nathan's message of salvation, even when he tries to speak Kikongo, does not necessarily strike his hearers as good news, but its opposite:

*Tata Jesus is Bangala! Declares the Reverend every Sunday
at the end of his sermon. More and more, mistrusting his
interpreters, he tries to speak Kikongo. He throws his head
back and shouts these words to the sky, while his lambs sit
scratching themselves in wonder. Bangala means something precious and dear. But the way he pronounces it, it
means the poisonwood tree. Praise the Lord, hallelujah, my
friends. For Jesus will make you itch like nobody's business.* [26]

And there is *baptiza*, Nathan's fixed passion:

*Batiza pronounced with the tongue curled just so means
"baptism." Otherwise, it means "to terrify." Nelson spent
part of an afternoon demonstrating to me that fine linguistic difference while we scraped chicken manure from the
nest boxes. No one has yet explained it to the Reverend. He
is not of a mind to receive certain news. Perhaps he should
clean more chicken houses.* [27]

What, however, makes Adah an even more interesting character
for the purpose of this essay is the fact that she is able to recognize and
locate her life within this complex and ambiguous narrative of
Nathan's mission. On leaving the Congo after the death of Ruth May,
she returns to Georgia with her mother, undergoes neurological thera-
py, and is thereby able to walk straight and ends up attending Emory
University and becoming a doctor and an expert in tropical disease.
But even as her life took on this completely different, now "normal"
biography, she is still able to recognize herself in Nathan's complex
mission. Years later, when the three surviving Price girls, now all
grown, meet in West Africa, Leah shares the latest news she has heard
from Brother Fowles and Celine concerning Nathan their father in the
Congo:

*They actually never got to look at him. I guess Father had
reached a certain point. He hid from strangers. But they
always heard plenty of stories about the white witch doctor
named Tata Prize. They got the impression from talking to
people that he was really old. I mean old, with a long white
beard. He'd gotten a very widespread reputation for turning himself into a crocodile and attacking children.* [28]

"The tales got wilder and wilder as the years went by," Leah continued. "That he'd had five wives who all left him, for example."[29] Adah
stopped laughing. "That is *us*," she said, "Nathan's five legendary
wives—they must have meant *us*."[30]

In another incident, when Adah is reflecting on her life, she writes:

> *I wonder whether they still think of him standing tall before*
> *his congregation shouting: "Tata Bangala!" I do. I think of*
> *him exactly that way. We are the balance of our damage and*
> *our transgressions. He was my father. I own half of his*
> *genes, and all of his history. Believe this. The mistakes are*
> *part of the story. I am born of a man who believed he could*
> *tell nothing but the truth, while he set down for all time the*
> *Poisonwood Bible.*[31]

That Adah is able to recognize herself within the story of Nathan's
complex mission is not only important because it reveals her skills of
attentiveness, but because it captures very well our challenge as
African Christians. Stated simply, the challenge is to recognize that
"Nathan's legendary wives—that is us," or which is the same thing: to
realize that we have now come to live within the household of Nathan
Price. That is why, by attending to the stories of the Price women, we
may be able to catch narrative glimpses of our own lives as well as the
characters formed by the complex narrative of mission in Africa.

3. Nathan's Legendary Wives—That is Us!

One aspect that makes *The Poisonwood Bible* such a delightful
story to read is that it is told from five perspectives. Nathan's four
daughters take turns (chapters) to tell the story, with Orleanna's own
impressions and recollections providing a link between the five main
sections of the book. In this way, the reader is able to get a firsthand of
how each of the Price women viewed, responded to, and negotiated the
delicate intersection between Nathan's mission and the realities of
Africa. But even more importantly, the reader is able to see, displayed
in their accounts, how each one's life came to be shaped within this
intersection.

In fact, viewed from this angle, the stories of the Price women
become *types* of characters, which Christianity continues to form in
Africans. For what Adah says of her sisters is true in many ways of

African Christians and our ongoing engagement with Christianity: "Carry us, marry us, ferry us, bury us: those are the four ways to exodus for now. Though to tell the truth, none of us has yet safely made the crossing. Except for Ruth May, of course."[32] That is why a quick look at the other characters of the Price women can prove to be highly instructive.[33]

ORLEANNA

"What is the conqueror's wife, if not a conquest herself?"[34]

Orleanna is the wife of Nathan Price and the mother of four daughters. Nathan neither listens to her nor takes her seriously. She is both sad and guilt-laden (especially after the death of her youngest daughter, Ruth May). In relation to Nathan's mission, she is in the background. Similarly, her impressions are not part of the main story of *The Poisonwood Bible*, but its backdrop, as the recollections of one who has been denied a voice and even memory. "Are we allowed to remember?" she asks.[35]

In many ways, Orleanna reminds one of the plight of Africa. As she herself admits, "In the end my lot was cast with the Congo. Poor Congo, barefoot bride of men who took her jewels and promised the Kingdom."[36] More specifically, one can see reflected in Orleanna's life the millions of African women who, like Orleanna, find themselves caught in the throngs of Africa's big and powerful stories. These stories include the stories of Christianity in Africa, the stories of African culture, and stories of Africa's politics and the world economy. In all these stories, African women are rendered into second-class citizens, and their particular gifts are passed over, misused, or simply taken for granted. Like Orleanna, they have no story of their own within these grand narratives. Orleanna speaks of them when she notes,

> *For women like me, it seems, it's not ours to take charge of beginnings and endings. Not the marriage proposal, the summit conquered, the first shot fired, not the last one either—the treaty at Appomattox, the knife in the heart. Let men write those stories. I can't. I only know the middle ground where we live our lives.*[37]

Ironically, it is in this middle ground of their lives—the sheer materiality and ordinariness of their labor and love as they look after their families and provide the basic demands of life, the very contribution that tends to be overlooked—that they build the Church from ground up. For instance, it was Orleanna who first brought the community of Kilanga together in celebration. They came not for Nathan's Easter sermon but for Orleanna's Easter picnic.

> It was mother who decided to contribute most of the flock
> for feeding the village, like a peace offering. On the morn-
> ing of the picnic, she had to start at the crack of dawn to get
> all those hens killed and fried up. At the picnic she walked
> through the crowd passing out thighs and drumsticks to the
> little children, who acted just a pleased as punch, licking
> their fingers and singing out hymns. Yet for all her slaving
> over a hot stove, Father hardly noticed how she'd won over
> the crowds . . . The picnic was festive, but not at all what
> he'd had in mind. It was nothing in terms of redemption[38]
> (emphasis added).

There is also something about Orleanna's relationship to Nathan that rings true in many African women's ambiguous relationship to the church. Orleanna writes the following concerning her attitude to Nathan:

> I feared him more than it is possible to fear a mere man.
> Feared Him, Loved Him, served Him, clamped my hands
> over my ears to stop His words that rang in my head even
> when he was far away, or sleeping.[39]

It is this complex, multiple, ambiguous relationship that African women theologians—Mercy Oduyoye, Musimbi Kanyoro, Teresa Okure, Musa Duke, Nyambura Njoroge, and others have only recently begun to draw our attention to through their writing and work.[40]

RUTH MAY

"I am muntu Africa; muntu one child and a million all lost the same day."[41]

Ruth May is the youngest daughter of Nathan and Orleanna. Her life is well-summed up by Leah: "She had the heart of a mongoose. Brave and clever. She was the chief of all children in Kilanga, including her sisters."[42] She loves the children of Kilanga, plays with them, and teaches them simple American children's games ("Mother may I"). They in turn, especially Nelson, teach her African games and how to sing to the chickens. She also loves Jesus dearly. When the village of Kilanga decided to have a vote on whether to retain Jesus Christ in the office of personal God, only Ruth May in the Price family voted for Jesus. But it is the same Ruth May who comes down with malaria and gets very weak, but gradually recovers. She, however, tragically dies at the hands of Tata Kuvudundu's malicious trick to scare the Price family away from Kilanga.

Reflected in Ruth May's innocence and tragic death are the lives of millions of African children, who die everyday due to such "stupid" and thus preventable causes like malaria, malnutrition, diarrhea, AIDS, rebel madness . . . the list is endless. And the tens of thousands of powerless and innocent children whose death is "accidental" (incidental), and constitutes just a number: a statistic in UN reports on world poverty: "30,000 children die from hunger-related causes and preventable diseases every day, most of them in Africa." These are Africa's Ruth May: "muntu one child and a million all lost on the same day."[43]

Also reflected in Ruth May's story are millions of Africa's innocent children, men, and women who lie in unmarked graves all over the continent—the victims of Africa's endless wars and civil unrest—in the Congo, Burundi, northern Uganda, Sudan, and Sierra Leone. Ruth May also resembles the tens of thousands of Rwandan Christians who during the genocide sought shelter in Churches, and who met their end within the same churches, killed by fellow Christians—some betrayed by their own priests.

If all of these Ruth May's have forgiven us ("I forgive you Mother"), they nevertheless constantly call us to a sense of humility and repentance.[44] "Yes, you are all accomplices to the fall, and yes, we are gone forever. Gone to a ruin so strange it must be called by another name."[45] Moreover, one cannot pretend that the Church's presence and mission has nothing to do with things like hunger and malaria. Yes, malaria, hunger, genocide, love, and innocence—as well as the tragic deaths of millions of Africa's Ruth Mays—are part of the complex narrative of Christianity in Africa that must at once be embraced and owned. Again, Ruth May reminds us, "every life is different because you passed this way and passed history. Everyone is complicit."[46]

RACHEL

"Stick out your elbows, pick up your feet, and float along with the crowd. The last thing you want to do is to get trampled to death." [47]

Rachel is the eldest of the Price girls, a "typical" teenager, interested in nothing but her own beauty and how she appears in the eyes of her peers. She is shallow, even though she now and again tries to hide it through attempts at sophisticated speech, which only produces comic and humorous flips of the tongue.

From the start, she is cynical about her father's mission to Kilanga, and so her only hope and desire is to go back to Georgia and carry on with her life. In the end, however, she is the only one of the surviving Price women who never returns to America—not even to visit. On fleeing the Congo, she lives briefly in South Africa, maneuvers herself into a series of sexual relationships-cum-marriages, before settling down as the owner and manager of the Equitorial, a hotel for Western tourists and businessmen in Brazzavile.

This simple sketch of her biography clearly demonstrates Rachel's pragmatic and self-centered approach by which she uses her body and others to obtain what she needs. She credits this practical wisdom to a small book—*How to Survive 101 Calamities*—which she once read back in Georgia:

> You just have to save your neck and work out the details later. Like the little book said: Stick out your elbows, pick up your feet, and float along with the crowd. The last thing you want to do is get trampled to death.[48]

It is with the same self-centered pragmatism that she views and deals with Africa:

> The way I see Africa, your don't have to like it, but you sure have to admit it is out there. You have your way of thinking and it has its, and never the train you shall meet. You just don't let it influence your mind. If there's ugly things going on out there, well, you put a good stout lock on your door

and check it twice before you go to sleep. You focus on get-
ting your own one little place set up perfect . . . . Other peo-
ple's worries do not necessarily have to drag you down."[49]

Rachel cannot therefore comprehend her sister's love for and marriage
to the African schoolteacher, Anatole:

Now Leah, though. That one I will never understand. After
all this time I can certainly work with the Africans as well
as anybody can, mainly by not leading them into tempta-
tion. But to marry one? And have children? It does not seem
natural. I can't see how those boys are any kin to me.[50]

Against this background, the fact that the men of Rachel's sexual
exploits are all white, rich, and "powerful"—a mercenary, a diplomat,
and a businessman—is telling, in that it shows her determination to
alienate herself with the colonial story as the only way to become "successful" in Africa. Rachel's sexual (exploitative) relationships with the
various white men, however, leave her barren and thus unable to conceive and give birth to new life. This fact alone shows that even though
Rachel's pragmatism and colonial vision can appear to be successful,
they can only ensure her own individual and selfish survival—but
remain barren in terms of life-giving possibilities or a viable future for
Africa.

Rachel easily reminds one of many African Christians who have no
deep or enduring commitment: neither to the future of Africa nor to
anything or anyone else, except their own survival and well-being.
Such individuals, because they have learned to align themselves to, or
have found a niche within the colonial story, dominate politics and
business in Africa, but in a way that makes graft, corruption, and
exploitation the end of the game. Others have simply given up on the
future of Africa. They are people with acute awareness of the challenges and hardships of life in Africa. But they have also seen many
who have been sacrificed or destroyed in selfless dedication to the
ideals of salvation, democracy, and human rights, or in an attempt to
improve the life of others in Africa. They have accordingly given up
on any such dreams. A rugged individualism and Rachel's practical
wisdom dominates their lives: "let others do the pushing and shoving,
and you just ride along. In the end, the neck you save will be your
own."[51]

But Rachel also easily resembles the many religious entrepreneurs who have become "successful" simply by seeking or learning to take advantage of the opportunities that Christianity opens up in Africa. They preach a gospel of success, health, wealth, and power. I cannot help but think of the growing number of Faith Gospel ministries in Africa, whose "seed faith" foundation brings in tremendous resources and turns the preachers into some of the most "successful" and wealthy entrepreneurs.[52] In fact, examined closely, a number of the popular literature of the Faith Gospel—e.g., Otabil's *Four Ways of Productivity: God's Foundation for Living*[53]—do not sound any different, and in fact, provide the same easy-to-follow, pragmatic, and self-centered guidelines to success as Rachel's favorite book: *How to Survive 101 Calamities*.

LEAH

"I am the unmissionary, as Adah would say, beginning each day on my knees, asking to be converted. Forgive me Africa, according to the multitude of thy mercies."[54]

Leah is the elder of the Price twins and the strong-hearted leader of the children. Of the Price women, Leah's views undergo the most change. As a child, she longs for nothing more than to be accepted and approved by her father. She struggles to follow in his footsteps, impressed by his religious passion and confidence, and always eager to come up with the "right" answers to his questions. Over the course of their stay in Kilanga however, Leah slowly becomes disillusioned with her father's brand of Christianity, thanks in great part to his tyrannical authority, domestic violence, and unbending self-righteousness. Thus, when Orleanna recovers from a month-long sickness, Leah is the first to notice a change in her mother's attitude, and to register a similar change shaping up within her.

> *For one thing, [mother] was now inclined to say whatever was on her mind right in front of God and everybody. Even father . . . I was shocked and frightened to see her flout father's authority, but truthfully, I could feel something similar moving around in my own heart. For the first time in my life I doubted his judgment . . . . All my life I've tried to set my shoes squarely in his footprints, believing if only I*

*stayed close enough to him those same, clean, simple laws
would rule my life as well . . . . Yet with each passing day, I
find myself farther away.*[55]

Years later she will register the change, now complete, even more
concretely:

*That exacting, tyrannical God of [my Father] has left me
for good. I don't quite know what crept in to take its place.
Some kin to the passion of Brother Fowles, I guess, who
advised me to trust in Creation, which is made fresh daily
and doesn't suffer in translation. This God does not work in
especially mysterious ways. The sun here rises and sets at
six exactly. A caterpillar becomes a butterfly, a bird raises
its brood in the forest, and a greenheart tree will only grow
from a greenheart seed. He brings drought sometimes, followed by torrential rains, and if these things aren't exactly
what I had in mind, they aren't my punishment either. They
are rewards, let's say for the patience of a seed. The sins of
my fathers are not insignificant. But we keep moving on. . .
reaching for balance.*[56]

Telling as this summary of Leah's "mature" faith may be, it still belies
the long journey that it has taken her to come to this stage. In her own
words, the journey has been nothing short of an ongoing conversion:
"I am the unmissionary . . . beginning each day on my knees asking to
be converted."[57]

While it is clear that the conversion is a conversion away from her
father's finger-wagging, fire-and-brimstone brand of Christianity, it is
what she converts to—"something kin to the passion of brother
Fowles"—that is instructive and needs to be elaborated. Even though
Brother Fowles only makes one direct appearance in the novel, his
memory is constantly evoked by his talking parrot, Methuselah. He is
the Catholic missionary who ran the Kilanga mission before the Price's
arrived. He has since left the mission after falling in love with and getting married to Celine, a Congolese woman with whom he now lives
and raises a family down the river from Kilanga. Asked by Nathan as
to the kind of work he is doing now, Brother Fowles answer is simple,
but revealing: "I rejoice in the work of the Lord . . . I do a little ministering. I study and classify the fauna. I observe a great deal, and probably offer very little salvation in the long run."[58]

A little salvation in the long run—that is what, in fact, Brother Fowles was able to offer to the village of Kilanga during his time at the mission, as is evident from this conversation between him and Orleanna about the village chief:

> Were you really on such good terms with   Tata Ndu?
> (Mother asked)
> "I respect him, if that's what you mean."
> But as a Christian did you really get anywhere with him?'
> Brother Fowles stood up and scratched his head, making his white hair stand on end . . . "As a Christian, I respect his judgments. He guides his village fairly, all things considered. We never could see eye to eye on the business of having four wives . . . ."
> He has more than that now, Leah tattled.
> "Aha, you see I was not a great influence in that department," [Brother Fowles] said. "But each of those wives has profited from the teachings of Jesus, I can tell you. Tata Ndu and I spent many afternoons with a calabash of palm wine between us, debating the merits of treating a wife kindly. In my six years here I saw the practice of wife beating fall into great disfavor. Secret, little altars to Tata Jesus appeared in most every kitchen, as a result."[59]

But it is clear that more than any *work* he does, or any little salvation he might offer, it is his love and admiration of the people of the Congo that characterize his life in the Congo. He admits:

> I have come to love the people and their way of thinking. . . . They are very religious people, you know . . . . Everything they do is with one eye to the spirit. When they plant their yams and manioc, they're praying. When they harvest, they're praying. Even when they conceive their children, I think they're praying.[60]

It is to this love, this "passion of Brother Fowles" that Leah has been converted, which is not essentially a form of activism, (religious or humanitarian) on behalf of Africa—not some kind of "native spirituality"—but basically an appreciation of, and identification with Africa's hopes, dreams, and frustrations. It is a presence, a particular way of "being at home" in and with Africa. It is a certain love and a way of being sustained by Africa, as Brother Fowles admits to Orleanna:

"We're branches grafted on this good tree. . . . The great root of Africa sustains us."[61]

What Leah's story makes obvious is the fact that coming to such passion is not automatic, but takes the form of a journey of, and is made possible by, friendship. This is the friendship that Leah shares with Anatole, the schoolteacher whom she eventually marries and with whom she gives birth to four "peanut-brown" children. For Leah, therefore, the very color of her children is a reminder not only of her journey with Anatole, but of the time and patience that the conversion to the passion of Brother Fowles required. She admits: "I look at my four boys, who are the colors of silt, loam, dust, and clay, an infinite palette for children of their own, and I understand that time erases whiteness altogether."[62]

What Leah's story also confirms is the courage required to sustain the journey of ongoing conversion. It is the courage that Leah embodies when she is finally able to stand up to her father, but also to challenge the patriarchal traditions of Kilanga, and thus win a vote that allows her to go hunting with the men. As it turns out, this is not just courage to stand firm in one's convictions; it is a commitment to stand with and for those marginalized by the systems, ideologies, or oppressive traditions. It is this commitment to the grassroots transformation of Africa that lands Leah's husband Anotole twice in Mobutu's prison, and inspires Leah to be critical of American foreign policy:

> Rachel informs me I've had my brains washed by a Communist plot. She's exactly right. I've been won by the side of schoolteachers and nurses, and lost all allegiance to plastic explosives. No homeland I can claim as mine would blow up a struggling distant country's hydroelectric dams and water pipes . . . and bury mines in every Angolan road that connected food with a hungry child. We have watched this war with our hearts in our throats, knowing what there is to lose. Another Congo. Another wasted chance running like poisoned water under Africa, curling our souls into fists. [63]

It is also clear that Leah's conversion is a commitment to the ongoing transformation of Africa's basic needs and hopes—realized through communal solidarity. Thus, Anatole and Leah end up setting up a co-operative farm across the border in Angola, on which they raise pigs and grow maize, yams, and soybeans. On the farm, Leah teaches classes in nutrition, sanitation, and soybeans, to "women who respectfully call me Mama Ngemba and ignore nine-tenths of what I tell them."[64]

One can see reflected in Leah and Anatole's life, the life of millions of African Christians who, like Leah and Anatole, are caught at the intersection of the social-political and religious ferment of many African countries; and who, like Leah and Anatole, are committed to each other, to their families, and to the ongoing transformation of their communities. But also reflected in the life of Leah is the Church, an African Church that has learned to define her mission and existence within the dialect of Africa's history, not as a mission of self-righteous dispensation of God's judgment (Nathan), but as a mission of presence, of being-at-home in and with Africa—one of learning to listen a great deal, and perhaps offer some salvation in the long run.

It is the Church of Desmond Tutu, a Church of courageous witness and of resistance during apartheid in South Africa, but also a Church committed to a future of forgiveness and reconciliation. It is therefore a Church that has learned to suspect the politics of racial, tribal, and national identity. It is a Church that "keep[s] moving on—searching for balance," for a new Christian identity, for a way of being church beyond a Western, African, tribal, or national identity. It is the Church of Andre Sibomana in Rwanda, who dared to denounce both the genocide and the atrocities of the post-genocide regime in Rwanda, at great personal cost.[65]

It is the Church of small things.[66] The Church of the village catechist who teaches five-year-old children to count from one to ten, to write their names, and to make the sign of the cross. It is a Church of nurses and health care workers, who assist mothers in labor and who spend time teaching the basic principles of hygiene to men and women who "forget nine-tenths of what they are told." It is the church of mothers and fathers who hold each other tightly through some nights, and on other nights stay up in hopeful and prayerful vigil for their sick children. It is the Church of priests and nuns who, like Brother Fowles, just do "a little ministering" but spend the greater part of their day in the mundane tasks of planting cabbages and soybeans, visiting families, teaching school children a civics or domestic science class, meeting with the village council, or celebrating Eucharist. . . . It is a church that "begins each day on its knees, asking to be converted" to a more visible presence within the local communities and a commitment to the

transformation of Africa's needs and hopes. It is a church that strives—
not to be "a powerful instrument of thy perfect will here" (Nathan), but
a humble presence; and hopes that through such presence and witness
she might offer some little salvation in the long run.

A CONCLUDING CONFESSION—
ONE FOR THE NEST BOXES

I hope it is now obvious that a work of fiction like *The Poisonwood
Bible* can evoke a rich conversation about Christianity in Africa, one
in fact, that can be far more interesting and productive than one generated around the homogenizing notion of African culture. Moreover,
what the reader might have noticed is how, in the current conversation,
the focus has shifted from the "faces of Jesus" and increasingly turned
to the reality of the *church*. For what the stories of the Price women
have revealed is not simply the example of *individuals* whose lives are
shaped by a particular missionary narrative, but *types* or ways of being
church in Africa. And so, from this perspective, Nathan's five legendary wives are but different faces of the church in Africa: Adah's is
the listening and attentive church; Orleanna's is the silent and silenced
church; and Ruth May's is the church of martyrs and victims. While
Rachel's is the Church of power and money-hungry charlatans, Leah's
is a Church of ongoing conversion.

I must confess, though, that this was a very rewarding revelation,
which became apparent to me only at the end. It was like working with
a problem you cannot exactly pin down. You know there is something
wrong with the particular set of issues you are dealing with, but are not
exactly sure what the problem is. When I started working on this paper,
I knew there was something misleading about the standard discussions
of "faces of Jesus in Africa." I tried to conceptualize the problem in
terms of the popularity of the notion of "culture" and how this notion
leads to very neat accounts of inculturation, which fail to display the
complex ways in which African Christians are facing the contradictions, challenges, and frustrations of everyday life. I was, however, not
fully satisfied with this explanation, for I was sure there was more at
stake, even though I could not put my finger on it. It is only now that
I realize that my basic uneasiness with the discussion of faces of Jesus
in Africa has to do with the manner in which this discussion tends to
obscure the nature and complex ways of being church in Africa.

What the brief look at the characters of *The Poisonwood Bible* has helped to make clear is that in order to provide a far more engaging discussion of Christianity in Africa, we need to shift the conversation from the neat walls of Christological translations into the murky waters of ecclesiological narratives. For it is in the life and witness of the Church; in the unstable and multiple histories, in her basic and ordinary witness—or as Adah would say, in the scratching of chicken manure from the nest boxes—that the true meaning of baptism (*batiza*) is revealed to us. But this means that once we enter the fray of history that the nest boxes are a part of, we might discover, just as Adah did, that pronounced a certain way, *batiza* means to terrify. Such a discovery would no doubt have a sobering effect, for it would indicate the possibility that for many in Africa, the Church might have become such a *terrifying* presence. It is this realization that engenders and calls for humility in terms of theological methodology. For in the end, it confirms that Nathan is right: "Jesus is *bangala*." But it also confirms that unless we are ready to confront the fact that the reality of Jesus in Africa is at once saving, terrifying, and itching, we should perhaps not babble in Jesus talk.

Notes

[1] Based on a revised lecture given at the University of Dallas in Texas (USA) and sponsored by the late Dr. William Farmer and the International Bible Commentary (IBC). April 16, 1999.

[2] See e.g., C.G. Baeta, ed. *Christianity and African Culture* (Accra:Conference Report 1995), as the proceedings of the 1955 Consultation on *Christianity and African Culture*; Kofi Appiah-Kubi and Sergio Torres, eds. "African Theology en Route: Papers from the Pan-African Conference of Third World Theologians," Accra 1977 (Maryknoll, NY: Orbis, 1979); For as good statement of this debate as it took place in relation to Black Theology see Mothabi Mokgethi, "African Theology or Black Theology: Toward an Integral African Theology," *Journal of Black Theology in Southern Africa* 8/ 2 (1994), 113–141.

[3] Kwame Bediako, *Christianity in Africa: The Renewal of a Non-Western Religion* (Maryknoll: Orbis, 1995).

[4] Robert Schreiter, ed. *Faces of Jesus in Africa*, (Maryknoll, NY: Orbis, 1998). Most of the essays in this volume also appear in Jesse Mugambi and Laurenti Magesa, eds. *Jesus in African Christianity: Experimentation and Diversity in African Christology*, (Nairobi: Acton Publishers, 1998).

[5] *Ibid.*, 52–53.

[6] *Ibid.*, 3.

[7] *Ibid.*, ix.

[8] *Ibid.*, 103–115.

[9] *Ibid.*, 105.

[10] *Ibid.*, 116–127.

[11] *Ibid.*, 8–12. For a more extended treatment of this image by Nyamiti see his, *Christ as Our Ancestor* (Harare: Mambo Press, 1986).

[12] *Ibid.*, 10–11.

[13] *Ibid.*, 8.

[14] This is the case even when the "African cultural experience" is extended, as it ought to be, beyond the quaint, traditional worldview of ancestors to take into account such realities as "African women's experience," suffering and poverty in Africa, or the marginalization experienced by many Africans today. In this respect, see the contributions by Nasimiyu-Wasike [70–84], Magesa [151–163] and Waliggo [164–180] respectively. It is the neat and easy insertion of Jesus as our hope, liberator, or co-traveler within whatever the African world is shown to be that I find problematic. For more on this theme see my "On What About . . . ?: Why Simply Making Jesus One of Us Will Not and Cannot Save Us," unpublished paper.

[15] In order to fully understand the interest and even popularity of the notion of "culture" in our time, one also needs to pay attention to Bernard McGrane's interesting observation that we live in a 20th century paradigm in which "culture" has become a way, the dominant way of understanding and talking about non-Western others. See Bernard McGrane, *Beyond Anthropology: Society and Its Other* (New York: Columbia University Press, 1989). In making this observation McGrane also helpfully notes how within this paradigm there seems to be a certain democratization of culture, but one that does not allow a critical engagement with the other. One's culture is just one among many, and so there is very little that one can really say about another's culture by way of critical engagement. This is perhaps one reason why talk about culture is popular in our time. The "other" in this case, the "Africans and their culture" are a fascination, particularly since their being different does not call into question the social, economic, and political inequalities that makes their world different from the world of the West. Instead, theirs is merely a cultural difference. For my extended discussion of McGrane's work see Katongole "Postmodern Illusions and the Challenges of African Theology," in *Modern Theology* 16/2 (2000), 237–254.

[16] See, for instance, John and Jean Comoroff, *Of Revolution and Revelation,* Vol 1. (Chicago University Press, 1991); Tinyiko Maluleke, "Christianity in a Distressed Africa" *Missionalia* 26/3 91998: 337. On hidden and public transcripts, see James Scott, *Domination and the Arts of Resistance,* (New Haven:Yale University, 1990). There is a lot that one finds helpful in these and similar characterizations of the encounter between the missionaries and Africa. One must be careful however not to view this complex encounter as an event of the past, something that happened during the missionary phase of Christianity, and from which we have since moved on. The claim I make in this essay is that it is this complex negotiation that characterizes the ongoing formations of African Christianity.

[17] Barbar Kingsolver, *The Poisonwood Bible* (New York: Harper Collins Publishers, 1998), p.334.

[18] *Ibid.*

[19] *Ibid.*

[20] *Ibid.*, 18.

[21] I am grateful to my colleague Teresa Berger for pointing out to me the connection between Nathan's colonial assumptions and attitude to Africa and his domestic vio-

lence. The theme of colonialism as rape, i.e., sexual violence is an old one. It is therefore quite telling that Nathan not only does violence to "Africa" but to the women in
his life.

[22] Kingsolver, 26–28.

[23] *Ibid.*, 62.

[24] *Ibid.*, 57.

[25] *Ibid.*, 172.

[26] *Ibid.*, 276.

[27] *Ibid.*, 214.

[28] *Ibid.*, 485.

[29] *Ibid.*, 488.

[30] *Ibid.*, 490.

[31] *Ibid.*, 533.

[32] *Ibid.*, 414.

[33] Another strength of Kingsolver's narrative is in its ability to render complex the
very notion of African culture. One only needs to think of the different and complex
ways the Africans—Tata Ndu, Nelson, Anatole, Mama Tataba and other women, Tata
Kuvudundu, etc.—interact with the Prices. In fact, an immediate impulse would be to
see these characters as representing various faces of Africa. In terms of Christian characters, however, it is the Price women, more than the African characters, who provide
more elaborate and concrete ways of being formed by or under the powerful story of
mission in Africa.

[34] *Ibid.*, 9.

[35] *Ibid.*, 495.

[36] *Ibid.*, 201.

[37] *Ibid.*, 383.

[38] *Ibid.*, 49.

[39] *Ibid.*, 192.

[40] See e.g., Mercy Amba Oduyoye, *Daughters of Anowa: African Women and
Patriarchy* (Maryknoll, NY: Orbis, 1997); Musimbi Kanyoro, ed. *The Will to Arise:
Women, Tradition, and the Church in Africa* (Maryknoll, NY: Orbis, 1992); Oduyoye
M. ed. *Transforming Power: Women in the Household of God* (Accra: Sam Woode,
1997); Kanyoro and Nyambura Njoroge, ed. *Groaning in Faith: African Women in the
Household of God* (Nairobi: Acton, 1996); Musa Duke, *Postcolonial Feminist
Interpretation of the Bible* (St. Louis: Chalice Press, 2000).

[41] Kingsolver., 537.

[42] *Ibid.*, 430.

[43] *Ibid.*, 537.

[44] *Ibid.*, 543.

[45] *Ibid.*, 537.

[46] *Ibid.*, 538.

[47] *Ibid.*, 405.

[48] *Ibid.*

[49] *Ibid.*, 516.

[50] *Ibid.*, 464.

[51] *Ibid.*, 516.

52 The Seed Faith idea ties the idea of God's blessings and one's success to an individual's financial contribution or deposit. The opening words of the sermon of Mensa Otabil, founder of the International Central Gospel Church (Ghana) quoted by Gifford, provide a good example of the theology behind the Seed Faith idea: "If you haven't deposited anything, you have no right to ask for anything . . . People think that you should give so that the church has money. No. The main purpose is that you enter a covenant so that God of Abraham, Isaac and Jacob will meet all your needs." See Gifford, *African Christianity: Its Public Role* (Bloomington, IN: Indiana University Press, 1998), p. 80.

53 Mensa Otabil, *Four Laws of Productivity: God's Foundation for Living*. (Accra: Altar International, 1992).

54 Kingsolver, 525.

55 *Ibid.*, 233–234.

56 *Ibid.*, 525.

57 *Ibid.*, 525.

58 *Ibid.*, 250.

59 *Ibid.*, 257–258.

60 Kingsolver maintains a website www.kingsolver.com dealing with her life and work, with an entire section dedicated to answering questions about *The Poisonwood Bible.* The dangers of relying on extra-fictional information notwithstanding, it is clear that for Kingsolver, Brother Fowles represents Christian mission in kinder voice. She notes: "In fact, my favorite character is Brother Fowles, whose role in the novel is to redeem both Christianity and the notion of mission . . . . Nathan Price is, indeed, an arrogant proselytizer, but he's not the only agent of Christianity here. His wife and daughters take different paths toward more open-minded kinds of spirituality, and I called in Brother Fowles specifically to represent Christian mission in a kinder voice." I am grateful to my student, Amy Bressler, who first drew my attention to the Kingsolver website in a seminar discussion, and whose discussions of the various characters of *The Poisonwood Bible* in a term paper helped to shape my own thinking.

61 *Ibid.*, 258.

62 *Ibid.*, 526.

63 *Ibid.*, 503.

64 *Ibid.*, 523–524.

65 Andre Sibomana, *A Hope for Rwanda: Conversations with Laure Guibert and Herve Deguine*, translated by Carina Tertsakian, (London: Pluto Press, 1997).

66 I borrow the expression and underlying inspiration from Arundhati Roy's acclaimed and national bestseller, *The God of Small Things* (New York: Harper Collins, 1997).

CHAPTER NINE

RACISM: CHRISTIAN RESOURCES
BEYOND RECONCILIATION

C hristian worship provides one of the best resources and contexts for Christians to unlearn race and resist racism. For
instance, the greeting which Christians receive and offer to one
another during worship is a witness to the fact that Christians are
drawn beyond themselves into the story of God's own life and self-sacrificing action in the world. It is by standing within this story that
Christians learn to see themselves and others as gifts who, in their bodily differences, are called to be the visible Body of Christ. In the act of
being greeted and of greeting one another in the name of the Trinity
they bear witness to this story. Accordingly, when Christians take worship not as an occasional act but as a way of life, they acquire
resources which enable them to see and relate to one another in ways
far more interesting and truthful than any recommendations for racial
reconciliation could ever be.

My appreciation of worship as the best context for a discussion on
race has been shaped by many factors, among which are my own
resistance to a newly-acquired racial identity, and a determined effort
to recover a vision and way of life beyond such an identity. And so, for
the reader to fully appreciate "where I am coming from," I thought it
helpful to begin with a personal story.

ON DISCOVERING RACE: A PERSONAL STORY

I did not know that I was black until the summer of 1991, when I
first came to the United States. That it took me so long to discover my
"race" was, however, never due to any confusion about my parentage
or doubts about my skin pigmentation. It is just that in Uganda "black"
is simply an adjective, and a black person is simply one with an unusu-
ally dark complexion. And since as far as complexion goes, I am
"brown" or "dark brown," I was never black. I was therefore surprised
on coming to the United States to discover that these distinctions were

not significant in the same sort of manner, and that I was simply black. Moreover, what I soon discovered was that here, black was not an adjective that operated among other adjectives to describe a person, but an ethically and ideologically coded designation of what a person is—in this case, my very identity.

To be sure, I do not remember if there was any particular incident or decisive moment at which I became black. In fact, during this first visit in the summer of 1991, I must have gotten away with a number of things that were outside the usual or normal range of expectations of black and white interactions. This was particularly the case since I happened to be assigned as summer resident priest at a rural, predominantly white parish in Indiana. And since I was not aware I was black, I just went about discovering America and American culture in the most innocent manner. And if people were extra nice to me, this did not strike me as odd. It simply confirmed my impression of Americans as generally very friendly people. In this way, Americans reminded me of the people back at home in Uganda.

I do, however, remember being amazed by the fact that even after a very short time at the church I served, everybody in the town seemed to know me. Whether at a Wal-Mart store, or at an ice cream parlor, or on an evening walk, I met people who greeted me with a friendly "Hi Father." I remember at first thinking to myself: everybody here must be Catholic, and so they must have seen me at mass. It is only when I asked one woman whether she came to St. Mary's and she said "no" that I was curious how she had gotten to know me. Her quick reply: "This is a small town, and word gets around very quickly." It had never struck me that I was the only "black" person in town.

This fact was brought home to me one afternoon when, as I prepared to take my driver's license test, I needed some practice in parallel parking. I chose a relatively quiet street in the neighborhood for this exercise, and when I was satisfied with my skills, headed back home. Just a couple of blocks away from the church, a police car pulled me over. The police officer was very polite, and when he had examined my documents and found nothing wrong, explained that he had received a call from a concerned neighbor who had seen a black person doing a couple of parking maneuvers in the neighborhood.

The discovery of myself as black continued and even became heightened when I went to study in Belgium in the fall of the same year. And even though I was never able fully to understand Flemish, I was aware of how frequently the word *zwart* came up in references to, or conversations about me. Not that all these references were racial in the negative sort of way. They just confirmed the extent to which race had become the dominant grid through which my life was read, and through which I was supposed to see my life. This discovery made me angry. For as far as I was concerned, black or *zwart* did not name anything about me—not even my skin color. It was just an identity that I was assumed to have; something I was supposed to be.

What I found particularly difficult to understand was the fact that all my characteristics, roles, and functions did not seem to be as significant as the fact that I was black or *zwart*. I was particularly shocked that my being a Christian among fellow Christians, or my being a priest in a predominantly Catholic country like Belgium did not make any difference. I was black and that greatly determined my social interactions, the church I went to, the type of housing that was open to me for rent, and even how well I did in some courses. To be sure, most of this was very subtle, even though there were other incidents where racism was more overt.

I remember, for instance, when Sam, another priest from Ghana who was in the same program with me, asked me to go with him to check out his new apartment. He had been shopping around for a while for an apartment, and had called a number of landlords whose ads he had seen in the paper. At detecting his African voice, the majority of them had told him that the apartment in question had just been rented out, even though the ad for the same apartment would appear in the paper the following day or week. Sam got a brilliant idea. He asked Rob, a Belgian student in our program, to call on Sam's behalf. Sure enough, the apartment was available. So Sam invited me to go over with Rob to check out the apartment. On seeing the three of us, the landlord realized the trick. And even though Rob immediately explained that he had called for the apartment, the landlord apologized for the mistake, but the apartment was not available.

I am sure there is nothing unique about my story, except perhaps in the sense that for me this was a novel experience, a recent discovery of what it means to be black. But this is perhaps what made me all the more determined not to accept this new identity of myself as a racialized person. For I soon realized that I was beginning to hate not only myself but others as well, for no other reason except their being black or white. It was then that I realized that I would either have to accept and learn to live with my new identity, or find ways to resist it. But even as I faced the challenge, the choice seemed to be clear. How

could I allow such a recent discovery to become the overriding characteristic for my self-understanding?

It is this personal biography that perhaps best explains why I have
come to see the need to move theological discussions beyond the
search for guidelines and principles that foster racial reconciliation.
For, helpful as many of these recommendations might be, they are
based on a realism that accepts race and racial identity as a fact.
Accordingly, their greatest relief seems to be one of providing insights
and skills (theological, ethical, political) to help us "manage" or deal
with the reality of race. However, given my story above, even as I
hoped for and expected justice and racial equality, I constantly found
myself longing for spaces and practices in which I could recover a sort
of pre-1991 racial innocence. Accordingly, it became increasingly
clear to me that, more than racial reconciliation, the far more urgent
ethical and theological challenge was the recovery of a vision and way
of life "beyond race."

But if I understood this to be the challenge, I also soon discovered
that the standard philosophical and theological discussions did not
offer much in terms of concrete resources with which to meet the challenge. For, where philosophical and theological discussions could shed
a light on the issue of race, their recommendations nevertheless still
fell short of providing *concrete* alternatives to, or resources for, a way
of life beyond race. A simple theoretical digression will help to make
this clear.

THE PHILOSOPHICAL AND
THEOLOGICAL DISCOURSE ON RACE

The Consolation of Philosophy

One can learn a great deal from the philosophical discourse on
race. In my case, for instance, it was my philosophy background that
helped me to see the connections between the notions of race, civilization, reason, progress—in a word, the connection between race and the
Enlightenment project. It is this connection that led me to see the
extent to which assumptions of race still underpin the social, political,
and economic institutions of Western civilization. More specifically,
philosophy helped me to see how the modern problem of race is connected to the modern accounts of the self and human flourishing. If
philosophy helped me to begin to make these connections, it also

helped to expose the arbitrariness of the notion of race. For instance, I found Hannah Arendt's attempt to connect race and imperialism highly instructive, especially her observation that both are grounded in practical economic interests.[1] Similarly, by connecting the notion of race to the "invention" of Africa as the dark, uncivilized other of European enlightenment, Mudimbe[2] was able to show how race classification is just one factor reflecting the anxiety at the heart of Western claims to "civilization." Thus, both Arendt's and Mudimbe's arguments helped me to see the deep connection between colonialism and race.

But for all these insights, philosophy was still far from providing skills and resources for a vision of life "beyond race." In fact, the best that philosophy seemed to offer in terms of relief were *theoretical* skills. No doubt, one could *do* a lot with these and similar intellectual insights. I remember, for instance, how, armed with such insights, my African colleagues and myself often found ourselves in a spirited conversation in which we discussed, debated, and eventually deconstructed "blackness" as simply an invention: a political and ethical construct meant to advance particular political and economic interests. But even with the consolation of such deconstruction, we were still without any concrete skills or practices with which to live out our lives beyond "the political and ethical construct" that we had discovered race to be. At the end of the day, we were all still "black" and my friend Sam could still not find an apartment.

THEOLOGY AND RACIAL RECONCILIATION

The challenge of providing concrete alternatives to racism and race categories is also one that theological discussions have tended to shy away from. For, in turning to theology, one is first confronted with the astonishing realization that the observation that James Cone noted in 1975 is still largely true in our day. That is, in spite of the fact that race and racism are a major social problem, white theologians have, on the whole, had very little to say against racism.[3] The silence may of course be an indication of the realism with which the mainstream of Western theology has come to accept race and racism as a fact about which nothing much can be done. It may also be, as Cone suggests, that the fact that white theologians have remained virtually mute on issues of race is because they have been unwilling to question their own cultural history, particularly the political and economic structures of Western societies. What the silence does, however, is to turn the theological discourse on race into just another area of special interest—one that black theologians are expected to pursue. My being asked to contribute an essay on racism in this volume may itself not be unrelated to this observation.

Secondly, one notes that theological discussions on race have been greatly dominated by recommendations for racial reconciliation. Whereas this might sound like a very concrete recommendation, one soon discovers that a great many of these theological discussions are not only abstract, they leave us at the level of principles and insights. For even when the discussions begin by making reference to Scripture and/or Christian tradition, the goal is quite often to draw from these traditions *ethical* implications or insights, which could be applied generally.

This is also perhaps the reason why, within many of these discussions, the problem of race is easily reduced to a general problem of difference, one that is common to all societies. Craig Keener's "The Gospel and Racial Reconciliation"[4] provides a good example. In this essay, Keener first notes that whereas differences in skin color and other physical features were noticed, but rarely understood in a prejudicial manner in the New Testament, "racism in the sense of various cultures viewing themselves as superior was widespread."[5] He then examines Paul's theology of reconciliation in order to show that the Gospel provides insights and guidelines in how the Christian can overcome this problem of "prejudice," and transcend "all other human barriers we have erected among ourselves."[6] I draw attention to Keener's essay because it offers a clear example of how, once the problem of racism has been reduced to a universal human problem, the Christian response cannot but itself be limited to one of discovering what *insights* the gospel can shed on this general problem. To the extent that a great many theological recommendations for racial reconciliation move in this manner, they leave us at the level of insights and principles, and do not draw attention to specific Christian practices, which might offer concrete skills of resistance and an alternative to racism.

Even more problematic, however, is the fact that the attempt to reduce racism to a general problem of difference and prejudice tends to obscure the particular history and assumptions that sustain racism as a distinctively modern problem. In the absence of any attention to that narrative, it is simply assumed that race is a natural category, and therefore, all one can hope for is tolerance or some form of racial reconciliation or harmony.

What my excursus in philosophy has allowed me to appreciate, however, is the fact that race is not a natural category, but one that is somehow connected to the modern accounts of the self and human flourishing. And so, by not questioning the category of race, theologies for racial reconciliation may unwittingly reproduce the same accounts of the self as those responsible for giving rise to the problem of racism in the first place.

This observation is connected to a wider problem facing theology in modern times: namely, that in an attempt to remain a respectable discipline, theologians often feel that we have to appeal to the modern accounts of culture, race, and history to provide us with an account of reality. But since it is these accounts that are responsible for giving rise to the problem of race in the first place, appealing to the same accounts leaves us with little or no resources with which to move beyond the limits that the vision of these accounts impose. This is one reason why I personally find the theologies of racial reconciliation not to be radical enough. For while these discussions offer insights and ethical guidelines on how to deal with or manage the problems of racism, they leave us within the same politics and a social history where race is still a dominant story.

But if, as I have noted, the challenge is one of recovering a vision and way of life beyond race, then what is required is a different story and a different set of practices that would not have to assume race or racial identity. If this sounds like a utopian or idealistic expectation, it is because Christian theology and ethics are by their nature idealistic in the sense that they reflect God, who constantly calls the Church to new imaginations of the real—of what is possible. Moreover, my own idealism was also made possible by my personal biography. For while I knew race and racism to be a fact in the West, I also knew as a matter of fact that it is possible not be black or white. In fact, what my personal story had led me to see is the fact that being black or white, or for that matter any other racial identity, was an acquired identity, which is to say, a *learned* vision of life and set of corresponding habits. This, I think, is what Cornel West has in mind when he notes that blackness has no meaning outside a system of race-conscious people and practices.[7]

This is what makes a Christian response to race not so much a matter of principles and insights, but one of *practices*. In other words, if racial identity is a matter of community, an alternative identity is not only possible, it is a matter of an alternative community, embodying different practices and a different vision of the self. If racism is at home within modern Western societies, then the Christian challenge to racism is really one of being able to step outside the vision of modern Western society, and find oneself part of a community and practices in which race and racial identity simply makes no sense. Christian worship provides precisely such an opportunity, in the sense that within the practice of Christian worship a new unique community is being constituted in a manner that both challenges and offers a concrete alternative to the story of race and racism.

CHRISTIAN WORSHIP AS A "WILD SPACE"

Such a claim needs to be qualified in at least two ways. First, we all are sadly aware that worship can be and has so often been one of the most segregated spaces. And so, far from offering an alternative to the cultural patterns of racism, Christian worship has often simply confirmed and even reinforced the racialized boundaries and interaction within modern society. That is why an appreciation of worship like we are calling for involves a reassessment of the relation of worship to modern culture. While worship has tended to provide an opportunity for a spiritual confirmation and affirmation of the dominant cultural patterns and values, I suggest that we see worship as site for imagining and embodying concrete alternatives to the dominant cultural patterns and values. In this way, Christian worship is able to provide Christians with the resources and possibilities for living out, and living out concretely, alternatives to the vision of modern society.

Secondly, the notion of "stepping outside" might strike many as encouraging a form of Christian sectarianism. Even without getting into the so-often misleading assumptions connected to this impression,[8] there is nothing about Christian worship that forces Christians to withdraw from engagement in their societies. What is meant instead is that through a practice like worship, Christians are able to develop the skills and practices required to engage critically with their societies, in other words, to live as "resident aliens"[9] within the societies they find themselves in.

More recently, I have found McFague's notion of "wild spaces"[10] a helpful way to characterize the practice of Christian worship. In an attempt to recover ethical existence in the face of a consumer-oriented economy and culture, McFague suggests the cultivation of wild spaces as a normative requirement if the individual is to resist, survive, or creatively reshape the draft of an all-too-powerful consumerist worldview. A wild space, according to McFague, is whatever does not fit the stereotypical human being or definition of the good life as defined by conventional culture. What is particularly significant, however, is that for McFague, a wild space is not the province of a self-sufficient way of life outside Western capitalist and consumer society. Rather, wild spaces are created or discovered in the rifts of that very culture.

> Imagine conventional Western culture as a circle with your world overimposed over it. If you are [a] poor Hispanic lesbian, your world will not fit into the conventional Western one. It will overlap somewhat (you may be educated and able-bodied), but there will be a large crescent that will be outside. That is your wild space; it is the space that will allow—and encourage—you to think differently, to imagine alternative ways of living. It will not only give you problems, but possibilities.[11]

I would like to suggest that Christian worship is precisely such a wild space, which allows— and encourages—[Christians] to think differently, to imagine and embody alternative ways of living. Worship enables Christians to break out of the *status quo* of conventional culture, but also offers resistance to it in ways that a new change in rules does not. For it is by standing within the wild space of worship that Christians can now see themselves in a different perspective. Such seeing, of course, is not theoretical, but is, in fact, made possible to the extent that the Christian is located within concrete practices, which reflect a different story of the self than that named by race.

And so, in the remaining part of this essay, I would like to draw attention to just one such practice of Christian worship: namely, the act of greeting, in order to highlight the conclusion that the greeting which Christians receive and offer to one another during worship provides resources for Christians to *unlearn race*, and come to embody a new pattern of life.

ON BEING GREETED IN THE NAME OF THE TRINITY

When Christians gather for worship, they are greeted and in turn take time to greet one another. The Catholic liturgy of the mass, for instance, begins with the priest greeting the congregation in these or similar words. "May the Grace of Our Lord Jesus Christ, the Love of God the Father, and the Fellowship of the Holy Spirit be with you. . . ."

Even though I have been quite familiar with this formula, I first began to fully appreciate its full theological significance on a 1997 visit to Malaysia, when on one afternoon, I was invited to participate in the celebration of mass at a Kampung (village) community outside Kuching. Mass began outside the church, with the priest greeting the congregation, and everyone in the congregation greeting everyone else. What I found particularly striking was not only the orderliness of the whole exercise, but the fact that we had to extend greeting not only to those next to us, but to each person in the congregation. For what happened was that the greeting was part of the procession into the church, whereby the congregation formed two lines—with the person at the end of each line passing through the formed lines and greeting everybody in the line. Even though it was quite a while before the last person got into the church, by that time we had all had a chance to touch, kiss, shake the hands, and look into the eyes of everyone else in the congregation.

I draw attention to this example not only because I do not know any other congregation that takes the practice of liturgical greeting as seriously, but also for the fact that this Kampung community is one of the most racially and ethnically diverse communities I have experienced. A simple survey confirmed that the congregation comprised Christians of Chinese, Malay, and Indian, as well as a host of *Orang Asli* (indigenous or tribal) backgrounds. Thus, the more I have had a chance to reflect on this experience, the more I have realized its profound theological relevance, and the rich resource which greeting provides for Christian ethics in the context of race.

BEYOND MODERN ANTHROPOLOGY

Ordinarily, greeting can be a good way to help people drop their guard and feel at home. Within the context of Christian worship, greeting does accomplish a similar goal. This was certainly the case at the mass at the Kampung. On a deeper level, however, what the greeting does is to help Christians drop the guard of their modern self. This is so important if we are to begin to imagine ourselves and others beyond racial categories. For I suspect that one of the reasons why racism is such an intractable problem for us is that it reflects the story of the modern self, particularly the constant anxiety at the heart of the modern project. The anxiety has something to do with our desire to become both autonomous and our own self-makers. For, having repudiated any story beyond its own choosing, the modern self must now seek to justify not only its own existence, but also the certainty of its knowledge, as well as the worthiness of its undertakings and values. However, with self-interest as the one and perhaps only story to live for, self-justification becomes both tenacious and ever-suspect.

This anxiety cannot but give rise to distinctive politics of power as control, and an economics of exploitation of people different from us in the name of self-interest and self-preservation. In fact, as McGrane points out, it is this constant anxiety that gives rise to practices in which the meeting with the other is policed by theories of race, history, or culture—all of which are meant to assure the modem self's place at the center of history, as the climax of civilization, or as the most advanced.[12] It is perhaps not surprising that the result of this self-arming has been a history of colonialism, imperialism, and slavery. What this history reflects, however, is nothing but the endless thrust of the desire for control and conquest of the modern self, a self haunted by the need to justify its own existence and place in history. Racism is just one aspect of this story.

That is also why, unless this story of the modern self is questioned, ethical recommendations for racial reconciliation may unwittingly reproduce the same politics of anxiety. That is what makes an ethics of "tolerance" problematic. For it reproduces a problematic form of inclusion by which power and privilege are extended but not questioned. In this way, white privilege may be extended to black folks without, however, questioning the underlying politics and accounts of the self and of human flourishing that are responsible for giving rise to the problem of racism in the first place. What is required if such a politics is to be resisted is an altogether different story of the self—a different politics in which the self is "relieved," so to speak, of the need to provide the grounds for its own existence or to prove its importance. The relief can only come to the extent that the self is not at the center of life. Christian worship is precisely the performance of this different story, which draws the self into the wider story of God's creation and redemption.

In other words, if modern anthropology, in which theories and the practices of racism are at home, is an "arming" strategy, Christian worship is a "disarming" practice. That is what being greeted "In the name of the Father, and of the Son, and of the Holy Spirit . . ." does. For the greeting is an invitation for the Christian to relax, as it were, in the knowledge that his or her life need no other grounds for its justification, since it is already justified and part of that new creation that is made possible by "the love of God, the grace of Son, and the fellowship of the Holy Spirit." Becoming thus aware of, and learning to relax in, this good news, Christians can now be aware of other Christians—not as strangers competing for limited resources, but as fellow pilgrims, fellow citizens of this new creation.

THE PERFORMANCE OF A CHRISTIAN ANTHROPOLOGY

The greeting at the start of worship places the Christian at the very heart of a Christian anthropology, or which is to say, the very heart of ecclesiology. For what the greeting announces is the fact that the Christian is part of a peculiar gathering, one that is based not in the self-interested accumulation of economic or political gains, but a gathering or assembly (*ecclesia*) of reconciled sinners, performed by the self-sacrificing love and forgiveness of God.

To put it differently, the story is not one of Christians gathering, but of being gathered, being assembled, of *being* greeted. The greeting at the start of worship announces the wonderful news that the Christian is the recipient and not the provider of this new dispensation. That Christians are greeted just goes to confirm that they are not the ones who initiate this story of grace, love, and forgiveness. In fact, the story is not about them. Rather, it is the story of what God has done and continues to do on their behalf—not just them, but God's whole creation. In other words, this is a story whose existence and truth precedes us. That is why the greeting is at the same time a reminder of the story of "in the beginning"—a beginning that reflects God's superabundance and goodness. For this is what the very name of Trinity names—the superabundance of love, fellowship, and communication as it exists within the three persons of the Trinity. It is into this superabundance of creation and fellowship that the Christian is invited and drawn by the act of being greeted "in the name of the Father. . . ."

Thus the greeting pronounces us as the gifts that we are. And having received the good news of our being gifts, we can learn to see others similarly as gifts. Thus, having been greeted in the name of God the Father, God the Son, and God the Holy Spirit . . . Christians can now

greet one another in the same name. In this way, the greeting becomes
a benediction, which is offered to the congregation, and which they, in
turn, offer to one another. But it also becomes an invitation to mimic
or model the same story of differences as embodied by God the Trinity.
This does not mean that we can now dismiss as irrelevant all differences, but rather it is an invitation to learn to name our differences and
particularities in the name of the Trinity. The act of greeting, whether
it is by kissing or shaking the hands of the one next to us, is the way
in which Christians make this conviction concrete.

Once the issue has been characterized in this manner, one realizes
that within the act of greeting the range of Christian theology from creation to eschatology is being played out. In other words, being greeted
and taking the time to greet one another in the name of God, the
Christian is standing between creation and eschatology; witnessing to
the peaceful abundance and differences within God's creation, while at
the same time anticipating the final display of the fullness of God's
love, fellowship, and grace in the whole of creation at the end of time,
when Christ will be all-in-all. In the meantime, Christians become part
of this new creation, this new gathering or assembly: a new community of worship, not just one that performs this act of worship, but one
for whom worship has become a way, *the* way of life.

A CHRISTIAN ETHICS

Greeting thus becomes a mode of being in the world, in the in-
between times; it is does not have ethical "implications," it *is* Christian
ethics. And as ethics, it announces and opens up a revolutionary future
in which, as McCabe says, "we do not merely see something new, but
we have a new way of seeing" God, the world, ourselves in it, and others.[13] Similarly, as Christian ethics, worship does not simply encourage or facilitate racial reconciliation. Rather, it institutes a whole new
social reality in which being black or white just makes no sense. That
is why worship itself is the revolutionary future, a "wild space" in
which a different story, a different performance, is being played out
and rendered visible in the world.

That is why it is significant that the greeting comes at the start of
worship. In fact, one reason why I found the practice at the Malaysian
Kampung so remarkable was that the greeting was the way, the only
way, that anyone could get into the church, thus listening to the word

of God and sharing the Eucharist. This in itself is highly significant, since it confirms that "greeting" is the concrete embodiment of a key Christian claim—namely, that we cannot know God; we cannot even hear his word rightly, let alone share his table, unless we have learned to greet each other, including the stranger, with the sign of peace. In fact, within the context of such greeting each other in the name of the Father the very concept of "stranger" is being challenged and redefined from a radically Christian perspective.

Significant as it is, the rite of Christian greeting cannot be isolated from the full context of Christian worship and presented as an "ethic" for racial reconciliation. In fact, the fact that greeting is located at the beginning of worship simply shows how it is this concrete practice that initiates us: draws us into the full politics and economics of what it means to be a worshipping community. Anyone able to stand the greeting should be willing and ready to go all the way. In the particular case of the Malaysian Kampung, this was perhaps the reason the worship did not end with the usual dismissal, but with an invitation to "fellowship." What I particularly found remarkable about the fellowship, apart from the fact that everybody stayed around, was the fact that all the cans of *Coca-Cola* that different people had brought in were opened and poured into one jug. It was from this one jug that the *Coca-Cola* was served using only one cup, which was passed on from one person to the next. As I thought about this practice, I found myself thinking how it would have been much easier, more time-efficient, and even more "hygienic" to hand each person a can of *Coke* (or invite one to pick one), since there were more than enough to go around. Only gradually was I able to see, in this "awkward" practice, as a form of resistance to the individualism inherent in a market economy that, for instance, neatly packaged *Coca-Cola* in cans and bottles are so convenient for *individual* consumption.

This is what is meant by the claim that greeting is both an invitation and a concrete embodiment of what it means to go all the way. For, through the act of greeting, the otherwise racially and ethnically diverse Kampung community found ways of moving beyond the dominant cultural identifications of being Malay, Indian, Chinese, Dayan, or Kadazan. At the same time, worship constituted a visible wild space, which allowed and encouraged resistance to other dominant stories, including resistance to the individualism of capitalistic consumption, even as they were already standing within the story of modern economics by drinking *Coca-Cola*.

That the entire gamut of Christian theology and ethics should be embodied within such a gesture as greeting just confirms how God is not abstract, but as concrete as the handshakes, voices, hugs, and kisses of a people who greet each other "in the name of the Father." And so, when abstracted from such concrete practices, God remains just an idea—a hypothesis to be believed or contested.

BEYOND DOCETISM: ON "TOUCHING COLOR"

We can highlight the point above by noting how Christian worship, the act of greeting in particular, provides Christians with an opportunity to be present to one another in ways that challenge the docetism that may very easily be masked by theologies of "racial reconciliation." Early Christian docetism was an attempt to downplay the significance of Jesus' bodily incarnation. Because the docetists felt that attributing full bodily incarnation to Christ would limit the claims to Jesus' divinity and attributes, they taught that Jesus' bodily incarnation was just an appearance which Christ had to assume in order to affect for us his saving operations.

Jennings is right to note that there is an unrelenting docetism that haunts the way Christians in the West deal with race, culture, and the problem of racism.[14] For even though racism is in great part an imagination involving bodies, the danger now is to claim an easy and quick "racial harmony"—one however that avoids the need to confront, touch, feel, and relate to bodies that are different from us. Thus, the temptation, as Jennings reminds us, is to claim: "I do not see anyone as black or white, just my sister or brother in Christ. There is no such thing as race. We are all one in Christ." Or we say, "We just need to learn how to forgive, respect, and live together and go on to the future." Or we say, "Where I was raised there were no black people. Therefore, race was and is not an issue for me."[15]

Such claims, however, are so often a reflection of our desire to see racial harmony without facing the need for the transformation of our usual forms of social existence and community. Moreover, the claim to color blindness may be, as Mary McClintock Fulkerson suggests,[16] just another strategy of condensation associated with liberal claims to tolerance, whereby the one who is "tolerant" can still position the other in his or her sphere of influence. In this way, claims to color blindness are just a way to avoid face-to-face bodied relation in situations of reciprocity. Without such bodied interaction, however, Christians cannot fully appreciate what it means to be the Body of Christ. That is why the practice of greeting within Christian worship is a good place to begin if we are to recover the significance of the body for Christian salvation.

This is another reason why I found the practice at the Kampung very significant, in that the greeting was so much about the body. It involved movement, touch, hugs, kisses, and handshakes. There was therefore just no way one could avoid touching and relating to other bodies. In so doing, however, a key conviction of Christian life was being played out—namely, that the body matters for Christian salvation, since as Christians we believe that we are saved in and through the body, our own bodies, but ultimately the Body of Christ. Such concrete bodily interaction is therefore a good way to learn what it means to be that very Body of Christ—the one Body of Christ which is made up of different members (bodies). And so, in the very act of Christian greeting, in kissing or touching other bodies, including those who look very different from one's own, one is being introduced to the very mystery of the Body of Christ.

Which means that in our modern time-conscious world, where greeting is often nothing more than a disinterested "hi," the challenge is at the same time one of recovering an embodied account and the practice of greeting like the one at the Malaysian Kampung. What is, however, even more important is the need to recover Christian discipleship as a practical way of life at the margins of the dominant cultures of our day. For I suspect that the fact that the Christian community in Malaysia learned to take worship so seriously has to do with the unique situation of their being a minority in a predominantly Muslim country. For finding themselves in a marginal (8% of the population) position, Christians in Malaysia may have no choice but to turn to their tradition and practices for resources with which to lead meaningful lives at the margins of the dominant culture. That is why the specific challenge facing Christians in the West, as well as in other cultures where Christianity is the dominant religion, has to do with the recovery of worship as a "wild space" that can foster an alternative imagination to the one of the dominant culture. This challenge is particularly urgent in the West, given the fact, as already noted, that worship here tends to reflect and reinforce the same neat racialized interaction of the dominant culture. In this respect, Dr. Martin Luther King Jr.'s comment that 11 o'clock is the most segregated hour in America is not only a true sociological observation—it is a deeply disturbing theological assessment of a Church that has long given up on the challenge to embody an alternative imagination. What makes King's observation even more disturbing is the realization that it is true not just of the Church in the West. For whereas the case of racism that we have been examining makes this obvious in relation to America, Martin Luther King Jr.'s observation reflects a more global phenomenon of a Christianity that has become comfortable—too much at home—within the dominant cultures of our time.

In Africa, for instance, similar versions of a cultural Christianity are so easily reproduced through an uncritical quest for inculturation. The effect is that here, too, instead of providing an opportunity for re-imagining African identities and societies from a Christian perspective, Christian worship tends to reflect and reproduce the same ethnic or tribal divisions within African society. This is also what leads us to suspect any attempts to encourage racially or ethnically homogenous congregations, even when their existence is justified in terms of a need or appreciation of cultural diversity or authenticity. For if what we have said about worship and greeting is true, there seems to be no greater challenge relating to our invitation to be the Body of Christ than to resist these new forms of segregation, which might easily ride on a postmodern celebration of culture. Such fascination with difference and culture might just be another way to assume a kind of superficial "racial diversity," one, that avoids the need to resist the dominant forms of our social and cultural existence.

CONCLUSION

By way of conclusion, I can only recount my own experience of the transformation that worship makes possible, which brings me to where I began my story. For, during the years I lived in Europe, I was lucky to belong to the St. Mary and St. Martha English-speaking parish of the university. It was through worship with and in this multi-cultural, multiracial congregation that I not only got a chance to meet people from all parts of the world, but also to recover somewhat the sort of pre-1991 racial innocence for which I so much longed. Through our weekly worship and the concrete greeting and interaction it provided, I was able to become part of a community for whom being black or white had ceased to be a defining or even interesting identity. This did not only allow a certain relaxation and lack of pretentiousness in our worship, it opened up possibilities for friendship based on what we discovered to be more interesting stories of our lives. This was the very same 'relief' that helped me to survive the summer of 1991, when I first discovered that I was black. For even as I discovered my race, I was lucky be part of the community of St. Mary's Parish. The opportunity to worship in and together with the white congregation of St. Mary's again proved to be one of the transforming spaces for both myself and my congregation. I remember, for instance, an elderly man who later tearfully confessed to me that I was the first black person whose hand he had shaken. Another man whispered to me at the end of mass how he had at first been reluctant to receive Communion from the hands of a black person. The most telling case, however, was that of Dorothy, a woman in her late 80s whom I had seen regularly and greeted at Saturday five o'clock mass. When I learned that she had been taken to a nursing home, I went down to visit her. She was very happy to see me, and excitedly called to her roommate: "Come and say hello to Fr. Emmanuel," she said. "Fr. Emmanuel is not a Negro. He is a priest!"

Through the greeting we receive and offer within Christian worship, we can, like Dorothy, begin to see each other not as strangers in competition for limited resources, but as gifts of a gracious God. For then we would already have discovered ourselves within a new imagination—on the road to a new and revolutionary future, which worship both signals and embodies. Part of this new future consists in discovering that there are more determinative, and far more interesting stories that we can tell about ourselves and about others than just being white or black.

Notes

[1] Hannah Arendt, *The Origins of Totalitarianism* (New York: Harcourt, Brace, 1951).

[2] Valery Mudimbe, *The Invention of Africa* (Bloomington, IN: Indiana University Press, 1988).

[3] Cone, James H., *The God of the Oppressed* (New York: Seabury Press, 1975), 45–53.

[4] Craig S. Keener, "The Gospel and Racial Reconciliation," in *The Gospel in Black and White*, ed. Dennis L. Okholm (Downers Groove, IL: Intervarsity Press, 1997), 117–130.

[5] *Ibid.*, 118.

[6] *Ibid.*

[7] Cornell West, *Race Matters* (New York: Vintage Books, 1993), 39.

[8] Emmanuel Katongole, *Beyond Universal Reason: The Relation Between Religion and Ethics in the Work of Stanley Hauerwas* (Notre Dame, IN: University of Notre Dame Press, 2000), 189–203.

[9] Hauerwas, Stanley, and Will Willimon, *Resident Aliens: Life in the Christian Colony* (Nashville: Abingdon Press, 1989).

[10] Sallie McFague, *Life Abundant: Rethinking Theology and Economy for a Planet in Peril* (Minneapolis: Fortress Press, 2001).

[11] *Ibid.*, 48.

[12] Bernard McGrane, *Beyond Anthropology* (New York: Columbia University Press 1989), p. 2–3.

[13] Herbert McCabe, *What is Ethics All About?* (Washington: Corpus Books, 1969), 75.

[14] Willie Jennings, "Wandering in the Wilderness: Christian Identity and Theology," in *The Gospel in Black and White*, ed. Dennis L. Okholm (downers Groove, IL: Intervarsity Press, 1997), 37–48.

[15] *Ibid.*, 47.

[16] Mary McClintock Fulkerson, "We Do Not See Color Here: A Case Study in Ecclessial Cultural Invention," in *Converging On Culture: Theologians in Dialogue with Cultural Analysis and Chriticism*, eds. Delwin Brown, Sheila Greeve Daveny and Kathryn Tanner (Oxford: Oxford University Press, 2001).

CHAPTER TEN

HAUERWASIAN HOOKS, STORIES, AND THE SOCIAL IMAGINATION OF "THE NEXT CHRISTENDOM"

My work . . . has been an attempt to make connections, to find the hooks, not only between scientists and theologians, but also between philosophy and theology, between the "past" and the "present" of our own lives, between the everyday and God. To discover "hooks" you first have to look and, just as important, you must be prepared to be surprised. Moreover, the endeavor to make connections is never finished because there will always be something else that needs to be said. What was "hooked" at one time can become "unhooked" at another . . . (Stanley Hauerwas).[1]

Writing an essay in honor of someone from whom you have learned everything you know about theology and ethics can be a tricky business. Apart from the feeling that such an essay cannot provide any new insights, there is also the fear of embarrassment, in that the essay may just confirm what a bad student one has been. But since for me Stanley Hauerwas has been more than just a mentor, but a wonderful friend, writing this essay is a joyful acknowledgment of the gift that Hauerwas and his work has been. I therefore, find no better way of acknowledging this than to remember how it all started—namely, how I got hooked by Hauerwas in the first place. I use the language of being "hooked," because I think that is exactly what happened given the fact that I was led to Hauerwas' work almost against my will. Moreover, as the epigram above shows, Hauerwas himself has admitted that finding hooks is indeed what his work is all about. And that a Catholic priest from Uganda, one moreover who wanted to be a philosopher, now finds himself a theologian and professor of World Christianity, is itself a good example of the type of hooks Hauerwas' work makes possible.

But I also hope that my story will confirm that to be hooked by Hauerwas is to be unhooked in a number of ways, thereby finding one-self in an odd space—at the margins—of the dominant cultural ways of looking at and dealing with the world. This is what makes Hauerwas a dangerous hook, but also, at least for me, a very interesting and exciting one, in that his work forces me to think about the challenge of theology and ethics primarily not in terms of being relevant to the world, but in terms of possibilities of new visions, and new imagina-tions of the world. I therefore hope that my story will help to highlight my interest and ongoing preoccupation with the notion of social imag-ination, and also why, given this interest, I have so much trouble with Jenkins' *The Next Christendom*.[2] For as I show in the second part of the essay, *The Next Christendom* both assumes and underwrites a Christianity that has long given up on the need to be an alternative vision or imagination of the world. First, however, my being hooked.

ON BEING HOOKED BY HAUERWAS

1. A Reluctant Hook

When I received a scholarship to Leuven (Louvain, Belgium) in the summer of 1991, it was to study philosophy. It was therefore with great reservations that I started reading Stanley Hauerwas' theological essays in the Fall of 1992. I had just read in a class on analytic philos-ophy, Harry Frankfurt's small book, *The Importance of What We Care About* and had found some of its insights on moral transcendence quite interesting.[3] I was therefore thinking of writing my M.A. dissertation on the topic of moral transcendence in light of some aspects of African culture, and so had gone to ask professor Frans De Wachter to be my thesis advisor. While De Wachter thought the topic was potentially interesting, he nevertheless felt that the "African culture" in my title put it beyond his competence as advisor. He therefore suggested that I think of a topic that might be (as he put it) "closer to us." His reply caught me off-guard, for I did not have any other topic right off the top of my head, certainly not one that was closer to mainstream European philosophy. I had just assumed that given Belgium's historical links with Africa, a topic that had to do with the African worldview would-n't sound so strange at the K.U.L. (Katholicke Universiteit Leuven) Higher Institute of Philosophy.[4]

Seeing that I was somewhat at a loss, De Wachter asked if I knew the work of Stanley Hauerwas, and casually remarked that Hauerwas seemed to be doing something interesting in the area of ethics. I had never heard of the name, but that afternoon, sitting at a library computer, I was amazed at the number of essays and books that showed up under a search of Hauerwas' name. Since almost none of these were available at the Higher Institute of Philosophy library, I was forced to make the journey to the Department of Theology library, where I read as many of Hauerwas' essays as were immediately available.

When I met with De Wachter a few days later, I had made up my mind. Stanley Hauerwas' reflection and writing were indeed interesting and provocative, but too "theological" for me. I had come to Leuven to do philosophy, and so for my dissertation I wanted to work on a philosopher, or some topic more recognizably philosophical. De Wachter, however, encouraged me to see that it would perhaps not be a waste of time to discover the "philosophical underpinnings" that sustained Hauerwas' provocative work in Christian ethics. Reluctantly I followed his recommendation, not being sure how or where the writing of an American theologian would lead me in terms of both my Ph.D. ambitions in philosophy, and my interest in African studies in particular.

As I ploughed through Hauerwas' work in an attempt to discover its philosophical underpinnings; I found his style of writing to be extremely engaging. In fact, a great deal of what he was saying regarding Christian morality reflected my own experience of the moral life. The sense of communal identity, an appreciation of virtue, a respect for tradition and authority, and, on the whole, a view of the universe as pervaded with spiritual and symbolic meaning—all notions that Hauerwas was calling for—were part of the moral heritage which, as an African, I simply took granted.

Incidentally, that was also what worried me about what Hauerwas was trying to do. For, given my philosophical background, I had learned to view these experiences of the moral life, stories, practices, traditions, and customs as simply a background, the *mere* content of what had to be transcended for one to arrive at the moral and rational point of view. And so, even as I found Hauerwas account of the moral life true to experience, I felt it was too down-to-earth, too concrete; it was the sort of ethics that would only make sense within a small community. And so, when I read Gustafson's critique of Hauerwas' work, it helped to conceptualize my uneasiness. Gustafson had noted that

234 A FUTURE FOR AFRICA

Hauerwas' emphasis on narrative could not but result into a form of theological fideism, whose social effect would be to force Christians to withdraw from the complexities of public life into a tribal ghetto.[5] I took this charge very seriously. All through my education in Africa, I had been taught to be on constant guard against tribalism, which seemed to be an ever-present reality which not only threatened peace and stability in Africa, but which was also connected to primitive and backward forms of life. In fact, the whole of my educational background, including the philosophical and theological training in the seminary, was premised on the need, both explicit and implicit, to advance from the bondage of tribal backwardness into the civilization of modernity and nation-state progress. I am sure my desire to study philosophy—a discipline that promised to lead one to discover the very nature and essence of reality—must itself have been somehow influenced by this conditioning. I was not excited about studying a theologian in the first place; now I became even less enthusiastic about the prospect of studying one that espoused a sectarian and tribalist perspective.

These concerns were part of the considerations I had on my mind when, after the completion of my Masters program, I proposed to shift my focus from Hauerwas to Kant. As far as I was concerned, with the notions of moral character, vision, narrative, and community, I had discovered the philosophical foundations of Hauerwas' work; and the rest, e.g., his stress on the church as a community in which these notions operated, were "merely" its theological content.[6] Accordingly, I mentioned to DeWachter that for my Ph.D. research I needed to move on to what I thought of as "the more philosophically challenging" issues of moral rationality in Kant. To be sure, I also believed that since the Kantian tradition provided the ethical impetus behind colonialism and a great deal of the modernizing rhetoric in Africa, working on Kant would be a step closer to understanding the challenges that face African societies.

De Wachter, however, insisted that I stay with Hauerwas' work and respond to the critical issues that arise out of the narrative-based account of ethics that Hauerwas provided.[7] When in the summer of the same year (1993) I had a chance to meet Hauerwas for the first time, and shared with him what I intended to do. He did not seem impressed. "Emmanuel," he said in his usual half joking, half serious manner, "the best way for you to take Kant seriously is to stay clear of him." Still, I was not sure. Matters were however, decided for me when I returned to Belgium in the fall and learned that I only had two more years' worth of scholarship. I could not embark on a completely new research project. I was stuck with Hauerwas. Now I had no choice but to read closely even those sections of Hauerwas' work which, in the Masters research, I had overlooked or simply glossed over as "mere theological content."

As I found myself in this odd situation of working on a theologian for a Ph.D. in philosophy, I just tried to make the best of it. And so, for the next three and half years of my stay in Leuven, I shuttled back and forth between the Institute of Philosophy and the Theology Department libraries. I even enrolled for a part-time Masters in Religious Studies, and was accordingly assigned a desk in the theology library, where I spent a lot of time. My fellow students in theology wondered whether I was still a philosopher, or if I had finally seen the light and converted to theology. Even though I myself did not think of what I was doing in terms of conversion, I was not sure that what I was doing counted as "interdisciplinary" studies either, given the fact that Hauerwas' work has never been considered part of the theological mainstream. I just tried to make sense of what Hauerwas was saying, and in the process found myself unable to fit into the disciplines of philosophy or theology—working at both their margins, but never fully belonging to either.

I have taken time to tell the story of my being hooked by Hauerwas because in many ways it helps to confirm that it is the experience of being an "outsider" (to European culture, on the one hand, and to the disciplines of theology and philosophy, on the other), which led me to see how deeply political Hauerwas' work is. As Hauerwas notes, the formation of Christian character does not take place in isolation but is made possible through stories, symbols, everyday interactions, and practices that are available to one as a member of a community. For Hauerwas, of course, it is through the church that Christians are formed into characters that reflect the story of God. As I struggled to make sense of this central theme in Hauerwas' work, I realized that what Hauerwas was saying in relation to the church and the formation of Christian identities was indeed true of all communities. It is then that it dawned on me that the formation of identity is what is always going on in all politics. All politics, I began to see, is based on stories which involve specific assumptions about the nature of the world, but which stories succeed in shaping particular expectations, identities, and characters in the world, which reflect those very assumptions.[8]

Once I made this connection, I realized how relevant Hauerwas' work was for understanding the social-political challenges in Africa. The discovery came as a very wonderful surprise for me, since one of the major reservations I had in working on an American theologian for my Ph.D. had to do with the fear that such a theologian would not advance my understanding of the challenges facing Africa. But with the connection between stories, identity, and politics, I was now beginning to see that behind the problematic state of politics in Africa are stories which involve assumptions about Africans and African societies, but which in turn shape African societies and Africans into patterns of hopelessness and violence. Accordingly, I was beginning to suspect that the problem of tribalism in Africa was not, as I had been made to understand, grounded in the natural or cultural differences of African peoples. It had greatly to do with the stories through which the nation-state politics imagined and continues to imagine African societies.[9]

At the same time, I was now able to see more clearly the political motivations behind the charges of "tribalism" and "sectarianism" that Gustafson and many others were raising against Hauerwas' work. Apart from the fact that these charges rested on questionable philosophical foundations, they originated from a serious realization that the position Hauerwas advanced could only marginalize the church from the dominant political imagination shaped by the story of Western liberal democracy. But that is precisely what I was finding to be most therapeutic about Hauerwas' work namely, the invitation to step outside the dominant political imaginations and formations, and realize how the world can, and does indeed, look different. In fact, in view of this invitation, I was beginning to see that the primary challenge of Christian social ethics in Africa was not how or if the church can contribute to secure the ever-illusory promises of democracy, human rights, and development—contributions that assume the political imagination of Nation-state politics. The challenge was one of providing different stories, which reflect a different vision of the world and a different way of being in the world. It is this primary interest in political imagination that has continued to shape my own theological preoccupation. What my own experience at the margins of both Western Civilization and of philosophy and theology may have helped to confirm is the fact that the hope and resources for an alternative social imagination are discovered and cultivated not on the back, so to say, but at the margins or within the cracks of the dominant stories that shape the dominant social-political imaginations.

More recently Hauerwas has provided a more extensive argument in this direction in the context of his 2001 Gifford Lectures. And so, to get a better handle on the political force of Christian convictions, and how these offer a novel way of looking and being in the world, it might be helpful to capture in brief outline the central argument of *With the Grain of the Universe*.[10]

2. The Church as Social Interruption:

In *With the Grain of the Universe* Hauerwas undertakes to overcome what Milbank had characterized as Christian theology's "false humility"[11]—the tendency by Christian ethics to allow its social contribution to be shaped and defined by the secular disciplines of political science, economics, and sociology. It is this tendency which gives rise to the project of "natural theology," which in effect, amounts to an attempt to divorce Christian claims about the world from the concrete practices, characters, and stories in which those stories are embodied. The project of natural theology, Hauerwas sets out to show in *With the Grain of the Universe*, is misconceived. Natural theology, he argues, "divorced from a full doctrine [and practice] of God cannot help but distort the character of God, and accordingly the world in which we find ourselves."[12]

Because the argument of *With the Grain of the Universe* seems to have a major epistemological focus, those unfamiliar with some of the epistemologically-centered discussions in philosophy of religion, or with the work of the individual authors discussed, may find the book both intimidating and cumbersome. However, as Hauerwas goes about to display the limitations of natural theology through the discussion of the work of William James and Reinhold Niebuhr, contrasted with the work of Karl Barth, the political implications become evident. Simply stated, Hauerwas' response to natural theology is shaped around three interconnected arguments. First, he notes that Christians do in fact make *claims* about the world. The truth of these claims, however, cannot be separated from the training in Christian discipleship, and therefore cannot be known unless it is embodied in faithful lives. For it is through such lives that one is able to see concretely what it means to conceive the world differently. Thus, the necessity of witnesses, and what makes John Howard Yoder, John Paul II, and Dorothy Day such crucial witnesses, is essential to the argument of *With the Grain of the Universe.*

Secondly, the fact that *claims* require embodiment shows that Christian claims about creation or the Resurrection, for instance, are not simply located within a social reality that is neutral or independently given. They constitute their own unique social reality. Quoting Yoder:

> *The point that apocalyptic makes is not only that people who wear the crown and who claim to foster justice by the sword are not as strong as they think—true as that is. . . . It is that people who bear crosses are working with the grain of the universe. One does not come to that belief by reducing social process to mechanical and statistical models, nor by winning some of one's battles for the control of one's own corner of the fallen world. One comes to it by sharing the life of those who sing about the Resurrection of the slain Lamb.*[13]

Thirdly, and what the above citation makes clear is that for those who profess the Cross and Resurrection of Christ, the world does indeed look different. Accordingly, the decisive social force constituted by the belief in the Cross and Resurrection cannot be in sustaining or stabilizing the politics of the day, or the requirements of negotiating the world as it is currently defined, but by its ability to form unique characters and patterns of life, which interrupt such politics. Thus, for Yoder, the life, death, and Resurrection of Christ as the most decisive event in history calls into existence a people committed to a life of self-giving and nonresistant love.[14] Similarly for John Paul II, affirming the truth that the Redeemer of man, Jesus Christ, is the center of the universe and of history makes the Christian a potential martyr.[15]

This brief overview of *With the Grain of the Universe*, sketchy as it is, helps to make obvious the political import of Christian claims. What also becomes evident is that for Hauerwas the political import happens not simply in terms of recommendations to secure justice, democracy, or peace within liberal politics; but in terms of concrete communities, capable of forming patterns of life that reflect a different knowledge and different desires than those formed by nation-state politics. Once this essential political nature of Christian claims is recognized, then it becomes evident that Christianity offers more than guide-lines or assistance on how Christians can cope with the existing social-political realities. It ushers in a new future—a revolutionary future, according to McCabe, in which "we do not merely see something new but have a new way of seeing; in which something is produced which could not be imagined in the old terms and which changes our whole way of envisaging what has gone before."[16] What the argument of *With the Grain of the Universe* helps to confirm is that one comes in contact with this revolutionary future by "sharing the life of those who sing about the Resurrection of the Slain Lamb." In other words, the church not simply preaches about or helps to usher in the revolutionary future. The church *is* the revolutionary future, or as Richard Hays, puts it, the Church is God's "demonstration plot" of a new future—a new social imagination concretely embodied.[17]

This seems to be like a long introduction, but I hope it makes clear why we need to think about the challenge of Christian social ethics pri-marily in terms of social imagination. More specifically, for the pur-pose of this essay, the extensive background helps to explain why I feel so uneasy about the shape of *The Next Christendom*. Both the way Philip Jenkins describes "the coming of global Christianity" as well as its dominant Pentecostal expression in the South reflect the story of a Christianity which has long given up on the need to interrupt the dom-inant political imagination, and thus the need to witness to a new future.

THE NEXT CHRISTENDOM:
A TALE OF TWO CHRISTIANITIES

In *The Next Christendom*, Philip Jenkins offers very good indica-tion of the shifts taking place within world Christianity, shifts which are helping to make the global South, Africa in particular, the new cen-ter of gravity of the Christian faith. While the number of Christians is rapidly shrinking in the North and West, Jenkins observes, a phenom-enal growth is taking place in the global South:

> *By the year 2025, there will be around 2.6 billion Christians, of whom 633 million will live in Africa, 640 in Latin American, and 460 million in Asia. Europe, with 555 million would have slipped to third place. African and Latin America would count for half the Christians on the*

planet. By 2050, only about one-fifth of the world's 3 billion
Christians will be non-Hispanic whites.[18]

With such and similar projections Jenkins shows that Christianity is not only experiencing exponential growth in the global South—Africa is at the center of this boom. For an African theologian this should be very good news, which confirms that Africa's hour of faith and confidence in the Gospel is finally here.[19] In fact, with the growing confidence in the prospects of Christianity in Africa, the Catholics among us can begin to entertain the hopes for an African pope.[20]

There are, to be sure, quite a number of aspects, apart from the overwhelming statistical evidence, that one finds instructive in Jenkins' study, and which seem to bolster confidence in a southern Christianity. For instance, against a postcolonial sensitivity that tends to dismiss Christianity in the South as the arm of Western imperialism, Jenkins defends the trends shaping southern Christianity as "genuine" Christianity, affected at the intersection of biblical translation and the adaptation to local tradition and thought-patterns.[21] Jenkins also provides very helpful indications of the reasons behind the success of Christianity in the South. He particularly notes how, in the wake of failed politics, the new churches provide functional alternative arrangements for health, welfare, and education.[22] As Jenkins notes, "to be a member of an active Christian church today might well bring more tangible benefits that being a citizen of Nigeria or Peru."[23] Thus, according to Jenkin's observation, what we experience in the South is not the usual expectation of a "spiritual" (pie in the sky) gospel, but a confident, fully embodied Christian expression whose influence is reflected in the social, political, and economic spheres of life.

1. The Two Faces of Christianity

While these and many other aspects seem to make *The Next Christendom* a very instructive study, I find some of its underlying assumptions and objectives questionable. Much of my uneasiness has to do with the neat North and South axis around which the story of world Christianity is told, providing for the many contrasts that Jenkins offers between the southern and the northern versions of the Christianity. I have no doubt that as a professor of history and religious studies, Jenkins' task is to describe the trends and the world as they are, and not as they should be. However, by assuming the categories of

North and South as the lens through which the story of world Christianity is read, he cannot help but underwrite an account of Christianity which simply reflects the existing social, economic, and political constellations. This is what gives rise, in Jenkins' work, to two distinct faces of Christianity, which have nothing or very little in common. For instance, in describing the growth of Christianity in the global South, Jenkins notes, "Christianity is thriving wonderfully among the poor and persecuted, while it atrophies among the rich and secure."[24] He also notes that in terms of theological and moral orientation, the members of a southern-dominated church are likely to more conservative, "stalwartly traditional or even reactionary by the standards of the economically advanced nations."[25] In these and many other contrasts in the book Jenkins depicts not only the trends shaping Christianity in the global South, but also how radically different this Christianity is from the northern version of Christianity.

Jenkins is aware that the social, economic, and cultural differences between the North and the South have contributed to the invisibility of southern Christianity. He notes, "for whatever reason, southern churches almost remain invisible to Northern observers."[26] My concern is that assuming, as Jenkins does, the categories of North and South as the lens for telling the story of Christianity cannot but further distance southern Christians from their northern counterparts. This is already evident in such examples as the 1998 Lambeth Conference. After the defeat of the statement on homosexuality, primarily with the near-unanimous voice of Asian and African bishops, Bishop Spong of Newark declared that "the African bishops have moved out of animism into a very superstitious kind of Christianity."[27] "I never expected," he noted, "to see the Anglican Communion, which prides itself on the place of reason in faith, descend to this level of irrational Pentecostal hysteria."[28]

Jenkins' own descriptions of Christianity in the South, shaped by the assumptions of modern sociology of religion, betray a similar distancing. He notes, "as southern Christianity continues to *expand* and *mature* it will assuredly develop a wider theological spectrum than at present, and stronger liberal or secularizing tendencies may well emerge."[29] In this and many other places, the clear indication is that as southern Christianity is simply the pale shadow of the more rational forms of Christian expression in the North, and as the former grows, matures, expands (all expressions that Jenkins uses), it will take on a more decisively northern appearance.[30]

It is accordingly obvious that as long as the prevailing geopolitical (north-south) categories are used as the primary lens through which the story of global Christianity is told, northern Christians will find nothing or very little to learn from their southern counterparts. On the contrary they might just see themselves as caught in an irresolvable competition and conflict of interests against their southern counterparts. Given theses geo-political lenses, it is not surprising that there is "increasing tension between what one might call a liberal Northern Reformation and the surging Southern religious revolution . . . No matter what the terminology, . . . an enormous rift seems inevitable."[31] Accordingly, the more Christians in the North assume the story of their white, rich, liberal, democratic nations, the more they will view the growth of southern Christianity, which is made up predominantly of poor, black, or brown Christians as a worrisome "darkening" of the Christian landscape, and even a political threat. Jenkins not only describes this threat, he assumes it. For, one of the aims of Jenkins study is to draw attention to the religious revolution shaping up in the South, and to warn governments in the North about the potential of fanaticism latent in the Christian Third World. He notes,

> Worldwide, religious trends have the potential to reshape political assumptions in a way that has not been seen since the rise of modern nationalism. While we can imagine a number of possible futures, a worst-case scenario would include a wave of religious conflicts reminiscent of the Middle Ages, a new age of Christian crusades and Muslim Jihads . . . . In responding to this prospect, we need at a minimum to ensure that our political leaders and diplomats pay as much attention to religions and sectarian frontiers as they ever have to the distribution of oilfields.[32]

When one looks at it from this point of view, it becomes clear why as an African theologian I find myself ill at ease within this story of "the Coming of Global Christianity," whose subtext is to warn "our political leaders and diplomats" about the religious revolution in the South.

To be sure, there might be a lot that is worrisome about the trends shaping Christianity in the global South, Africa in particular (see below). I am not sure, however, that the "Christian Third World," as Jenkins calls it, will ferment a new Counter-Reformation; a new "Council of Trent,"[33]—one that will pose the greatest challenge to Western capitalism or, as Jenkins identifies it, the "McWorld."[34] What

I find particularly disturbing however, is the fact that the assumptions of *The Next Christendom* seem to want to insure that no such challenge emerges out of global Christianity. If this is indeed the case, then not only Christians in the South, but Christians (period) should view Jenkin's *The Next Christendom* with a very critical eye.

2. The Political Imagination of a Global Christianity?

I am suggesting that *The Next Christendom* is bad news for Christians not simply because it assumes the existing North—South dichotomies shaped by the economic and political realities of late capitalism, but because it seeks to secure this current vision of the world against any possible interruption from Christianity. To be sure, Jenkins is aware that "religious trends have potential to reshape political assumptions and imaginations." But that is what, according to him, needs to be reigned in. He notes that within the new Christian synthesis shaping up in the South there might be "many people for whom political loyalties might be secondary to religious beliefs," and "these are the terms in which people [will] define their identities."[35] Moreover, these identities may give rise to supranational affiliations and connections, which in turn, give rise to a new cultural reference in which the "Christian world of the South could easily find unity in common religious beliefs."[36] It is precisely such a prospect that Jenkins finds troubling for that would mean that that in the twenty-first century, "religion [would] replace ideology as the prime animating and destructive force in human affairs, guiding attitudes to political liberty and obligation, concepts of nationhood, and of course, conflicts and wars."[37]

I personally doubt that this will happen, given the fact that the dominant trends shaping Christianity in the South are themselves neatly located within the imagination of nation-state politics and economics (see below). But the fact that Christianity has the potential to give rise to such transnational identities, associations and communities is what Christians ought to find exciting. Such communities would not only embody a new future beyond the current North-South, rich-poor, liberal-conservative polarization; they would be the source of new identities and visions of life beyond our usual racially colored visions. In noting the shift in world Christianity, Jenkins postulates that the majority of believers will be neither white nor European nor Euro-American, and adds that "very soon the phrase a 'white Christian' may

sound like a curious oxymoron."[38] Whereas Jenkins means this as a
warning about the future, I hope this comes to pass, and very soon too!
I do not of course by this claim mean that white folks should cease to
be Christians. Instead, I am drawing attention to the need to imagine
Christianity in terms of concrete communities in which such labels as
white, black, African, American, and, so forth, have ceased to be the
primary identities in which we view ourselves and the world. Such
communities would not only reflect the radical sense of catholicity,
they would give rise to a new Christendom, in the sense of the
Republica Christiana—"as an overarching unity, and a focus of loyalty transcending mere kingdoms or empires."[39] According to the New
Testament these communities are the bearers of a revolutionary future,
one that reflects God's never-tiring effort to bring together a new community (*ecclesia*) in which the old identities of being a Jew, Greek,
male, female . . . have faded in the light of a new loyalty arising out a
common baptism (Gal 3: 27–28).

Such a revolutionary future does not come about by sheer numer-
ic projections. It happens in the form of concrete communities that
have learned to view the Death and Resurrection of Christ as the most
decisive event in history—one that interrupts the story of the *McWorld*,
—and is thus able to embody an alternative vision of the world to the
one structured by the north-south geopolitical interests. To the extent
that Jenkin's *The Next Christendom* assumes those geopolitical and
socio-economic definitions and seeks to protect them from any such
interruption, I find its assumptions problematic. It is for the same reason that I find the dominant trends of Pentecostalism shaping
Christianity in the global South, Africa in particular, to be equally
problematic.

3. Blessings and Success in a Postcolonial Africa.

In *The Next Christendom*, Jenkins rightly notes that Pentecostalism is fast becoming the dominant Christian expression in Africa.[40]
Pentecostalism is a wide and complex phenomenon that defies any
easy generalization. This is particularly true of Pentecostalism in
Africa. There are however, a number of elements—the call to be "born
again," emphasis on the gifts of the Holy Spirit, healing, expectation
of miracles, signs, and wonders, charismatic expression, etc.,—that cut
across many Pentecostal churches in Africa. The more closely one
examines these elements as well as the influence they exercise within

the mainline churches, the more one discovers that far from providing a critical challenge to the dominant political culture, these elements simply locate Pentecostalism at its center. That is why, at least in terms of political imagination, the "Christian Third World" may not be as markedly different from its northern counterpart, as it might first appear.

The above conclusion may sound surprising in light of Jenkins' work, especially since, as I noted above, one of the goals of Jenkins' study is not only to describe the new Christian synthesis shaping up in the South, but to display how different these forms of Christianity are from the northern versions of it. He particularly notes the medieval outlook and premodern sensibilities of the churches in the South. The new churches, Jenkins notes,

> . . . preach deep personal faith and communal orthodoxy, mysticism, and Puritanism, all founded on clear scriptural authority. They preach messages that, to a Westerner, appear simplistically charismatic, visionary, and apocalyptic. In this thought-world, prophecy is an everyday reality, while faith-healing, exorcism, and dream visions are all basic components of religious sensibility. For better or worse, the dominant churches of the future could have much in common with those of medieval or early modern European times. On this evidence, a southern Christian future should be distinctly conservative.[41]

Given such a description, it may come as a surprise to realize that for many Africans, Pentecostalism nevertheless represents a form of modernity. This is not only true, it helps to confirm that in many ways the Pentecostal synthesis in Africa nicely locates itself within the dominant imagination of postcolonial politics and economics in Africa, and quite often reproduces its patterns, more strikingly its modernity, and its illusory promises of success and prosperity. No where is the reproduction more evident than in what might be called the Bonnke factor within African Christianity.

Reinhard Bonnke and his "Christ for all Nations (CfaN) ministry provides a good example of the type of Pentecostal-Charismatic synthesis that is on the rise in Africa.[42] Bonnke's travels and crusades across Africa attract hundreds of thousands, and in some places millions of attendants. The crusades, which in Bonnke's words serve as a sort of "Holy Spirit Evangelism in Demonstration"[43] are characterized by night-long sessions of praise and healing, interspersed by Bonnke's charismatic preaching. In his preaching Bonnke expounds his popular theme—Africa shall be saved/Africa is being saved—and offers promises of deliverance, miracles, and of blessings—themes that reflect the influence of the prosperity Gospel. Bonnke is not the only one—he is just a more obvious example of prosperity Gospel preaching, for as Gifford and many others have noted, the prosperity Gospel characterize many of the charismatic churches in Africa.[44]

To be sure, the relation between the prosperity Gospel and the Pentecostal-Charismatic synthesis for which Bonnke is just one example is a complex one and requires a full study of its own. I do, however, find the essay by David Maxwell helpful in trying to understand why the prosperity gospel seems to be the key subtext in much of the new forms of Pentecostal Christianity in Africa.[45] According to Maxwell, two doctrines of the prosperity Gospel—the doctrine of the Spirit of poverty, and the doctrine of talents—help to click the connection between the dominant economic and political culture with the dominant Pentecostal expectation of "being delivered from the past." With the doctrine of "the Spirit of poverty," Maxwell notes, preachers are able to explain the prevalence of poverty in terms of bondage with the past, from which one needs to be delivered.[46] With the doctrine of talents, they exhort the born again to give since it is only when they invest their talents with God can they expect God to ensure their own accumulation—which in turn confirms their having been delivered from the bondage of the past.

I find Maxwell's analysis is helpful, and is quite consistent with Birgit Myers observation the "need to break with the past," as it operates within African Pentecostalism, is quite often "the flip side of becoming modern in social, economic, and political aspects."[47] What both analyses confirm, is the fact that since Pentecostalism locates itself within them, it cannot provide a critical challenge to the social and economic realities of a post-colonial Africa. In fact, the notions and categories in which Pentecostal Christianity trades—deliverance from the past, a focus on immediacy, promises of success and prosperity—are the same expectations that the political and economic culture in Africa tends to encourage. In this connection, the version of Christianity that makes Bonnke and similar Charismatic preachers popular in Africa is one that promises a "redemptive uplift"[48] that simply reflects the aspirations of a modern prosperous Africa. The Jesus one meets within Bonnke's crusades is not a Jesus who questions and challenges the social and political structures of the time, but one who helps the Christian to be among those who benefit from them. He is a super-natural wonder-worker whose death has won (once for all) the blessings which those who are born again enjoy, and thus become successful in a world shaped by the post-colonial carriers of modernity.

Once the issue has been put in this way, it becomes clear that Bonnke's version of Pentecostal Christianity is not an isolated phenomenon, but an example of the type of Christianity that is increasingly becoming a dominant cultural force in Africa. Part of its popular appeal, as the above analysis shows, has to do greatly with its being "relevant" to the social, economic, and political realities of Africa. I therefore find it misleading to refer to this type of Pentecostal-Evangelical synthesis as a form of "liberation theology."[49] On the contrary, I think the words of a Latin American theologian quoted by Don Miller, provide a more apt assessment. Asked about the high profile of Pentecostalism in Latin America, the theologian is quoted as saying: "Liberation theology opted for the poor, but the poor opted for Pentecostalism."[50] His observation, I think, is true in many ways about African Christianity today. The observation not only points to the current popularity of Pentecostalism, it involves a subtle but incisive indictment of its limitations. For what the remark involves is a realization that if liberation theology sought to evaluate, question, and challenge the economic social conditions that rendered so many people poor, no such possibility exists within Pentecostalism. Instead, within the type of Pentecostal-Evangelical Christianity preached by the likes of Bonnke, born again Christians are encouraged to be among those who benefit from the economic-political order. That is of course what makes this version of Christianity questionable and even "dangerous" in terms of its political imagination. For even when it purportedly seeks to stay clear of any direct political involvement, it remains deeply political. Gifford is thus right when he notes:

> By focusing so narrowly on supernatural causes it diverts attention from the economic or political causes of so much reality—it hardly encourages critical analyses of the economic interests or forces shaping societies. With its emphasis on personal healing, it diverts attention from social ills that are crying out for remedy. Its stress on human wicked-

*ness and the fallen nature of the world is no incentive to
social-economic, and constitutional reform. By emphasiz-
ing personal morality so exclusively, it all but eliminates
any interest in systemic or institutionalized injustice. By
making everything so simple, it distracts attention from the
very real contradictions in the lives of so many in [South]
Africa.*[51]

To be sure, there are many positive aspects connected to the Pentecostal-Evangelical synthesis shaping up in Africa—the lively services;
a renewed interest in scripture; the element of personal transformation;
the nurturing of new ministries and leadership skills, particularly
among the youth, etc.[52]—which need to be taken seriously. My aim
here has been to draw attention to the political-economic imagination
within which the emerging forms of African Christianity are located.
The critical point that I have sought to highlight is that once Christianity has assumed the political and economic imagination of postcolonial Africa, then it cannot provide a critical challenge to these
political and economic realities of Africa in terms of offering an alternative vision of society and human flourishing. On the contrary, once
African Christianity in the form of the Pentecostal appeal is hooked
onto the political and economic imagination of a postcolonial Africa
with its illusory promises of prosperity, then it will inevitably not only
reflect and reproduce the same imagination, but will, sooner or later,
come to be marked by the same patterns of violence, corruption, and
"culture of eating"—as is characteristic of the political and economic
culture of a postcolonial Africa.[53]

CONCLUSION

This has been a long discussion, but one that helps to show why I
find myself doubly disappointed by the shape of *The Next Christendom*. First, by the way in which Jenkins sets up the story of world
Christianity in terms of a contrast between North and South, and secondly, by the "success" of Christianity in Africa, made possible, in
part, by the great appeal of Pentecostalism. Both forms of disappoint-
ment however, are directed to the same account of Christianity that is
located within, and reflects the political and economic realities of the
day. What I have tried to show in this essay, indeed throughout the
entire book, is that to the extent Christianity locates itself within these

stories, it loses its ability to question or point a way beyond the radical contrasts of the economic and political realities of the "McWorld." More specifically, in the case of Africa, our analysis has confirmed that among the factors that that are helping to turn Pentecostalism into a dominant cultural force in Africa is a version of Christianity which promises "miracles" necessary to succeed in a postcolonial Africa.

How do we go on from here? *We can accept the world as it as, and try to provide ways in which Christianity can be relevant to such a world.* This is the realism that accepts as given the realities of the "McWorld" and of a postcolonial Africa, and allows our vision of Christianity to be shaped by and within these realities. *Or, we can aspire to a different kind of realism, one that acknowledges that the world as it is the product of stories; stories shape not just a vision of the world, but concrete expectations and identities within the world.* This means acknowledging the fact that since different stories shape different worlds, the Christian story can and does shape a different world, for those who "sing about the Resurrection of the slain Lamb." It is the new realism that Hauerwas' work has been writing about and describing as the task of Christian social imagination. Even though our discussion here has been theoretical, the task of social imagination is itself very concrete. For what Stanley Hauerwas has also shown is that this task happens in terms of concrete communities—churches—capable of forming habits and lives that portray a different logic and a different vision of the world. Such communities are the bearers of a revolutionary future. Since I have been hooked by this new realism, I expect the story of world Christianity to be about such communities, drawn from across the nations. I also hope that the story of world Christianity be one that highlights the signs, practices, and everyday witness through which the communities called church are concretely able to interrupt both the story of liberal capitalism as it shapes the "Mc World" of the West and the illusory promises of prosperity in a postcolonial Africa.

Notes

[1] Stanley Hauerwas, "Hooks: Random Thoughts By Way of a Response to Griffiths and Ochs," *Modern Theology* 19/1 (2003): 89–101 [90].

[2] Phillip Jenkins, *The Next Christendom: The Coming of Global Christianity* (Oxford: Oxford University Press, 2002).

[3] Frankfurt Harry G., *The Importance of What We Care About* (Cambridge: Cambridge University Press, 1988).

[4] It had been, after all, a Belgian white father missionary, Fr. Placide Tempels, who had inspired the modern discussions about the nature and possibility of African philosophy by his seminal essay on *La philosophie Bantou* (Elizabethville, 1945). English translation, *Bantu Philosophy* (Paris, Presence Africaine, 1953).

[5] James Gustafson, "The Sectarian Temptation: Reflections on Theology, the Church, and the University," *Proceedings of the Catholic Theological Society*, 40 (1985): 83–94.

[6] Emmanuel Katongole, "The Agent's Perspective: A Study of Stanley Hauerwas' Moral Philosophy," Unpublished Masters thesis, Higher Institute of Philosophy, K.U. Leuven, June 1993.

[7] It was only at the formal dinner following my doctoral defense that De Wachter confessed why he desperately wanted me to work on Stanley Hauerwas. He had read a couple of Hauerwas' essays and found his claims both provocative and outrageously wrong. He needed, as he put it, "ammunition with which to counteract the misleading claims" which Hauerwas was making about ethics. He hoped that my research would come up with such ammunition. However, as he confessed at the dinner, working with me had only succeeded in wining him over, if not so much to Hauerwas' side, to begin to appreciate the tradition-based nature of the moral life. De Wachter's confession was particularly telling, and confirmed how we quite often find our lives inscribed in narratives not of our making, but that in the process of negotiating those limitations, we may discover that our lives and the lives of others have been permanently transformed, hopefully, as in this case, for the better.

[8] For a more extensive treatment of the relation between stories and politics, see my *Beyond Universal Reason: The Relation Between Religion and Ethics in the Work of Stanley Hauerwas* (Notre Dame, IN: Notre Dame University Press, 2000), 214–251.

[9] The case of Rwanda provides a most compelling confirmation of this claim. Much has been written about the Genocide of 1994. What is particularly striking in trying to understand this horrific event is how, in the light of the hamitic story told by European colonialists and embodied within the pre- and later postcolonial state, Rwanda in effect became two different tribes—Hutu and Tutsi—united in their animosity toward each other. For an excellent discussion of the role of the Hamitic story in forming the Hutu and Tutsi as political identities see, Muhamood Mamdani, *When Victims Become Killers: Colonialism, Nativism, and the Genocide in Rwanda.* (Princeton: Princeton University Press, 2001).

[10] Stanley Hauerwas, *With the Grain of the Universe: The Church's Witness and Natural Theology* (Grand Rapids, MI: Brazos Press, 2001).

[11] *Ibid.*, 17.

[12] *Ibid.*, 15.

[13] *Ibid.*, 17.

[14] *Ibid.*, 219.

[15] *Ibid.*, 227–230.

[16] Herbert McCabe, *What is Ethics all About?* (Washington, DC: Corpus Books, 1969), 77. McCabe's observation makes part of his extended argument of ethics as language. In order to learn to speak a language, one needs to participate in the community in which that language is spoken. If Jesus, as the word, is the self-communication

of God and the meaning of human history, then in order to learn to speak in this manner one would need to participate in that new society of which Jesus is the harbinger and inaugurator.

[17] Richard B. Hays, *Moral Vision of the New Testament: A Contemporary Introduction to New Testament Ethics* (New York: Harper Collins, 1996).

[18] Phillip Jenkins, *The Next Christendom*, 3.

[19] See for instance, Kwame Bediako, *Christianity in Africa: The Renewal of a Non-Western Religion* (Maryknoll, NY: Orbis Books, 1995).

[20] For my extended reflection on the prospects of an African pope see my "Prospects of Ecclesia in Africa in the 21st Century," *Logos* 4/1 (2001), 179–196.

[21] *Ibid.*, 108–124.

[22] *Ibid.*, 73.

[23] *Ibid.*, 76.

[24] *Ibid.*, 260.

[25] *Ibid.*, 7.

[26] *Ibid.*, 4.

[27] *Ibid.*

[28] *Ibid.*, 121.

[29] *Ibid.*, 7, emphasis added.

[30] In his response to Donald Miller's report on the *Emergent Patterns of Congregational Life and Leadership in the Developing World: Personal Reflections from a Research Odyssey* (Duke Divinity School: Pulpit and Pew Research Reports, Winter 2003), Daniel Alshire, Executive Director, Association of Theological Schools in the United States and Canada betrays the same distancing. While describing the growth and dynamism of Christianity in the South as just "yet one more face, of which there have been many, and of which there will be many more," he notes: "I am not sure how instructive they are for organized Christianity in North America, with its different history, different culture, and itself the heir of another powerful emergent religious sentiment" (p. 26.).

[31] Philip Jenkins, "The Next Christianity," *The Atlantic Monthly*, (October 2002), 53–68 (p. 54).

[32] Jenkins, *The Next Christendom*, 13.

[33] Jenkins, "The Next Christianity," 64.

[34] Jenkins, *The Next Christendom*, 6.

[35] *Ibid.*, 10.

[36] *Ibid.*, 11.

[37] Jenkins, "The Next Christianity," 55.

[38] Jenkins, *The Next Christendom*, 3.

[39] *Ibid.*, 10.

[40] *Ibid.*, 7, 67 et passim.

[41] *Ibid.*, 8.

[42] See http://www.cfan.org.

[43] Paul Gifford, "Africa Shall be Saved: An Appraisal of Reinhard Bonnke's Pan African Crusade," *Journal of Religion in Africa* 17/1 (1987), p. 64.

[44] See Paul Gifford, *African Christianity: Its Public Role* (Bloomington IN: Indiana University Press, 1988), pp. 39–44 et passim.

[45] See David Maxwell, "Delivered from the Spirit of Poverty: Pentecostalism, Prosperity, and Modernity in Zimbabwe," *Journal of Religion in Africa* 28/3 (1998), 350–373.

[46] The teaching can be summarized as follows: "Africans are poor, not because of structural injustice, but because of a spirit of poverty. Even though they are born again, only their soul has in fact been redeemed. Ancestral spirits, along with their pernicious influence, remain in their blood. These ancestors were social and economic failures during their own lifetimes. Misfortune is passed from generation to generation via demonic ancestral spirits." Maxwell, "Delivered from the Spirit of Poverty," 358.

[47] Birgit Myer, "Make a Complete Break with the Past: Memory and Postcolonial Modernity in Ghanaian Pentecostalist Discourse," *Journal of Religion in Africa* 28/3 (1998), 316–349 [317].

[48] Maxwell, "Delivered from the Spirit of Poverty," 354.

[49] Omenyo, "The Charismatization," 23.

[50] Donald Miller, *Emergent Patterns*, 6.

[51] Gifford, "Africa Shall Be Free," 86.

[52] Overall, Miller's *Emergent Patterns* (1–24) provides one of the most positive assessment of the prospects of the Pentecostal-Evangelical synthesis in the Developing world.

[53] In *African Christianity*, Gifford provides ample evidence of this in relation to Christianity in Ghana, Uganda, Zambia, and Cameroon. The case of Zambia is particularly telling. The irony is that president Chiluba's attempt to declare Zambia a Christian state just created a situation in which the economic realities of Zambia's political world came to be nicely reflected and reproduced within the Christian churches. See, Gifford, *African Christianity*, 181–245. For my extended argument on nation-state performance on the church see my "Mission and Social Formation: Searching for an Alternative to King Leopold's Ghost," in *African Theology Today*, ed. E. Katongole (Scranton, PA: University of Scranton Press, 2002), 121–146. See also Chapter Six on "Kannungu and the Movement for the Restoration of the Ten Commandments in Uganda."

BIBLIOGRAPHY

Aguilar, Mario. *The Genocide in Rwanda and the Call to Deepen Christianity.* Eldoret, Kenya: Gaba Publications, 1998.

Appiah-Kubi, Kofi, and Sergio Torres, eds. *African Theology in Route: Papers from the Pan-African Conference of Third World Theologians.* Maryknoll: Orbis, 1979.

Arendt, Hannah. *The Origins of Totalitarianism* New York: Harcourt, Brace, 1951.

Avirgan, Tony, and Martha Honey. *War in Uganda: The Legacy of Idi Amin.* Westport, CT: Lawrence Mill & Co., 1982.

Baeta, C.G., ed. *Christianity and African Culture.* Accra: Conference Report, 1995.

Banura, Gerald. "A Critical Evaluation of the Kannugu Tradegy," *The Kannugu Cult-Saga: Suicide, Murder, or Salvation?* Eds. Kabazzi-Kisirinya, Deus Nkuruziza, and Gerald Banura. Kampala: Department of Religious Studies, 2000.

Barrett, David. "AD 2000: 350 Million Christians in Africa." *International Review of Mission* 59 (1970): 39–54.

Barrett, David. *World Christian Encyclopedia.* Oxford: Oxford University Press, 1982.

Bediako, Kwame. *Jesus in Africa: The Christian Gospel in African History and Experience.* Akropong, Ghana: Regnum Books, 2000.

Bediako, Kwame. "Five Theses Concerning the Significance of Modern African Christianity: A Manifesto." *Transformation* 13 (1996): 20–29.

Bediako, Kwame. *Christianity In Africa: The Renewal of a Non-Christian Religion.* Maryknoll, NY: Orbis, 1995.

Bediako, Kwame. "Understanding African Theology in the 20th Century." *Themelios* 20 (1994): 14–20.

Bediako, Kwame. "Cry Jesus: Christian Theology and Presence In Modern Africa." *Vox Evangelica* 23 (1993): 7–25.

Bediako, Kwame. "Jesus in African Culture." *Evangelical Review of Theology* 17 (1993): 56–64.

Bediako, Kwame. *Theology and Identity: The Impact of Culture upon Christian Thought In the Second Century and in Modern Africa.* Oxford: Regnum Books, 1992.

Bediako, Kwame. *Jesus in African Culture: A Ghanian Perspective.* Accra, Ghana: Asempa Publishers, 1990.

Bediako, Kwame. "The Roots of African Theology." *International Bulletin of Missionary Research* 13 (1989): 58–65.

Beherend, Heike. *Alice Lakwena and the Holy Spirits: War in Northern Uganda, 1986–1997*. Kampala: Fountain Publishers, 1999.

Blyden, Edward W. *Christianity, Islam and the Negro Race*, Edition 2, with an Introduction by the Hon. Samuel Lewis. New York: Black Classic Press, 1998.

Bowen, Roger. "Rwanda - Missionary Reflections on Discipleship and the Church After Rwanda," *Anvil* 13/1 (1999): 33–44.

Budde, Michael, and Robert W. Brimlow, eds. *The Church as Counterculture*. Albany: State University Press of New York, 2000.

Cassimir, Ronald. "The Politics of Popular Catholicism in Uganda," *East African Expressions of Christianity*, ed. Thomas Spear and Isaria N. Kimambo. Nairobi: East African Educational Publishers, 1999: 248–274.

Cavanaugh, William T. *Torture and Eucharist: Theology, Politics, and the Body of Christ*. Oxford: Blackwell Publishers, 1998.

Cavanaugh, William T. "The World in a Wafer: A Geography of the Eucharist as Resistance to Globalization." *Modern Theology* 15/2 (April, 1999): 187.

Chirimuuta, Richard and Rosalind. *AIDS, Africa and Racism*. London: Free Association Press, 1998.

Chittister, Joan. "New World, New Church: Political, Pastoral, or Prophetic." *Catholic Studies* 22 (1992): 1–11.

Comaroff, John L. and Jean. *Of Revelation and Revolution: Christianity, Colonialism, and Consciousness in South Africa*, vol. 1. Chicago: University of Chicago Press, 1991.

Cone, James H. *The God of the Oppressed* New York: Seabury Press, 1975.

Conrad, Joseph. *Heart of Darkness*. New York: Dover Publications, 1990.

Davison, Basil. *The Black Man's Burden: Africa Under the Curse of the Nation-State*. Oxford: James Currey, 1992.

deCerteau, Michel. *The Practice of Everyday Life*. Berkely, CA: University of California Press, 1988.

DeTemmerman, Els. *Aboke Girls: Children Abducted in Northern Uganda*. Kampela: Fountain Publishers, 2001.

Diawara, Manthia. *In Search of Africa*. Cambridge: harvard University Press, 1998.

Dowdall, Terry. "Psychological Aspects of the Truth and Reconciliation Commission," in *To Remember and To Heal*, ed. Botman, Russel and Robin Peterson. Cape Town: Human and Rousseau, 1996: 31–32.

Dube, Musa W. "Consuming a Colonial Time Bomb: Translating Badimo into 'Demons' In the Setswana Bible." *Journal of the Study of the New Testament* 73 (1999): 33–59.

Dube, Musa W. Postcolonial Feminist Interpretation of the Bible. St. Louis: Chalice Press, 2000.

Eagleton, Terry. *The Illusions of Postmodernism*. Oxford: Basil Blackwell, 1996.

Éla, J. M. *African Cry*, (Maryknoll, NY: Orbis, 1986). Translation of the French original *Le Cri de L'homme Africain* (Librarie Editions L'Harmattan, Paris 1980).

Éla, J. M. *My Faith as an African*. (Maryknoll, NY: Orbis, 1995). Translation of the French original *Ma Fol d'Afracain* (Editions Karthala, Paris, 1985).

Fanon, Frantz. *The Wretched of the Earth*, trans. Constance Farrington. NewYork: Gorve, 1968.

Fiala, C. "Dirty Tricks: How the WHO Gets Its AIDS Figures," *New African* (1998): 36–38.

Foucault, Michel. *The Archeology of Knowledge*, trans. A. M. Sheridan Smith. London: Tavistock Press, 1972.

Foucault, Michel. *Power/Knowledge: Selected Interviews and Other Writings*, ed. C. Gordon. Brighton: Harvest Press, 1980.

Frankfurt, Harry G. *The Importance of What We Care About*. Cambridge: Cambridge University Press, 1988.

Friedman, Jonathan. "Beyond Otherness," *Telos* 71 (1987): 161–170.

Fulkerson, McClintock Mary. 2001. "We Do not See Color Here: A Case Study in Ecclesial Cultural Invention," in *Converging on Culture: Theologians in Dialogue with Cultural Analysis and Criticism,* eds. Delwin Brown, Sheila Greeve Daveney and Kathym Tanner (Oxford: Oxford University Press, 2001), 140–158.

Gatwa, Tharcisse. "Resisting Democracy in Rwanda: Genocide and Reconciliation," *Reformed World* 48 (1998): 190–201.

Gatwa, Tharcisse. "Victims or Guildy? Can the Rwandan Churches Repent and Bear the Burden of the Nation for the 1994 Trajedy?" *International Review of Mission* 88 (1999): 347–363.

Gibellini, Rosino, ed. *Paths of African Philosophy*. Maryknoll, NY: Orbis, 1994.

Gifford, Paul. *African Christianity: Its Public Role*. Bloomington: Indiana University Press, 1998.

Gifford, Paul, ed. *The Christian Churches and the Democratization of Africa*. Leiden: E. J. Brill, 1995.

Gifford, Paul. "Africia Shall be Saved: An Appraisal of Reinhard Bonnke's Pan African Crusade," *Journal of Religion in Africa* 17/1 (1987): 64.

Gray, John. "Where There is No Common Power," *The New Statesman* (Sept. 24, 2001).

Gourevitch, Philip. *We Wish to Inform You That Tomorrow We Will Be Killed with Our Families: Stories from Rwanda*. New York: Farrar, Straus, and Giroux, 1998.

Gustafson, James. "The Sectarian Temptation: Reflections of Theology, the Church, and the University," *Proceedings of the Catholic Theological Society* 40 (1985): 83–94.

Hauerwas, Stanley. "Hooks: Random Thoughts By Way of a Response to Griffiths and Ochs," *Modern Theology* 19/1 (2003): 89–101.

Hauerwas, Stanley. *With a Gain of the Universe: The Church's Witness and Natural Theology*. Grand Rapids, MI: Brazos Press, 2001.

Hauerwas, Stanley. "The Christian Difference: Surviving Postmodernism," *Cultural Values* 3/2 (April, 1999): 164–181.

Hauerwas, Stanley. *Against the Nations: War and Survival in a Liberal Society*. Nashville: Abingdon Press, 1991.

Haurewas, Stanley and Will Willimon. *Resident Aliens: Life in the Christian Colony.* Nashville: Abingdon Press, 1989.

Hauerwas, Stanley. *The Peaceable Kingdom: A Primer In Ethics*. Notre Dame: University of Notre Dame Press, 1983.

Hauerwas, Stanley. *A Community of Character: Toward a Constructive Christian Social Ethic*. Notre Dame: Notre Dame University Press, Z 1981.

Haynes, Stephen. "Never Again: Perpetrators and Bystanders in Rwanda," *Christian Century* (Feb. 27 - March 6, 2002): 30 –35.

Hays, Richard. *The Moral Vision of the New Testament: A Contemporary Introduction to New Testament Ethics.* New York: Harper Collins, 1996.

Hebblethwaite, Peter. "In Rwanda, 'Blood is Thicker than Water' - Even the Waters of Baptism," *National Catholic Reporter* (June 3, 1994): 11.

Hegel, G.W. F. *Lectures on the Philosophy of History*. New York: Dover Publications, 1956.

Hoschild, Adam. *King Leopold's Ghost: A Story of Greed, Terror, and Heroism in Colonial Africa*. Boston: Houghton Mifflin, 1998.

Hooper, Edward. *The River. A Journey to the Source of HIV and AIDS.* New York: Little, Brown and Company, 1999.

Jameson, Frederic. *Postmodernism, or The Cultural Logic of Late Capitalism*. Durham, NC: Duke University Press, 1991.

Jenkins, Phillip. *The Next Christendom: The Coming of Global Christianity*. Oxford: Oxford University Press, 2002.

Jenkins, Phillip. "The Next Christianity," *The Atlantic Monthly*. October, 2002.

Jennings, Willie. "Wandering in the Wilderness. Christian Identity and Theology," in *The Gospel in Black and White*, ed. Dennis L. Okholm Downers Grove, IL: Intervarsity Press, 1997: 37–48.

John Paul II. Post-Synodal Apostolic Exhortation: "Ecclesia in Africa," in *The African Synod: Documents, Reflection, Perspectives.* African Justice Network. Maryknoll, NY: Orbis, 1996: 233–286.

Jones, Gregory. "Geographies of Memories," *Christian Century*, August 30 - September 6, 2000: 874.

Jones, Gregory. "Healing the Wounds of Memory," *Journal of Theology* 103 (Summer 1999): 35–51.

Jones, Gregory. *Embodying Forgiveness: A Theological Analysis.* Grand Rapids: Eerdman's, 1995.

Kabazzi-Kisirinnya, Nkurunziza Deudedit, and Gerard Banura, eds. *The Kannugu Cult Saga, Suicide, Murder or Salvation.* Kampala: Makerere University, 2002.

Kanyandago, Peter. "The Role of Culture in Poverty Eradication," in Carabine and Reilly, eds. *The Challenge of Eradicating Poverty in the World: An African Response.* Nkozi: Uganda Martyrs University Press, 1998: 119–152.

Kanyoro, Musimbi, and Nyambura Njoroge, eds. *Groaning in Faith: African Women in the Household of God.* Nairobi: Action, 1996.

Kanyoro, Musimbi, ed. *The Will to Arise: Women, Tradition, and the Church in Africa.* Maryknoll, NY: Orbis, 1992.

Katongole, Emmanuel, ed. *African Theology Today.* Scranton, PA: University of Scranton Press, 2002.

Katongole, Emmanuel. "Globalization and Economic Fundamentalism in Africa," in *The Cries of the Poor in Africa: Questions and Responses for African Christianity*, ed. Peter Kanyandago. Kisubi: Marianum Publishing, 2002: 57–78.

Katongole, Emmanuel. "Mission and Social Formation: Searching for an Alternative to King Leopold's Ghost," *African Theology Today*, ed. Katongole. Scranton, PA: University of Scranton Press, 2002.

Katongole, Emmanuel. "Prospects of Ecclesia in Africa in the 21st Century." *Logos* 4(1) (2001):179–196.

Katongole, Emmanuel. "Postmodern Illusions and the Challenges or African Theology: The Ecclesial Tactics of Resistance." *Modern Theology* 16(2) (2000): 237–254.

Katongole, Emmanuel. *Beyond Universal Reason: The Relation Between Religion and Ethics in the Work of Stanley Hauerwas.* Notre Dame: University of Notre Dame Press, 2000.

Katongole, Emmanuel. "African Christian Theology Today: On Being a Premodern Modernist." Unpublished, 1998.

Katongole, Emmanuel. "African Renaissance and Narrative Theology in Africa" *Journal of Theology for Southern Africa,* 102 (1998): 29–40.

Katongole, Emmanuel. "Clinton's 'New Deal' for Africa: Salvation or Nightmare?" *Tomwa* 8/1 (1998): 7–11.

Katongole, Emmanuel. "Theological Perspectives on Poverty," *The Challenge of Eradications of Poverty in the World: An African Challenge*, eds. Deidre Carabine and Martin O'Reilly. Nkozi: Uganda Martyrs University, 1998.

Keane, Fergal. *Season of Blood. A Rwandan Journey.* London: Penguin Classics, 1996.

Keener S. Craig. "The Gospel and Racial Reconciliation," in *The Gospel in Black and White*, ed. Dennis L. Okholm. Downers Grove, IL: Intervarsity Press, 1997: 117–130.

Kingsolver, Barbara. *The Poisonwood Bible.* New York: Harper Collins Publishers, 1998.

Kolini, Emmanuel. "Towards Reconciliation in Rwanda," *Transformation* 12/2 (1995): 12–14.

Kritzinger, J. "The Rwandan Tragedy as Public Indictment of Christian Mission: Missiological Reflections of an Observer," *International Review of Missions* 88 (October 1999): 347–363.

Kyemba, Henry. *A State of Blood: The Inside Story of Idi Amin.* New York: Ace Books, 1977.

Linden, Ian. "The Church and Genocide: Lessons from the Rwandan Tragedy," *The Reconciliation of Peoples*. Geneva: WCC Publications, 1997: 43–55.

Longman, Timothy. "Christian Churches and Genocide in Rwanda," *In God's Name: Genocide and Religion in the 20th Century*, ed. Omer Bartov and Phyllis Mack. New York: Berghahm Books, 2001: 139–160.

Longman, Timothy. "Christianity and Democratization in Rwanda," *The Christian Churches and the Democratization of Africa: Studies of Religion in Africa*, ed. Paul Gifford. Leiden: E. J. Brill, 1995.

Lyotard, J. F. *The Postmodern Condition: A Report on Knowledge*, trans. G. Bennington and B. Massumi. Minneapolis: University of Minnesota Press, 1984.

Maluleke, Tinyiko. "Christianity in a Distressed Africa: A Time to Own and Own Up." *Missionalia*, 26 (1998): 324–340.

Maluleke, Tinyiko. "In Search of the True Character of African Christian Identity: A Review of the Theology or Kwame Bediako." *Missionalia*, 25(2) (1997): 210–219.

Maluleke, Tinyiko. "Half a Century of African Christian Theologies: Elements of the Emerging Agenda for the 21st Century." *Journal of Theology for Southern Africa*, 99 (1997): 4–23.

Maluleke, Tinyiko. "A Review of J.N.K. Mugambi's 'From Liberation to Reconstruction.'" *Missionalia* 24 (1996): 472–473.

Maluleke, Tinyiko. "Black and African Theologies in the New World Order: A Time to Drink from Our Own Wells." *Journal of Theology for Southern Africa*, 96 (1996): 3–19.

Maluleke, Tinyiko. "Recent Developments in the Christian Theologies of Africa: Towards the Twenty-first Century." *Journal of Constructive Theology*, 2(2) (1996): 33–80.

Mamdani, Muhamood. *When Victims Become Killers: Colonialism, Nativism, and the Genocide in Rwanda.* Princeton, NJ: Princeton University Press, 2001.

Martin, John. "Rwanda: Why?" *Transformation* 12/2 (1995).

Maxwell, David. "Delivered from the Spirit of Poverty: Pentecostalism, Prosperity, and Modernity in Zimbabwe," *Journal of Religion in Africa* 28/3 (1998): 350–373.

Mbeki, Thabo. "African Renaissance: Statement of the Deputy President Thabo Mbekl." *Pretoria* (August 13, 1998).

Mbiti, John. "Christianity and Traditional Religions in Africa." *International Review of Mission,* 59(236) (1970): 438.

Mbiti, John. *African Religions and Philosophy.* Garden City, NY: Anchor Books, 1970.

McCabe, Herbert. *What is Ethics All About?* Washington: Corpus Books, 1969.

McFague, Sallie. *Life Abundant: Rethinking Theology and Economy for a Planet in Peril.* Minneapolis: Fortress Press, 2001.

McGrane, Bernard. *Beyond Anthropology* New York: Columbia University Press, 1989.

Mda, Zakes. *Ways of Dying.* Oxford University Press, 1995.

Melvern, Linda. *A People Betrayed: The Role of the West in Rwanda's Genocide.* New York: St. Martin's Press, 2000.

Miller, Donald. *Emergent Patterns of Congregational Life and Leadership in the Developing World: Personal Reflections from a Research Odyssey.* Durham, NC: Duke Divinity School, Pulpit and Pew Research Reports: 2003.

Mofokeng, Takatso. "Black Christians, the Bible, and Liberation," *Journal of Black Theology in Southern Africa* 2/1 (1988): 34–42.

Mokgethi, Mothabi. "African Theology or Black Theology: Toward an Integral African Theology," *Journal of Black Theology in Southern Africa* 8/2 (1994): 113–141.

Moltmann, Wendel. *The Women Around Jesus.* New York: Crossroads, 1987.

Moreira, Alberto. "The Dangerous Memory of Jesus Christ in a Post-Traditional Society," *Concilium* 4 (1999).

Morris, Jack. "A Lesson from the Massacre of Foreign Tourists in Uganda," *America* 180/19 (May 1999): 12–14.

Mudimbe, V.Y. *The Idea of Africa.* Bloomington: Indiana University Press, 1994.

Mudimbe, V.Y. *The Invention of Africa: Gnosis, Philosophy and the Order of Knowledge.* Bloomington: Indiana University Press, 1983.

Mugambi, J.N.K. *From Liberation to Reconstruction: African Christian Theology After the Cold War.* Nairobi: East African Education Publishers, 1995.

Mugambi, J.N.K. *Critiques of Christianity Within African Literature*. Nairobi; East African Education Publishers, 1992.

Mugambi, J.N.K., and Laurenti Magesa, eds. *Jesus in African Christianity: Experimentation and Diversity in African Christology*. Nairobi: Acton Publishers, 1998.

Myer, Brigit. "Make a Complete Break with the Past: Memory and Postcolonial Modernity in Ghanaian Pentecostalist Discourse," *Journal of Religion in Africa* 28/3 (1998): 316–349.

Ngabirano, Max. "National Justice: A Challenge to the Great Lakes Region of Africa," *Afer (African Ecclesial Review)* 43/45 (2001): 229–251.

Nzachayo, Paul. "Religion and Violence: Outbreak and Overcoming," *Religion as a Source of Violence?* Ed. Beuken Wimand Karl-Josef Kushel. Maryknoll, NY: Orbis Books, 1997: 11–22.

Nyamiti, Charles. *Christ as Our Ancestor*. Harare: Mambo Press, 1986.

Oduyoye, Mercy Amba. *Daughters of Anowa: African Women and Patriarchy*. Maryknoll, NY: Orbis, 1997.

Oduyoye, Mercy Amba, ed. *Transforming Power: Women in the Household of God*. Accra: Sam Woode, 1997.

Olok-Apire, P. A. *Amin's Rise to Power: The Inside Story*. London: Lawrence and Hill, 1983.

Otabil, Mensa. *Four Laws of Productivity: God's Foundation for Living*. Accra: Alter International, 1992.

Parratt, John. "Reinventing African Christianity." *African Theology Today*. Grand Rapids: Eerdmans, 1995.

p'Bitek, Okot. *Song of Lawino land Song of Ocol*. London: East African Writers Series, 1994.

Pirouet, Louise. "Religion in Uganda under Amin," *Journal of Religion in Africa* 11 (1980): 13–29.

Postman, Niel. *Amusing Ourselves to Death: Public Discourse in the Age of Show Business*. New York: Penguin Books, 1985.

Power, Samantha. "Bystanders to Genocide," *Atlantic Monthly*, (Sept., 2001).

Prunier, Gérard. *The Rwanda Crisis 1959 – 1994. History of a Genocide*. Kampala: Fountain Publishers, 1995.

Richburg, Keith. *Out of Africa: A Black Man Confronts Africa*. New York: Harvest Books, 2002.

Rieff, David. *A Bed for the Night: Humanitarianism in Crisis*. New York: Simon and Schuster, 2002.

Ritzer, George. *The McDonaldization of Society: An Investigation into the Changing Character of Contemporary Social Life*, revised ed. Thousand Oaks, CA: Pine Forge Press, 1996.

Rorty, Richard. *Contingency, Irony, and Solidarity*. Cambridge, MA: Cambridge University Press, 1989.

Roy, Arundhati. *The God of Small Things*. New York: Harper Coliins, 1997.

Ryan, Patrick. "The Roots of Muslim Anger," *America* (Nov. 26, 2001): 14.

Said, Edward. "Representing the Colonized: Anthropology's Interlocutors," *Critical Inquiry* 15 (1989): 205–225.

Sanneh, Lamin. *Encountering the West: Christianity and the Global Cultural Process: the African Dimension.* Maryknoll, NY: Orbis, 1993.

Sanneh, Lamin. *Translating the Message: The Missionary Impact on Culture.* Maryknoll, NY: Orbis, 1989.

Sanneh, Lamin. *West African Christianity: The Religious Impact.* London: C. Hurst, 1983.

Sanneh, Lamin. "The Horizontal and the Vertical in Mission: An African Perspective." *International Bulletin of Missionary Research,* 7(4) (1983): 165–171.

Sanneh, Lamin. *The Scars of Death: Children Abducted by the Lord's Resistance Army in Uganda.* Human Rights Watch, 1997.

Schaberg, Jane. "How Mary Magdalene Became a Whore." *Biblical Review* 7, (October 1992) 30–37; 50–52.

Scheer, Gary. "Rwanda: Where was the Church?" *Evangelical Missions Quarterly* 31 (1995): 324–326, 328.

Schreiter, Robert, ed. *Faces of Jesus in Africa.* Maryknoll, NY: Orbis, 1998.

Scott, James. *Domination and the Arts of Resistance.* New Haven: Yale University Press, 1990.

Shenton, Joan. *Positively False. Exposing the Myths around HIV and AIDS.* New York: I. B. Tauris, 1998.

Sibomana, Andre. *Hope for Rwanda: Conversions with Laure Guibert and Herve Deguine,* trans. Carina Tertsakian. London: Pluto Press, 1997.

Simopoulos, Nicole. "David's Kingdom: The Congo's Inferno. An Examination of Power from the Underside of History," *Bulletin for Contextual Theology in Southern Africa and Africa* 4/3 (1979): 9–25.

Speke, John Hanning. *Journal of the Discovery of the Source of the Nile.* New York: Harper and Brothers, 1864.

Surin, Kenneth. "Certain 'Politics of Speech': 'Religious Pluralism' in the Age of the McDonald's Hamburger," *Modern Theology* 7/1 (1990): 68–100.

Taylor, V. "The Future of Christianity," in *The Oxford Illustrated History of Christianity,* edited by John McManners. Oxford: Oxford University Press, 1990: 628–685.

Taylor, V. *A Timely Message fro Heaven: The End of the Present Times.* Rukungiri, 1996.

Tuhirire, Chris, Gerald Banura and Joseph Begumanya. "Kannugu Research Team's Report," *The Kannugu Cult-Saga: Suicide, Murder, or Salvation?* Eds. Kabazzi-Kisirinya, Deus Nkuruziza, and Gerald Banura. Kampala: Department of Religious Studies, 2000: 40.

Villa Vicencio, Charles. *A Theology of Reconstruction: Nation Building and Human Rights.* Cape Town: Phillip, 1992.

Weber, Max. *The Protestant Ethic and the Spirit of Capitalism.* London: Routledge, 1992. German original 1904–1905.

West, Cornel. *Race Matters* New York: Vintage Books, 1993.

West, Gerald O. *Biblical Hermeneutics of Liberation: Modes of Reading the Bible in the South African Context.* Pietermaritzburg: Cluster Publications, 1991.

Wrong, Michela. *In the Footsteps of Mr. Kurtz. Living on the Brink of Disaster in Mobutu's Congo.* New York: Harper Collins, 2001.

Young, Josiah. *African Theology: A Critical Analysis and Annotated Bibliography.* London: Greenwood Press, 1993.

Index